Logical Relations in Discourse

The Summer Institute of Linguistics

Volume Editor

Rhonda L. Hartell

Production Staff

Bonnie Brown, Managing Editor
Laurie Nelson, Production Editor
Rhonda L. Hartell, Compositor
Hazel Shorey, Graphic Artist

Logical Relations in Discourse

Eugene E. Loos

Editor

The Summer Institute of Linguistics

© 1999 by the Summer Institute of Linguistics, Inc.
Library of Congress Catalog No: 98-61616
ISBN: 1-55671-040-2

Printed in the United States of America
All Rights Reserved

08 07 06 05 04 03 02 01 00 99 10 9 8 7 6 5 4 3 2 1

No part of this publication may be reproduced, stored in a retrieval system, or transmitted in any form or by any means—electronic, mechanical, photocopy, recording, or otherwise—without the express permission of the Summer Institute of Linguistics, with the exception of brief excerpts in journal articles or reviews.

Copies of this and other publications of the Summer Institute of Linguistics may be obtained from:

International Academic Bookstore
Summer Institute of Linguistics
7500 W. Camp Widsom Rd.
Dallas TX 75236-5699

Voice: 972-708-7404
Fax: 972-708-7433
Email: academic_books@sil.org
Internet: http://www.sil.org

Contents

Preface vii

Logical Connectives, Relationships, and Relevance 1
    Ernst-August Gutt

The Grammar of Sentence Conjunctions in St. Lucian French Creole 25
    David B. Frank

Connectives and Clause Combining in Banggi 37
    Michael E. Boutin

A Look at Two Ifè Connectives 67
    Marquita Klaver

A Pragmatic Analysis of a Failed Cross-Cultural Communication 73
    Barbara J. Sayers

A Beginning Look at Brahui Connectives 113
    David A. Ross

'If' in Capanahua 195
    Eugene E. Loos

A Noncategorical Approach to Coherence Relations: Switch-Reference
    Constructions in Mbyá Guaraní 219
    Robert A. Dooley

Proposed Tests for the Validity of an Analysis of Logical Connectives 243
    Eugene E. Loos

Preface

Logical relations between propositions are an elusive subject matter about which little research was available at a workshop in 1989, and it remains so today; most of the work in this volume was done between 1989 and 1991, but we trust that the reader will find the papers useful in 1999, also.

There has been no agreement about how logical relations should be defined, how they should be analyzed, what should or might be included, or in which part of the grammar or lexicon they should be treated. Linguistic research has largely focused on sentence structure but logical (interpropositional) relations have not fit in well with a formal representation of sentence structure. When morphemes can be identified markers of logical relations, they tend to be relegated to the lexicon as lexemes without further analysis. Discourse analysis, which by definition covers more than the sentence, does not usually address the knotty problems involved in identifying elusive relations that have no explicit marker. Translation, oriented discussions have sought to establish a way to reach equivalence of structure or message between languages but when the language types are mismatched, translators have lacked analytical criteria that produce results comparable with the advances made in sentence structure.

Logical relations are difficult to grapple with because (1) often the markers for presumed logical relations are also signals for other kinds of grammatical or semantic functions; (2) in many languages there are no overt phonological markers at all; instead, sequential ordering or other cues are the communicative element; and (3) sometimes not even sequential ordering is crucial; rather, context and the semantic content of the phrases or clauses that constitute the propositions provide the clues the addressee uses to construe the intended relationship between the propositions.

When the workshop began, we assumed no refined definition of LOGICAL RELATIONS other than that logical relations are taken to be explicit or presumed SEMANTIC RELATIONSHIPS between propositions or between a speaker

vii

viii

or hearer and propositions expressed by clauses, sentences, or groups of sentences in a discourse. LOGICAL CONNECTIVES on the other hand are overt markers such as *for, because, and, if, then,* and *therefore* that the speaker uses to code a logical relation; the addressee is expected to interpret the markers as cues about how to infer associations between the propositions. The range of phenomena turned out to be much broader than we anticipated. Interpersonal and interpropositional relations in speech are intertwined.

Whether logical relations are expressly encoded, extracted from linguistic patterns, or inferred from extralinguistic cues, they are important to the coherence of a discourse. Participants in the workshop found that linguists need to pay more attention to how language is processed by the listener, using pragmatic, psychological, and sociolinguistic information. It is such information that makes it possible to explain the well-formedness of a text or to understand why the text should be interpretable at all as a meaningfully offered and accepted communication.

Understanding logical connectives or a lack thereof has been a problem for dictionary compilers and translators, because we accept the principle that assigning meaning to a form ought to be grounded on regularities of syntactic structure, regularly perceived semantic associations, and/or common pragmatic use. We sought to find at least partial solutions to three aspects of the problem: (1) identification: how do we discover what we have not yet found; (2) treatment: how do we describe what we have found; and (3) argument: how do we explain what we think we have found so as to convince a critical observer, or even a sympathetic one?

The articles in this volume attempt to treat some of these aspects and are offered for readers' appraisal.

Eugene E. Loos

Logical Connectives, Relationships, and Relevance

Ernst-August Gutt

1. Introduction

In April 1989 Eugene Loos and Ivan Lowe conducted a linguistic workshop designed to tackle a number of important questions in the area of logical connectives in discourse, such as the following:

> What are the essential typological syntactic and semantic features that must/should characterize each connective in any language for a relationship between propositions to be acceptably defined?

> What are the pragmatic characteristics of a designated connective?

> What kinds of data should field workers seek in order to present convincing evidence that what they claim to be a particular logical connective is, in fact, that?

In the first two weeks of the seminar, the participants were introduced to the RHETORICAL STRUCTURE THEORY developed by Mann and Thompson (1986, 1987), and also to relevant aspects of the communication theory currently being developed by Kathleen Callow (1998) in her book *Man and Message*.

Rhetorical structure theory looks at texts primarily from the analyst's point of view and is intended to provide "a linguistically useful method for describing natural text" (Mann and Thompson 1987:1). It does not make explicit claims as to whether this analysis reflects what goes on in people's minds when they communicate.

Callow's presentation differed from this in that she was interested in what goes on in the speaker's mind rather than in possible ways of describing a text. Consequently, the relationships her theory proposes to hold between the different parts of a text are meant to reflect a psychologicalreality in the speaker's mind.

I believe that Callow's position is preferable because by changing the question from What is the best (most appropriate, most elegant) way of analyzing the relationships in a text? to How does the communicator relate the propositions in his mind?, the issue becomes a psychological, hence an empirical one, rather than one of finding the best description for a set of phenomena, in whatever terms that is to be evaluated, such as elegance, completeness, simplicity, and so forth.

What both rhetorical structure theory and Callow's approach have in common is the reliance on a set of relations, thought to hold either between text parts or between propositions and chunks of propositions. This brings us to the central topic of this workshop: how do we know in any given case that there **is** such an interpropositional or rhetorical relation, and that it is of type X rather than Y? The current understanding is that both approaches need to define sets of relationships that are wide enough to cover all possible relations that speakers can use in texts. At the same time, the relations need to be defined in sufficiently explicit terms to differentiate them clearly from one another.

The fact that even with the more explicit definitions given in Mann and Thompson (1987) it often proved difficult in the workshop to determine why a particular example was analyzed as exhibiting relation X rather than Y seems to suggest that the task is not an easy one. This difficulty is further evidenced by the existence of a number of different schemes of relations that have been proposed in the past, such as in Ballard et al. (1971), Beekman and Callow (1974), and its further developments reflected in the semantic structure analysis approach, e.g., Callow (1982), Pike and Pike (1977), Longacre (1983), and others.

It is at this point, I believe, that the relevance theory of communication developed by Sperber and Wilson (1986) can be of considerable value because it offers the possibility of solving the problem by going one step further: there is good evidence that relevance theory can account for these various relationships *without necessarily having to refer to them as theoretical constructs in their own right*. In other words, relevance theory does not need to define a set of such relationships in order to account for our intuitions about them. This article seeks to demonstrate this possibility with examples taken from Silt'i, an Ethio-Semitic language spoken in Ethiopia. As we shall

Logical Connectives, Relationships, and Relevance

see, this approach also allows a clearer understanding of how logical connectives work.[1] Furthermore, we shall find that relevance theory helps us to gain a much richer understanding of the speaker-intended interpretation than relation-based approaches give us.

Before we can turn to examples, however, we will need to look at some basic notions of relevance theory.

2. Theory sketch

In this section I can only give the briefest sketch of relevance theory; a few more notions will be introduced as we go along. For more detailed information the reader is referred to Sperber and Wilson (1986).[2]

2.1 Ostensive-inferential communication and the principle of relevance

The starting point of relevance theory is a question: How do people manage to communicate? How is it possible for me as communicator to induce you to entertain thoughts that I have?

At a very general level, the answer is that a communicator produces a stimulus that makes evident (1) that he intends to convey some thoughts, and (2) what those thoughts are. In other words, the communicator behaves in a way that provides EVIDENCE of his intention to communicate certain thoughts, and it is the audience's task to INFER from the evidence provided what these thoughts are. This means that communication is viewed essentially as an INFERENTIAL PROCESS. Communication succeeds when the audience's inferences lead it to the thoughts which the communicator intended to convey. For example, suppose you are at a party with a friend. You notice that it is time to go home. So when your friend is looking at you, you catch her eye and direct her attention to the clock on the wall by conspicuously looking there yourself. The conspicuous nature of behavior will induce your friend to infer that you want to communicate something, and she will try to infer from it what it is that you want to convey. Thus, she will notice that you are drawing her attention to the clock and will try to infer what you are

---

[1] For a very insightful and much broader treatment of discourse connectives in general from a relevance-theory point of view see Blakemore (1987) with data from English and Blass (forthcoming) with data from Ghanaian and other languages.

[2] Relevance theory approaches communication from a somewhat different perspective than many of us are used to. It may be tempting to translate the concepts of relevance theory into one's own framework. As I know from my own experience, however, this is not a straightforward matter, and it may be better to first of all concentrate on understanding relevance theory on its own terms, and then try to relate it to other models later on.

intending to communicate by that. One possible inference would be that you intend her to take note of what time it is, which may lead to the further inference that you might think it time to go home, and so forth.

Note that we are not normally conscious of this inference process; it works very fast and is something that our mind takes care of subconsciously. We will usually have some awareness of the RESULTS of this process, but the process itself goes on below the level of consciousness. There are, of course, instances when our interpretation efforts rise to consciousness, but that is usually only when there are problems.

Of course, you could also have communicated by using some verbal stimulus, e.g., by saying, "Look at the clock" or "Look what time it is." Again your friend would then have to infer what thoughts you wanted to communicate from your utterance. In either case, the basic process would be the same: one infers from people's behavior, both nonverbal and verbal, what they intend to communicate.[3]

Communication thus involves inference, and inference involves information processing, but information processing is something we do and hence costs some mental effort: the audience needs to carry out inference, it needs to access information from memory, i.e., carry out memory searches; and in the case of verbal communication it also needs to carry out linguistic decoding, which is not for free either.

Life is not all work, however: there are also benefits, and these are defined in terms of CONTEXTUAL EFFECTS. Put simply, contextual effects can be thought of as gratifying changes in one's knowledge. I will say more about these changes in §3.2.2, but crucially contextual effects are achieved not by the utterance alone, but by the inferential combination of the utterance with the contextual knowledge of the audience. This captures two basic intuitions: first, it accounts for the fact that one does not usually consider it very rewarding to be told something one was well aware of already; the information presented has to make some difference. Second, it captures the further intuition that in communication it is not enough for the information to be new; it must rather link up with knowledge already present in some way.

The main points so far, then, are these: communication is rewarding, it brings contextual effects, but there is also a cost attached to requiring mental processing effort. This relation between contextual effects and the processing effort needed to derive them is defined as RELEVANCE: the relevance of

---

[3] If the utterances mentioned are intended to convey the message that it is time to go, then they would constitute what has come to be known as indirect speech acts. However, this does not mean that inference plays a role only in INDIRECT SPEECH ACTS. Rather, as Sperber and Wilson (1986) have shown, inference is basic to all verbal and nonverbal instances of human communication.

Logical Connectives, Relationships, and Relevance

an utterance will be the greater the more contextual effects it has, and the less processing effort it requires. It will be smaller the fewer contextual effects it has and the more processing effort it requires to achieve those effects.

And now we are ready for the crucial point: relevance theory proposes that by beginning an act of communication, a communicator automatically communicates the following presumptions: first, that there will be adequate contextual effects, and second, that these effects will be derivable with minimal processing effort on the audience's part. Put in less technical language, by claiming the audience's attention, the communicator claims that what he intends to convey will be rewarding, and that he has made it as easy as possible for the audience to receive this reward. This presumption is assumed to follow from our human nature, and relevance theory refers to it as the PRINCIPLE OF RELEVANCE.[4]

This principle is important because it explains how communication overcomes certain inherent problems. For example, as Kathleen Callow also pointed out in her presentation, for successful communication it is necessary for the hearer to have just the right context; communication cannot be successful unless the hearer actually uses the contextual information envisaged by the communicator. In relevance theory, this follows from the fact that communication necessarily requires the inferential combination of what is expressed with contextual information; and if the audience does not use the contextual information envisaged by the speaker, it is likely to come up with the wrong interpretation. Therefore, since it is in the speaker's interest that the audience will get it right, he will naturally try to clue them in about the right context, if he is in doubt that they can access it.

Thus, Callow gave the example that if she wanted to talk to her husband about an individual called Phil who was not a very close friend of theirs, she would probably introduce her actual remark by saying, "You know Phil at church? Now he...." She also noted that in the case of a very good friend this would not be necessary.

In relevance theory, this behavior is explained by the principle of relevance: when hearing the name Phil, the hearer will have to find a referent in memory to assign to this name. The speaker can, of course, leave that task completely to the hearer without giving him further clues, and if the referent is highly accessible in memory at the time of speaking, then this might well be the best strategy. Thus, information about people very close to us is probably highly accessible at most times, and it would be wasting the audience's

---

[4] As Sperber and Wilson (1986) show, this single principle takes care of all that the four maxims suggested by Grice (1975) were meant to do.

6   Ernst-August Gutt

processing effort to give further information about an individual that the audience would have thought of right away anyhow.[5]

At other times, however, the speaker will assist the audience in finding the right context in order to ensure that they arrive at the intended interpretation. He can do so not only by prefacing his utterance with preliminary remarks like the one just considered, but in many other ways. As we shall see, logical and other connectives are valuable devices for this purpose.

From the perspective of the communicator this may be clear enough, but given that we can never know any other person's thoughts directly, how can the audience ever be confident that they have got things right, both with regard to the context envisaged by the speaker and the interpretation as a whole? Even if they arrive at some interpretation what reason do they have to believe that it is the interpretation the speaker had in mind?

Thus, if you draw my attention to the clock on the wall, how can I tell whether you intend to convey to me that it is a very expensive clock or that it is time to go?

The answer lies in the principle of relevance: there is never more than one interpretation that is consistent with the principle of relevance. There can be only one such interpretation, because as soon as the audience has arrived at an interpretation that the communicator could have expected to have adequate contextual effects without requiring unnecessary processing effort, the interpretation process will stop. There may be other possible interpretations that might have adequate contextual effects, but they would no longer be optimally relevant because of the additional processing effort they require. Of course, there may be no interpretation that is consistent with the principle of relevance; in this case one will need further clarification of what the communicator meant or else it will remain unclear what he had in mind.

Therefore, the criterion of consistency with the principle of relevance entitles the audience to assume that the first interpretation that they find to be consistent with the principle of relevance is the one that the communicator intended to communicate. Thus, as soon as the audience has arrived at an

---

[5] In the literature, it is sometimes said that communicators do not express information already known to the audience because this is unnecessary. Relevance theory shows that it is not only unnecessary but detrimental to the success of the communication act: it makes the audience spend processing effort without increasing the contextual effects, and hence reduces the overall relevance of the utterance. This explains our feelings of irrelevance when someone starts clueing us in about a person who is actually well known to us. (Often we tend to cut such introductions short by saying, "Oh, I know Phil.") On the other hand, expressing known information is not always inappropriate, reminders being an obvious example. Relevance theory can account for these cases as well: it can be consistent with the principle of relevance to express known information if, for example, it would cost the audience more effort to find that information in memory than to derive it from a verbal reminder. For further discussion see Sperber and Wilson (1986:149ff.).

Logical Connectives, Relationships, and Relevance 7

interpretation that seems to have adequate contextual effects for the amount of processing effort invested, the audience can stop processing and assume that it has arrived at the intended interpretation. It need not look any further.

With regard to context selection this also means that the audience will use the contextual information most highly accessible to them first before spending more processing effort on going further afield. In other words, if someone starts talking to you about Phil, and what is said about this individual has adequate contextual effects on the assumption that it is your brother, then you will simply assume that this is indeed the Phil he means. Occasionally, it happens that the communicator was actually thinking of another person; in that case what he says about that individual will, sooner or later, cease to yield adequate contextual effects with the information you have about that individual. This lack of adequate contextual effects makes itself felt as 'not making sense': things don't seem to link up in the right way. In this way relevance theory offers an account of the notion of making sense and of its importance in communication.

2.2 The role of logical connectives

Since the nature of communication is seen to involve the inferential combination of what is said with certain contextual pieces of information, it is not difficult to see that connectives that establish logical relationships can be of great value in communication.[6] Let us illustrate this point briefly with an English example, taking the famous example from Grice (1975:161): "He is an Englishman; he is, therefore, brave."

This example is discussed from a relevance theory point of view in Blakemore (1987:82). She proposes that English *therefore* is used to "introduce a proposition that is derived as output to a synthetic inference rule." This means that it instructs the audience to treat the proposition marked by *therefore* as the conclusion to an argument in which a synthetic inference rule has applied. What is a synthetic inference rule? It is simply an inference rule that "...takes two separate assumptions as input" (Sperber and Wilson 1986:104).

This means the speaker expects the hearer to construe an argument of the kind in (1) that has at least two separate premises and yields the assumption 'he is brave' as a conclusion.

---

[6] I use the term LOGICAL here with some reservation since it can easily be misunderstood as referring to matters of standard logics only. It would perhaps be better to use the wider term INFERENTIAL here, but since the workshop referred to them as logical connectives, it seems best to follow that terminology here. Cf. also footnote 17.

8   Ernst-August Gutt

(1)   Premise 1:   ?
       Premise 2:   ?
       Conclusion: He is brave.

The task of the hearer is to find highly accessible contextual assumptions
that will complete this argument.

One of the most highly accessible contextual assumption is, of course,
the one just processed: He is an Englishman; so it would be an obvious
candidate for serving as one of the premises.

(2)   Premise 1:   He is an Englishman.
       Premise 2:   ?
       Conclusion: He is brave.

But what about premise 2? This is not difficult to supply either: a very
simple assumption that yields *he is brave* as a valid conclusion is: All Englishmen are brave.

So, the completed argument would be as in (3).

(3)   Premise 1:   He is an Englishman.
       Premise 2:   All Englishmen are brave.
       Conclusion: He is brave.

What is the point of using *therefore* here? By explicitly instructing the
audience to construe *he is brave* as the conclusion to an argument in the
context of the proposition *he is an Englishman*, the speaker narrows down or
constrains the various ways in which the utterance could have been related
to contextual assumptions; in other words, it imposes a CONSTRAINT on the
relevance of the utterance.[7] Thus, by using *therefore*, the speaker strongly
suggests to the audience to supply premise 2, *all Englishmen are brave*, as a
contextual assumption, because there are hardly any other, highly accessible
assumptions that could fill that part of the argument. This means that the
speaker is strongly implicating the truth of premise 2, in addition to that of
premise 1 and the conclusion. Such particular assumptions, which the hearer
is expected to supply in order to arrive at the speaker-intended interpretation,
are called STRONG IMPLICATURES. (In this case we are dealing with an
IMPLICATED PREMISE.)

---

[7] Note that the phrase "constraint on relevance" does not refer to a lessening of the degree
of relevance; on the contrary, constraints on relevance can be seen as increasing the relevance
of an utterance in that they aid the audience in finding the intended interpretation. For an extended treatment of this notion see Blakemore (1987).

Logical Connectives, Relationships, and Relevance 9

Consider by contrast what would have happened if the speaker had omitted *therefore*, saying simply: He is an Englishman; he is brave.

Here the audience would have no clear guidance as to how these two propositions are to be treated. It can, of course, treat them as premise and conclusion of an argument; however, this is not a necessary interpretation of the evidence. If, for example, it did not seem likely to the audience that the speaker actually believes *all Englishmen are brave*, then the audience would be entitled to look for a different interpretation. Thus it could simply be part of a listing of characteristics, without any intended implication that the bravery is seen as a consequence of being English. Perhaps that interpretation might still come to the mind of the audience; however, since the speaker has given no indication that the utterance should be interpreted in this particular way and other contextual assumptions lead to adequate contextual effects, the evidence that the communicator intended the audience to use this particular assumption is very weak. Such assumptions are, therefore, referred to as WEAK IMPLICATURES.

This is another important feature of relevance theory: it does not necessarily expect that propositions are either communicated or not communicated, but it assumes that they can be communicated with varying degrees of strength: the more essential a particular assumption is to establishing the optimal relevance of an utterance, the more strongly that particular assumption is communicated or implicated. The less essential it is to the interpretation process, the less strongly it is implicated. In other words, implicatures can differ in degree of strength. Thus, we can see that the use of logical connectives is well-motivated for guiding the audience to the speaker-intended interpretation: not only do they help the audience to access the speaker-intended context, but they also enable the communicator to strongly communicate particular contextual assumptions without having to spell them out.

3. Toward understanding pragmatic connectives in Silt'i

3.1 Preliminaries

The examples I want to look at are taken from the Silt'i language. Some of the examples are dealt with in more detail in the paper "Toward an analysis of pragmatic connectives in Silt'i" (Gutt 1988) presented at the Eighth International Conference of Ethiopian Studies in 1985. That study was exploratory rather than exhaustive, and I have not been able to do much more in this area since then. So the results presented here should be taken as preliminary rather than final. I think the analysis proposed is a reasonable

10 Ernst-August Gutt

one, but I am more interested in demonstrating the approach than arguing particular, language-specific points.

3.2 The problem

In Silt'i there is an affix, -m, whose meaning is rather hard to pin down. In many instances it seems to make little difference to the meaning, and could be translated best by 'and'. In other instances, its influence can be felt more strongly and seems to correspond to something like 'either' or 'neither' in English. Sometimes it seems to convey the meaning of 'also' or 'too'. At other times again it seems much stronger, amounting to something like 'even', sometimes acquiring almost a concessive sense, especially in conditional clauses.

Since the purpose of this presentation is not to argue for a particular analysis, but to make some basic points, I will not go into all these different uses here, but will deal only with the first two. So for now I will just briefly illustrate the first two uses: those that seem to correspond to English 'and', on the one hand, and something like 'either' on the other.

The first passage in (4) is part of a fable where a mouse has just given birth to nine little mice, and the cat comes to convey her good wishes on the delivery. The cat opens the conversation.

(4)   *5 mayraam*   *tashiillima*   *taawt'aash*   *baateet*
      Mary   youˆbeingˆwell   mayˆsheˆbringˆyouˆout   sheˆsaidˆtoˆher

        6 ufrimte   *aaw ashnam maayraam*   *taanbirash*
        theˆmouseˆm   yes   youˆm   Mary   mayˆsheˆmakeˆyouˆlive

        baateet   *7 adanimteenga*   *abbi*   *luufrite*   *bay*
        sheˆsaid   theˆcatˆmˆagain   then   toˆtheˆmouseˆtoˆher   comeˆon

        inde yesh   *innate*   *ayb*   *sici*   *waldamii*   *ihe*
        o.k.   here   this   milk   drink   theˆchildrenˆm   I

        liinzinsh   *baateet*
        letˆmeˆholdˆforˆyou   sheˆsaidˆtoˆher

5. "May Mary make you well," she (the cat) said to her. 6. And the mouse said, "Yes, and may Mary make you live/prolong your life." 7. And then the cat said again to the mouse, "Okay, come on, here drink this milk; and let me hold the children for you."

Logical Connectives, Relationships, and Relevance

The other sample passage in (5) is part of one of the various fables where the hyena (thought of as male) tricks the donkey (thought of as female). In this particular fable, the hyena challenges the donkey to a fight. Since the donkey is much stronger she pins the hyena twice. Each time the donkey gets off the hyena, letting him get up. However, the hyena cunningly claims that he had actually let himself drop to the ground voluntarily for the donkey. On these grounds he demands that the donkey, too, should let herself drop to the ground for the hyena. The stupid donkey does so, but the hyena doesn't let her get up again and eats her instead.

The part we are interested in is the final argument: the donkey is being held down by the hyena, but argues that the hyena should get off since she herself got off twice from the hyena. The hyena rejects this demand.

(5) *tee   jigg   bay   aabbeemee   bagadala*
     you(f)   quiet   say(f) my^father^m   when^he^threw^down

    alnak'aan   *baalaane*   *inkitkit ashaane*
    he^did^not^get^off he^said^and   tearing up

    baleet   *ileen*
    he^ate^her one^says

"Shut up, you! My father didn't get up either when he threw someone down!" he (the hyena) said, tore her (the donkey) to pieces, and ate her, they say.

3.2.1 Formulating a hypothesis. Just dealing with these two uses, the tempting solution would be to say either that there are two homophonous suffixes *-m,* or that the suffix *-m* has two distinct senses, one marking a conjunctive relationship and the other something like an alternative relationship. However, Ivan Lowe pointed out in his introductory lectures that it is not the most helpful way to begin one's analysis: by assuming a complex solution from the start one may miss a possible simpler solution. In fact, my analysis started from the minimal assumption that there is only one *-m* which has only one meaning, and this meaning corresponds to the inferential properties of " ∧ " (logical 'and').[8] In the interpretation process it

---

[8] This is not to suggest that connectives must always have one sense nor that there cannot be homophones. As will become clearer below, however, there is no reason to suspect that relationship-based accounts involve unnecessary multiplicity of meaning.

12   Ernst-August Gutt

amounts to an instruction to the audience to conjoin the proposition marked
by *-m* with another proposition.[9]

In the course of the analysis I came to postulate the following syntactic
properties: *-m* is suffixed to the leftmost subconstituent of the focused constituent of a sentence or to the sentence as a whole.[10]

3.2.2 Testing the hypothesis in context.

One way to test such a
hypothesis within the framework of relevance theory is to check whether the
hypothesis allows for an interpretation consistent with the principle of
relevance for passages containing *-m*.

The use illustrated in (4) is not all that exciting: it seems that the *-m* in
all cases is syntactically associated with the sentence as a whole and adds
the proposition expressed to the information processed previously. In logic,
the conjunction of two propositions in logic by *and* entitles one to infer that
both of the conjuncts are true. This may not seem very significant at this
point, but it does have pragmatic value, as we shall see below.

Example (5) is more interesting. It seems that here *-m* is associated with
a focused constituent, i.e., *abbee* 'my father'. It would go too far to present
the relevance-theoretical account of focus here in detail. What is important
here is that the distinction between focus and background makes a difference
as to how the respective pieces of information contribute to relevance: the
focused constituent pinpoints that piece of information that makes for relevance,
i.e., that is intended to have contextual effects. The background, by contrast, has
no contextual effects of its own but contributes to relevance by making more
accessible contextual assumptions needed for interpreting the utterance.

Technically, a background entailment of an utterance with focus is obtained by substituting the focused constituent by a semantic variable. Now
the sentence we want to concentrate on is (6).

(6)   *aabbeemee   bagadala   alnak'aan*
       my^father^*m* when^he^threw^down (a victim) he^did^not^get^off
       My father didn't get up either when he threw someone down.

---

[9] As Blakemore (1987) and Blass (1990) have shown, connectives and particles tend
to work by imposing such constraints on the relevance, hence on the interpretation of the
utterances.

[10] I am not entirely satisfied with the formulation of these synthetic conditions. It may be
possible to eliminate the disjunction here if one assumes that the focus can extend to the sentence as a whole. Furthermore, there is some evidence that *-m* is not attached to the leftmost
constituent when the focus is on a whole subordinate clause. However, since these syntactic
details do not affect the thrust of the general argument, I will not pursue them now.

Logical Connectives, Relationships, and Relevance 13

If the focused constituent is *aabbeemee*, then the next background entailment is: [X] *bagadala alnak'aan* 'X when^throws^down (a victim) X^not^get^off' where X represents a semantic variable that can range over individuals, perhaps best represented by English 'someone'. Note that the background is not itself a complete proposition: first, because of the variable X, and second because time reference has not been assigned yet, so that a better paraphrase in English might be: 'when someone throws (a victim) down he (does not) get off'.[11]

Now by definition the background entailment does not achieve relevance in its own right. But why, then, is it there at all? As will be recalled, relevance depends not only on the contextual effects achieved, but also on the amount of processing effort spent. It is this second factor that is operational here: the background entailment contributes to the overall relevance of the utterance by making some of the contextual information more accessible, and hence by reducing the processing effort.

And this is how it works: though not a complete proposition in itself, the background entailment does provide a schema or blueprint which the audience can complete to fully propositional form with comparative ease.

As we said above, essentially two pieces of information are missing from the entailment: the variable must be replaced by a referent. One of the most highly accessible referents is, of course, the hyena, so it becomes the most obvious candidate. With regard to time reference, since the hyena has just got the donkey on the ground at the time of speaking, the most accessible time reference is that of the time of speaking. So the proposition can easily be completed into 'when the hyena throws (a victim) down he does not get off'. With the conjunction in effect, we get the partial interpretation 'when the hyena throws (a victim) down he does not get off' and 'when the hyena's father got (a victim) down he did not get off'.

The fact that *aabbee* is focused furthermore means that it is the relevance-establishing part of the utterance, and so the audience will concentrate on this concept for contextual effects. One important feature of mental concepts in the relevance-theoretical framework is that they are assumed to be associated with different "entries" in memory, one of which is the so-called encyclopedic entry. The encyclopedic entry of a concept contains all sorts of information a person has come to collect about the referent to which it refers, and when a concept is being thought about (mentally represented), the encyclopedic entry is opened up and the information contained there

---

[11] This follows from the assumption that the logical form of an utterance is incomplete in a number of ways, including the exact time reference; thus, a sentence in the simple past tense can refer to virtually any point of time in the past. The time appropriate to that particular utterance is worked out pragmatically by consistency with the principle of relevance. Since the background is an entailment of logical form, it also has no fixed time reference yet.

14   Ernst-August Gutt

becomes available for use. Now it seems that one assumption associated with the concept father in Silt'i seems to be something like 'like father, like son', or more formally: If father does X, then son does X.

So now the set of propositions in (7) is available.

(7)   Utterance: When the hyena's father threw (a victim) down he did not
                     get off
       Contextual assumption 1:   and when the hyena throws (a victim)
                                    down he did not get off
       Contextual assumption 2:   If the father did X, then the son does X.

As can be seen, contextual assumption 2 and the proposition expressed in the utterance constitute an inferential argument of the form in (8).

(8)   Premise 1: If father did X, then son does X.
       Premise 2: The father did not get off when he threw down (a victim).
       The son does not get off when he throws down (a victim).

Now this is all very well, but what reason would an audience who derived this interpretation have to believe that it had found the right, i.e., speaker-intended interpretation?

The answer is that it is entitled to assume this if this interpretation is the first one that comes to mind and seems consistent with the principle of relevance.

As far as coming to mind first is concerned, the interpretation suggested seems to be a good candidate in that it involves only assumptions that can be assumed to be highly accessible to a Silt'i audience.

To be consistent with the principle of relevance, the interpretation has to yield adequate contextual effects. What contextual effects does this interpretation achieve? To answer this question, we need to have a closer look at contextual effects.

Contextual effects can be of three kinds: they can consist in the addition of contextual implications, in the cancellation of contextual assumptions, and in the strengthening of contextual assumptions. Contextual implications are defined as implications that are not derivable from the utterance alone, nor from the context alone, but only from an inference that uses premises from both. Put in less technical terms, the contextual implications of an utterance lead to new insights that are related to what one already knew.

Cancellation of contextual assumptions results when there is a contradiction between two assumptions, then one of them may get erased from memory. Put simply, this accounts for our intuition that it is relevant to discover where one has been wrong.

Logical Connectives, Relationships, and Relevance 15

The effect of strengthening existing contextual assumptions has to do with the fact that we do not just believe or not believe certain propositions to be true, but we can hold them true with varying degrees of confidence, or strength. Thus we are fully convinced of the truth of some assumptions, e.g., that there is a sun, but we may be less confident about the truth of the statement that early man had a lower intelligence than modern man. Therefore, one way of context modification lies in the possibility of altering the strength with which assumptions are held to be true.

Our example here seems to involve both the cancellation of one contextual assumption and the strengthening of another. When the donkey agreed to drop to the ground for the hyena, it did so no doubt on the assumption that the hyena would let her get up again. So at that point she entertained a thought, that is a contextual assumption, like "The hyena will get off me". When the hyena gave no indication that he would get off the donkey, however, another thought was likely to enter the donkey's mind, "The hyena will not get off me." Thus, the donkey would have come to entertain two mutually contradictory assumptions. What happens in such cases? Relevance theory proposes that in this case our mind compares the relative strength of the two contradictory assumptions, and if one of them is weaker than the other, then it will be erased from the mind, and so the contradiction will be resolved.

What, then, about the comparative strength of the two assumptions involved in our example? As the donkey's request indicates, her belief that the hyena would get up was based, rather naively, on a notion of fairness: since the donkey got off, so would or should the hyena.

The assumption implicated by the hyena, however, seems much stronger because it is not simply asserted, but presented as the conclusion of an argument the premises of which seem to be quite strong: there would be little doubt that the hyena's father never let a victim go of a good will, and the truth of the idea 'like father, like son' would certainly not be doubted either.[12] So the likely result is the erasure of the contextual assumption: The hyena will get off. In other words, the hyena's reply is designed to remove any doubt in the donkey's mind about its intentions. It is certainly not going to get off; the fate of the donkey is sealed.

At the same time, contextual assumption that the hyena would not get off him—probably not really fully believed by the donkey at first—would now be considerably strengthened, again because of the argument structure and the strength of the premises on which it is built.

---

[12] Relevance theory assumes that the strength of the conclusion of an argument depends on the strength of the weakest premise.

16 Ernst-August Gutt

Thus, the interpretation we arrived at would at least have the two contextual effects of cancelling one contextual assumption and strengthening another. In this way it would at least satisfy the minimum requirement for relevance.

So it seems that we have arrived at a fairly plausible interpretation of this utterance, assuming nothing more about -*m* than that its meaning corresponds to that of logical 'and', and that syntactically it can be associated with focus.[13]

3.2.3 Interpretation and rhetorical relationships.

We have proposed an analysis of the speaker-intended interpretation of this utterance without any reference to RHETORICAL or INTERPROPOSITIONAL RELATIONSHIPS. How then does relevance theory relate to these notions? After all, we do have intuitions about them. For example, the way we just analyzed the story seems to suggest a hereditary, almost causal, relationship: sons inherit their fathers' natures, so the hyena's behavior is causally conditioned by its natural traits; it actually couldn't behave otherwise. In other words, the thrust of the argument might be seen to be: How can I help eating you up? I am simply acting in accordance with the nature I inherited from my father.

This might not be the only possible interpretation, however. We might feel that the hyena is giving some kind of moral justification: it is right to follow one's father's example, therefore, it is morally justifiable for the hyena to eat the donkey.

Since we can and do have such intuitions, where do they come from and how can we account for them in the relevance theory framework?

The answer seems to be that these intuitions simply reflect what particular contextual assumptions we use in the interpretation process. Let us begin with the intuition that there is a cause-effect relationship. One of the contextual assumptions we assumed to be involved here was (contextual assumption 2 in (7)) 'If the father did X, then the son does X'.

We first assumed this assumption to simply reflect a popular belief, as expressed in the proverb 'Like father, like son'. It is, however, possible that more is involved; it is possible that people believe more specifically that heredity is involved here, that is, that the son inherits the nature and behavior of the father: If the father did X, then by the laws of heredity the son will do X. This belief assumes that the father's nature is the natural cause of the

---

[13] It should be noted that in our discussion we have interpreted the hyena's utterance from the point of view of his audience, i.e., of the donkey. If we continued to interpret it from the perspective of the storyteller's audience we would find further contextual effects; thus, the naivete of the donkey in assuming that the hyena would let her go would almost certainly have the effect of strengthening and solidifying the cultural assumption that donkeys are stupid, and conversely that hyenas are clever.

Logical Connectives, Relationships, and Relevance

son's nature, and it is this assumption that gives rise to the impression that a cause-effect relationship might be involved here.

What about the impression of a justificatory relationship? This would have arisen if, in addition perhaps to the assumption of natural cause, the assumption 'If the father did X, then it is right for the son to do X' was also highly accessible.

Together with the other propositions already introduced, this would allow the conclusion 'It was right for the hyena not to get off the donkey'. Which of these various assumptions would be implicated and with what strength would be determined by consistency with the principle of relevance against the context envisaged by the communicator.

This account is significant for our discussion in a number of respects. First, it shows that the interpropositional relationships we intuitively felt to be there are not semantic clues to help us find the intended interpretation; rather they are possible abstractions we can make about the interpretation itself once we have found it. In other words, the interpropositional relationships do not determine the meaning of the utterance, but can be derived from it.

Second, these relationships were not signalled or encoded by the connective itself. Rather, they follow from an interpretation that arose from the complex interaction of the proposition expressed by the utterance, of the constraint on relevance imposed by the connective -m, and of certain contextual assumptions, all interacting under the criterion of consistency with the principle of relevance.

This is not to say that languages cannot ever use connectives to encode such specific relationships. There is no reason why they should not. This is a language-specific, lexical matter rather than one of concern for a general theory of either semantics or communication.

And this brings us to the third point: there is no need to assume that there is a closed set of interpropositional relationships, either for one language or universally for all languages, that allows us to adequately describe how the various units of texts relate to each other. As we saw in our example, the link between the propositions is achieved inferentially by specific contextual assumptions. This, in fact, explains why relationship typologies find it so difficult to provide adequate categories: there is no reason why contextual assumptions should fall into such categories.

Fourth, relational typologies fall short of bringing out the intended interpretation; they focus on general abstractions but do not reconstruct the interpretation with its specific contextual assumptions. Consider the typical relationship-based analysis of the utterance, "The car is clean, so John must have washed it" (Larson 1984:306) in (9).

18   Ernst-August Gutt

(9)   Grounds: The car is clean,
        Conclusion: (so I conclude that) John must have washed it.

This analysis does not show a valid inference: the proposition 'the car is clean' by itself does not entail that 'John must have washed it'. Rather, what is minimally needed is another premise like:[14] If the car is clean, John must have washed it.

When an assumption like premise 1 is supplied, the inference becomes valid.

(10)   Premise 1:   The car is clean.
        Premise 2:   If the car is clean, John must have washed it.
        Conclusion: John must have washed the car.

It seems somewhat implausible, however, that premise 2 would be available as a ready-made contextual assumption. It is more likely that there is another complex argument in the place of premise 2, that starts from the general, obvious assumption: If the car is clean, someone must have washed it.

On the basis of other contextual information the speaker inferred that the individual someone was John rather than anybody else. Perhaps the speaker knew that John was the only person around who could have washed the car, or he saw John's watch lying besides the implements that had been used for washing the car, and so forth. The use of the modal *must* indicates that this assumption goes back to inference rather than direct observation.

The importance of reconstructing these implicit inferences can be seen when we try to explain why one cannot simply link up any two propositions by *so* to create a grounds–conclusion relationship. Consider: A meteorite exploded, so my baby brother must have dirtied his nappies [diapers] again. Though nonsensical, this example could easily be analyzed in terms of relationships as in (11).

(11)   Grounds: A meteorite exploded,
        Conclusion: (so I conclude that) my baby brother must have dirtied his nappies again.

---

[14] The qualification MINIMALLY NEEDED means that by this one assumption the argument could be completed. As I point out later, however, this assumption itself is more likely the conclusion to another sequence of inferences.

Logical Connectives, Relationships, and Relevance 19

The analysis does not show up in any way that this interpretation is implausible. If we try to approach it inferentially, however, we see that it minimally implicates something like the argument in (12).

(12)   Premise 1:   Whenever a meteorite explodes, my baby brother dirties his nappies.
       Premise 2:   A meteorite exploded.
       Conclusion: My baby brother must have dirtied his nappies again.

Now according to relevance theory, by inducing the hearer to construct this argument, he expects him to supply the implicated premise 1 or a set of inferentially equivalent assumptions; however, at least with our cultural background, premise 1 itself is not a plausible assumption, nor does there seem to be a plausible argument that would be inferentially equivalent to it. Thus, the reason why we find it implausible, is that we are unable to supply plausible assumptions that would be necessary to interpret the utterance along the lines indicated by the speaker. Thus, relevance theory can help us to distinguish between plausible and implausible interpretations: implausible interpretations involve implausible assumptions.

If all this is correct, then what the analysis of connectives requires is not the development of a set of relationships; rather, we need to discover what semantic, and perhaps also syntactic, properties these connectives have and how they contribute to an interpretation consistent with the principle of relevance, against the contextual knowledge of the audience.[15]

In the next section I want to draw attention to three practical ways of testing hypotheses about the properties of connectives.

---

[15] It may be objected that my own analysis of -m relies on an interpropositional relationship, that is, the logical relationship established by 'and'. Hence, are we not just reducing the number of interpropositional relationships to a smaller, more basic set, perhaps equivalent to the basic operations of standard logics? First, Sperber and Wilson (1986:87) do not assume that there is a "radical distinction between concepts such as *and*, *if...then*, and *or*, which are regarded as proper logical concepts, and concepts such as *when*, *know*, *run*, *bachelor*, which are considered nonlogical. Following another tradition, we regard these other concepts as also determining logical implications. Which concepts do or do not have logical entries, which rules these contain...are all matters for empirical investigation." Thus, relevance theory does not assume there to be a small set of logical relationships in the first place.

Second, some argumentative connectives do not encode a logical or inferential relationship at all. For example, Blakemore (1987:141) shows that *anyway* can indicate "that the proposition it introduces is relevant in a context that does not include the immediately preceding remark." This meaning is not reducible to any more basic, logical relationship, and there is no reason why it should be. As pointed out already, the meaning of such connectives is largely a matter of language-specific semantics.

3.3 Testing hypotheses about connectives

3.3.1 Testing hypotheses in texts. We have just looked at one way of testing one's hypothesis about the meaning of a logical connective: apply the hypothesis to some given text or text portion and see if it allows for an interpretation that is arguably consistent with the principle of relevance, making use only of the notions supplied by the theoretical framework. If no such interpretation can be proposed, then the assumed meaning of the connective may be wrong.

Suppose, for example, that we found occurrences of -*m* where no interpretation consistent with the principle of relevance could be construed on the assumption that the meaning of -*m* corresponded to that of logical 'and'. This would naturally suggest that our hypothesis is inaccurate, and we would have to look for a better one.

3.3.2 Testing the context-accessing function. Relevance theory allows us to test our hypotheses in another way: by exploiting the fact that a connective may have a context-accessing function. Thus, according to our analysis in its focal use, -*m* should suggest a certain kind of context to the audience.

Below is a little experiment I did that seems to corroborate the hypothesis that -*m* is focus-associated. In this experiment I gave the sentences in (13) one by one to three native Silt'i speakers.

(13) a. *wut'at ayaam laam liyookb ulbaarag heeda*
     Monday day cow he^to^buy Ulbarag he^went
     On Monday he went to Ulbarag to buy a cow.

    b. *wut'atim ayaam laam liyookb ulbaarag heeda*
      Monday-*m* day cow he^to^buy Ulbarag he^went
      Also on Monday he went to Ulbarag to buy a cow.

    c. *wut'at ayaam laamim liyookb ulbaarag heeda*
      Monday day   cow-*m* he^to^buy Ulbarag he^went
      On Monday he went to Ulbarag to buy also a cow.

    d. *wut'at ayaam laam liyookbim ulbaarag heeda*
      Monday day cow he^to^buy^*m* Ulbarag he^went
      On Monday he went to Ulbarag also to buy a cow.

Logical Connectives, Relationships, and Relevance

e. *wut'at   ayaam   laam   liyookb   ulbaaragim   heeda*
Monday   day   cow   heˆtoˆbuy Ulbarag-*m*   heˆwent
On Monday he went also to Ulbarag to buy a cow.

I did not provide them with any contextual information, but as we considered each sentence, I asked the test person whether it communicated to him anything beyond what was actually said, and if so, what. Their answers, given independently of one another, are summarized in (14).

(14) a. No interpretation given beyond the information expressed in (13a).

b. He seems to have gone previously.

c. He wanted to buy something else besides a cow or he had gone previously and now went again to also buy a cow.

d. He has also other business. (The K'ibbat dialect speaker inadvertently used (13c) when referring to (13d), and one other speaker said that he preferred (13c) instead of (13d).)

e. The K'ibbat dialect speaker rejected (13e). The other informants interpreted it as suggesting that he had gone elsewhere before.

Now it is not hard to see that the answers differ according to the position of the suffix *-m*, and as I try to show in my paper (Gutt 1988), the differences correlate well with the predictions of relevance theory with regard to the focus-background distinction. Thus, in (13b) *-m* marked the time phrase *wut'at ayaam* 'on Monday' and in (14b) we find this replaced by another time phrase: 'previously'. In (13c) *-m* marked the direct object *laam* 'cow', and in (14c) we find the substitution 'something else besides a cow', and so forth.

To briefly examine just one of these examples, (13b) could have the underlying structure *[wut'at-m ayaam] laam liyookb ulbaarag heeda*. Here the focused constituent would be the time phrase *wut'at ayaam* 'on Monday', with the *-m* suffixed to its leftmost subconstituent *wut'at* 'Monday'. Variable substitution at the focus yields the background entailment *[X] laam liyookb ulbaarag heeda*. The X is meant to indicate an appropriate semantic variable, ranging in this case over time expressions. By using the focused sentence (13b), the speaker induces the hearer to look for a contextual proposition corresponding closely to the background entailment, but with some value of X substituted at the focus. This seems to be borne out by the fact that in our example the informants suggested that the person had gone 'previously'.

22   Ernst-August Gutt

This brief sketch may suffice here to give an idea of how one can test whether or not a connective constrains the use of contextual assumptions in a particular way. For further discussion of the data itself the reader is referred to Gutt (1988).

3.3.3 Testing by predicted failure of communication.

Relevance theory accounts not only for regular, normal communication, but it explains communication breakdowns as well. In accordance with this, I tried to think of an utterance where the presence of -*m* would be predicted to lead to a breakdown of communication. What sort of case could that be?

According to relevance theory, the focused constituent must be the relevance-establishing part of the utterance. But suppose one construed an example where the focused information is already highly accessible in the context. In that case, the focal use of -*m* should be felt to be inappropriate. If this prediction turned out to be true, it could be taken as supporting evidence that the analysis is likely to be true.

I used the utterances in (15) to test the hypothesis.

(15) a. *safiiya   saalo   araashin   irasoot   ishlaan   baat*
          Safiiya Salo   farmer^he^is to^plough   he^can   she^said
          Safiya said, "Salo is a farmer; he can plough."

      b. *safiiya   saalo   araashin   irasootam   ishlaan   baat*
          Safiiya Salo   farmer^he^is to^plough-*m* he^can   she^said

As can be seen, the two utterances differ only in the occurrence of -*m* in the (15b). Yet the three informants to whom the data were presented independently of each other rejected (15b) while accepting (15a). This seems to confirm our prediction, and can be accounted for along the following lines.

Interpreting -*m* as focally-used, we obtain the underlying representation *[irasoota-m] ishlaan* and the background *[X] ishlaan*.

According to focus theory and by consistency with the principle of relevance, the increment of information that one needs to add to the background [x] *ishlaan* in order to obtain the underlying representation [irasoota] *ishlaan* must be the main point, i.e., the context modifying element, of the utterance. As the example has been construed, however, that underlying representation is immediately preceded by *saalo araashin* 'Salo he^is^farmer'.

In Silt'i culture, this would normally entail very obviously that Salo is able to plough; this is a stereotyped assumption stored in the encyclopedic entry of *araashi* 'farmer'. Furthermore, according to relevance theory, the content of the immediately preceding utterance constitutes a highly accessible context for the utterance under consideration. Taken together this means

Logical Connectives, Relationships, and Relevance

that there is a highly accessible context for the underlying representation that contains what is supposed to be its main point. In other words, the focused part, which should establish the relevance, is, in fact, already a highly accessible contextual assumption. Under these conditions, the audience would find it difficult to arrive at an interpretation consistent with the principle of relevance, and it is this difficulty which can be taken as the underlying cause of the speakers' rejection of this example.[16]

4. Conclusion

In summary, we see that relevance theory offers us a cognition-based framework that can help us to arrive at a relevance-based reconstruction of the speaker-intended meaning. Any such reconstruction is open to falsification by the criterion of consistency with the principle of relevance. These reconstructions of the speaker-intended meaning allow us to test hypotheses about the semantic (and other) linguistic properties of connectives, both in running text and by experimentation. There is no need to look for or develop a set of interpropositional relationships in order to spell out how the various utterances of a text relate to each other.

References

Ballard, D. Lee, Robert J. Conrad, and R. E. Longacre. 1971. The deep and surface grammar of interclausal relations. Foundations of language 7:70–118.

Beekman, John and John Callow. 1974. Translating the word of God. Grand Rapids: Zondervan.

Blakemore, Diane. 1987. Semantic constraints on relevance. Oxford: Blackwell.

Blass, Regina. 1990. Relevance relations in discourse: A study with special reference to Sissala. Cambridge: Cambridge University Press.

Callow, John. 1982. A semantic structure analysis of Second Thessalonians. Dallas: Summer Institute of Linguistics.

Callow, Kathleen. 1988. Which came first, man or message? Notes on Translation 2(3):1–23.

---

[16] The test results need not be as straightforward as this; in fact, in a second test the informant reactions seemed to disagree. Even this disagreement provided valuable clues about the interpretation process and could be accounted for in terms of relevance theory. For details see Gutt (1988).

———. 1998. Man and message. Lanham, Md.: Summer Institute of Lingusitics and University Press of America.

Grice, Paul. 1975. Logic and conversation. In Peter Cole and Jerry L. Morgan (eds.), Syntax and semantics, 3:41–58. New York: Academic Press.

Gutt, Ernst-August. 1988. Toward an analysis of pragmatic connectives in Silt'i. Proceedings of the Eighth International Conference of Ethiopian Studies, Addis Ababa, 26–30 November 1984, 1:665–78. Huntingdon: ELM Publications.

Larson, Mildred L. 1984. Meaning-based translation: A guide to cross-language equivalence. Lanham: University Press of America.

Longacre, Robert A. 1983. The grammar of discourse. New York: Plenum Press.

Mann, William C. and Sandra A. Thompson. 1986. Rhetorical structure theory: Description and construction of text structures. Information Sciences Institute Reprint Series ISI/RS-86–174. Marina del Rey: University of Southern California.

———. 1987. Rhetorical structure theory: A theory of text organization. Information Sciences Institute Reprint Series ISI/RS-87–190. Marina del Rey: University of Southern California.

Pike, Kenneth L. and Evelyn G. Pike. 1977. Grammatical analysis. Dallas: Summer Institute of Linguistics and The University of Texas at Arlington.

Sperber, Dan and Deirdre Wilson. 1986. Relevance: Communication and cognition. Oxford: Blackwell

The Grammar of Sentence Conjunctions in St. Lucian French Creole

David B. Frank

The sentence is commonly considered to be an independent unit in the grammar of any language. While it is true that the kinds of sentences that linguists make up to illustrate their theories usually appear to be independent and complete, in the real world, sentences are connected to each other by various means. Sentence grammarians tend to ignore cohesive devices, such as sentence conjunctions, which link one sentence to another, because they don't fit neatly into their theories. One way to really find out what kinds of facts a linguistic theory needs to account for is to take naturally-occurring language data as the basis for devising theories. This article is a study of sentence conjunctions—the words or phrases that denote relationships between sentences—in St. Lucian French Creole texts. It is part of a more comprehensive study undertaken with the goal of understanding how logical relations are expressed in the language and how discourse is structured.[1]

---

[1] I wish to thank Paul and Cindy Crosbie for collecting and processing some of the data used in this study. I also wish to thank Catherine Rountree, who performed a semantic analysis of the Crosbies' data, which helped me in doing this grammatical analysis. And I especially wish to thank the following persons for providing the texts that are analyzed here: Michael Ambrose, Wilfred Auguste, Benny Ghirawoo, Cletus Henry, May Joseph, Mano Leon, Francis Marcion, and Mary Tobierre.

26   David B. Frank

Viola Waterhouse (1963), in her article 'Independent and Dependent Sentences', has pointed out that some sentences cannot be seen as independent. She discusses several types of dependent sentences, but the type that I wish to focus on in this article is her ADDITIVE type. An additive dependent sentence, according to Waterhouse, involves "a sequence-marking particle or phrase, such as *therefore, moreover, consequently, on the other hand,* and the like" (p. 45). Thus, this article is actually a study of additive[2] dependent sentences. In order to distinguish among different types of dependent sentences of this sort, I have benefitted from Halliday and Hasan's (1976) analysis of cohesion in English discourse, the comprehensive analysis of English grammar by Quirk et al. (1972), and a study of universal semantic relations by Beekman et al. (1981).

Five types of conjunctive relations between sentences

There are five major types of conjunctive relations between sentences in St. Lucian French Creole. Another way of saying this is that there are five major additive dependent sentence types. These five types of relations between sentences are made explicit through the use of a particular conjunction or set of conjunctions, and are as follows: additive (made explicit through the use of *osi, épi,* or *èvèk*); sequential (*apwé, then*); contrastive (*mé*); resultative (*kon sa, ében, so*); and causal (*paskè*). These five categories and examples will be described in the following sections.

Additive

An additive relation between sentences simply means "Here is some more information." The use of the sentence conjunction *osi* 'also' signals that the sentence it is attached to has an additive relation to what has gone before it in the stream of speech as in (1).

(1)   *jou apwémidi sala, lè mwen wivé lakay, mwen twouvé fwè mwen té ja la. osi gwanmanman mwen épi gwanpapa mwen té ja la*

        That afternoon, when I arrived home, I found my brother was already there. *Also*, my grandmother and my grandfather were already there.

---

[2] That is, "additive" in the way that Waterhouse uses the term. In this article I have a more specific use for the term additive than Waterhouse has.

Grammar of Sentence Conjunctions in St. Lucian Creole 27

Although the use of the sentence conjunction *osi* is the clearest indication that an additive relationship is in effect, the conjuctions *épi* or *èvèk,* both meaning *'and',* are more commonly used to mark an additive sentence.

(2) *mé i té ja kwiyé tèlman, jis tan i vin anwé. i pwen ti manmay-la, i mennen'y mouté lakay manman'y.* **evèk** *madanm-lan wété épi vwa'y anwé pou jis tan i mò*

But she had already cried so much that she lost her voice. She took the little child, she brought her up to her mother's home. *And* the woman remained without her voice until the time she died.

A third possibility for an additive sentence might begin *with èk lòt bagay-la sé sa* 'and another thing is this'. And a fourth very common possibility in natural speech is that the additive relationship is not expressed formally through the use of any conjunction or phrase, as in (3), taken from a text where a man is telling his father why he should not go out at night.

(3) *piski abwézan ou pa jenn kon ou té yé. ou pa ka byen wè klè ankò. kouway-la ou té ni-an ha pèd. ou sa tonbé adan an kannal si ou alé òswè*

Because now you are not as young as you used to be. You can no longer see very well. The strength you used to have is already lost. You could fall into a ditch if you go out at night.

In (3), every sentence after the first has an additive relationship to what goes before. The speaker is making a list of reasons why his father should not go out. The additive relationship in this case is not signalled through the use of a conjunction, but *osi* or *èvèk* could very well have gone at the beginning of each of these additive sentences. The lack of a conjunction where it might have gone in examples like this is called ASYNDETON. As Quirk et al. (1972:550) explain in reference to English,

> The term coordination is used by some grammarians for both syndetic coordination—when explicit indicators of coordination are present—and asyndetic coordination—when the relationship of coordination is not marked overtly... Not all juxtaposed words, phrases or clauses are manifestations of asyndetic coordination. The possibility of inserting the coordinator is evidence that the construction is asyndetic coordination.

Quirk et al. use the concept of asyndeton to explain the relationships between words, phrases, or clauses, and its use here is extended to apply to relationships between sentences as well.

A formula could be devised for describing what I call the additive sentence type. This sentence type involves a sentence nucleus optionally in combination with an additive sentence conjuction.

(4)   additive sentence = (additive sentence conjunction) sentence nucleus

This formula states that an additive sentence is comprised of an optional additive sentence conjunction and a sentence nucleus. If the additive sentence conjunction is not present, then it is implicit, and it could just as well be present. The set of additive sentence conjunctions includes *osi, épi, èvèk,* and *èk* (a variant form of *èvèk*). Of this set, *osi* is the most diagnostic for determining whether a particular sentence is of the additive sentence type.

Sequential

A sequential relationship between sentences is very similar to an additive relationship. In this case, there is a time ordering between the referential content of a pair of sentences. This sequential ordering is made explicit, or can at least potentially be made specific, through the use of a sequential sentence conjunction such as *apwé* or *then* as in (5):[3]

(5)   *manman pléwé an chay sé moun-an oliwon vini.* **apwé** *manman bay ti manmay-la an tas dité èk on chaplé an kou'y*

The mother cried so much that all the people around there came. *Then* the mother gave the little child a cup of tea and a rosary around her neck.

Though *apwé* could be glossed 'then', it could alternatively be seen as an abbreviated form of the phrase *apwé sa* 'after that', which can also serve as a sequential sentence conjunction.

Another possibility is that a sequential sentence conjunction could occur with *èvèk* or *épi* (discussed above). The excerpt in (6) from a narrative text about an automobile accident illustrates several of the possibilities.

---

[3] *then* is borrowed from English. The use of this recent borrowing from English is actually more common than the use of the more traditional *apwé,* which is derived from French.

Grammar of Sentence Conjunctions in St. Lucian Creole

(6) *loto-a glisé asou an woul douvan-an èk dèyè'y an lézè pou an bon distans, épi i tounen viwé fasad vyé fò.* **a menm di tan** *i antwé adan an kannal asou lòt koté chimyen-an, épi i volé mouté èk tounen asou do'y. i tonbé an kannal-la asou an go wòch épi tèt li anfondwé....* **ek apwé tout sa,** *anyen pa wivé nou....* **apwé** *sa mwen wè sé dyé ki fè miwak sala wivé mwen / pou i moutwé mwen an lison épi pou i kwiyé mwen viyé.* **apwé** *mwen kité doudou-a épi mwen fini èk kalité lavi sala èk mwen viwé an chimyen dyé*

The car skidded on one of the front wheels with its rear in the air for a good distance, and it turned around facing Vieux Fort. *At the same time* it entered into a ditch on the other side of the road, and it flew up and turned on its back. It fell in the ditch on top of a big rock with its roof caved in... *And after all that,* we weren't hurt... *After that,* I saw it was God who made this miracle happen to me, so he could teach me a lesson and so he could call me back. *Then* I left my girlfriend and I finished with that kind of life and I returned to God's road.

Example (6) illustrates the following: 1) *apwé* and *apwé sa* can both be used to explicitly mark a sequence; 2) *èk* can optionally precede the sequential sentence conjunction, as in *èk apwé tout sa;* 3) *a menm di tan* 'at the same time' is another sequential sentence conjunction; and 4) sometimes a sequential relationship is encoded on the sentence level, as in the first sentence in which there is as sequential relationship between two clauses.

The fact that *èk, èvèk,* or *épi* could occur with a sequential sentence conjunction does not help define the sequential relationship between sentences, except that it shows that the additive and sequential sentence types are closely related: none of these three conjunctions could occur at the beginning of a contrastive or causal sentence (described below). What distinguishes the additive and sequential sentence types is that a sequential sentence conjunction could not occur at the beginning of an additive sentence, even together with *èvèk,* etc., and so in this respect the additive sentence type is defined negatively.

A sequential sentence conjunction is sometimes absent in examples of sequential sentences. The conjunctions *èk, èvèk,* or *épi* may be present, or there may be no sentence conjunction at all. In either case, the sequential sentence will be considered asyndetic. Example (7), from a hortatory text in which a father is warning his son not to try to cross the road by himself, illustrates this.

30 David B. Frank

(7) *an machin kay pété bouden'w, épi ou kay mò, épi ou pa kay wè ni manman'w ni papa'w ankò. epi yo kay pwen'w. yo kay mété'w. yo kay fè an twou. yo kay téwé'w anba tè-a. epi yo kay kouvè'w épi tè. épi ou yonn kay wété la*

A truck will burst your belly, and you will die, and you will not see either your mother nor your father again. And they will take you. They will put you down. They will make a hole. They will bury you under the ground. And they will cover you with earth, and you alone will remain there.

Each sentence of (7) after the first one *could* have begun with *apwé* or one of the other sequential sentence conjunctions. Thus they are considered to be asyndetic sequential sentences. A formula for the sequential sentence type is given in (8).

(8) sequential sentence = (sequential sentence conjunctions) sentence nucleus

The set of sequential sentence conjunctions includes *apwé, then* (both meaning 'then'), *apwé sa* 'after that', *lè sala* 'at that time', and *a menm di tan* 'at the same time'. The last of these is actually in a different subcategory from the rest, since it denotes simultaneity rather than sequence.

Contrastive

The contrastive relationship between sentences is actually a cover term for at least two semantically distinguishable relationships: contrast and con‑ traexpectatation. These two are not distinguished in the grammar, however: both are expressed through the use of the contrastive sentence conjunction *mé* 'but'. A purely semantic analysis such as Beekman et al. (1981) would distinguish between contrast and contraexpectation, but a grammatical analysis such as the present one confines itself to grammatical structure, i.e., the cooperation between grammatical form and grammmatical meaning. Examples (9) and (10) show the contrastive relationship between sentences.

(9) *so lapen sépawé'y èk lapen ba'y dé gwo èvèk i bay lapen dé piti. **mé** still bètafé p'òkò té satisfé*

So Rabbit divided it and Rabbit gave him two big ones and he gave himself two little ones. *But* still Firefly was not yet satisfied.

Grammar of Sentence Conjunctions in St. Lucian Creole 31

(10) *lapen just lévé. i pwan tout bagaj pwéson bètafé-a èk i alé lakay li épi'y, èvèk bètafé wèsté san pwéson. mé lapen té ni tout pwéson-an*

Rabbit just got up. He took all Firefly's fish and he went to his home with it, and Firefly remained without any fish. *But* Rabbit had all the fish.

In (9), the second sentence has a logical relationship of contraexpectation to the first. In (10) the relationship is simple contrast. In both, the second sentences are examples of contrastive sentences, with the relationship expressed through the use of the contrastive sentence conjunction *mé*.

Again, sometimes the relationship is asyndetic, as in (11).

(11) *i chaché ti manmay-la, i kwiyé, i bat tout wazyé, i bat gwan bwa ka chaché'y. i pa wè'y*

She looked for the child, she called, she searched through the bushes, she searched through the forest looking for her. She didn't see her.

The structure of a contrastive sentence can be expressed in a formula as in (12).

(12) contrastive sentence = (contrastive sentence conjunction) sentence nucleus

In other words, a contrastive sentence consists of a sentence nucleus often, but not always, preceded by *mé*. If this contrastive sentence conjunction is not present in a particular example, it is implied.

Resultative

The set of resultative sentence conjunctions includes *kon sa, ében, so,*[4] and *alò*, which have distinguishable glosses in other contexts, but in their use as sentence conjunctions they all mean 'so' (more or less). Resultative sentence conjunctions all serve to mark and introduce a resultative sentence. The logical relationships expressed through a resultative sentence include at least three kinds: reason-result, grounds-conclusion, and plan-execution. Though these three kinds of relationships are distinguishable semantically,

---

[4] *so* is more commonly used than the others listed here. Again we see that St. Lucian speakers of French Creole seem to prefer to use a sentence conjunction borrowed from English rather than the more traditional counterpart derived from French. The same holds true for certain other functors.

32 David B. Frank

they are not distinguishable grammatically; they are all expressed through what is called a resultative sentence in this article. The examples in (13)–(15) show this relationship.

(13) *ek dòktè-a gadé mwen. i èkzanminé mwen. i pa jwenn anyen mwen ni.* **kon sa** *i vwéyé mwen lopital*

And the doctor looked at me. He examined me. He didn't find anything wrong with me. *So* he sent me to the hospital.

(14) *tig an bwa jik atchwèlman. i p'òkò sa viwé pyès koté.* **eben** *si ou vlé ti, sé an bwa ou kay ni pou aché'y*

Tiger is in the woods to this day. He cannot return anywhere. *So* if you want Tiger, it is in the woods you will need to search for him.

(15) *bètafé, lapen di, konpè èspéyé mwen. mwen ka vini. mwen ka alé lòt bo-a la. mwen kay pwan dé bagaj mwen té wè èk mwen ka vini.* **so lè** *lapen alé, bètafé ka èspéyé*

"Firefly," Rabbit said, "Compère, wait for me. I am coming. I am going to the other side there. I am going to take a few things that I saw and I am coming." *So* when Rabbit went, Firefly was waiting.

In (13)–(15) there is a reason-result relationship between the final sentences and the preceding context. In (16), taken from a text about the supernatural, the logical relationship is one of grounds-conclusion.

(16) *i menm ka di mwen menm bagay-la wivé'y. i la ka goumen èk yon bagay tout lannwit-la.* **kon sa** *sé menm bagay-la ki té ka bat nou toulédé-a*

He himself is telling me the same thing happened to him. He is there fighting with something all night long. *So* it is the same thing that was beating up both of us.

A plan-execution sequence also falls under the category resultative. Plan-execution involves a direct or indirect quotation followed by an action that functions as the outcome of the quotation.

Grammar of Sentence Conjunctions in St. Lucian Creole 33

(17) *then bètafé di, eben mwen ka pwan klété mwen. so bètafé mété klété'y
òf, èvèk then lapen pa ni klété*

Then Firefly said, "Well, I am taking away my light." *So* Firefly
turned his light off, and then Rabbit didn't have any light.

A plan-execution relationship seems fairly different, semantically speaking, from a reason-result or a grounds-conclusion relationship, but there is a
recurring pattern that the same set of sentence conjunctions that marks a
result or a conclusion also marks the execution in a plan-execution pair.

The analysis of these resultative sentence conjunctions is complicated by
the fact that they can also function as discourse particles to mark the beginning of a new part of a narrative as in (18). The functions of discourse particles, however, is outside the scope of the present article.

(18) *on jou bonmaten bò senkè papa mwen tann an chyen, an bagay ka
goumen èk sé chyen nou-an dòwò-a, épi chak lè i lévé ay gadé,
bagay-la ka ni tan kouwi. la té ni jaden owon-an èk bagay-la ka ni tan
ay séwé anba jaden-an. chak lè i viwé antwé andidan, an bagay la ka
bat sé chyen-an ankò. goumen ka alé. so an lè papa mwen di i kay sav
si i majò pasé'y*

One morning at about five o'clock my father heard a dog, a thing
fighting with our dogs outside, and each time he rose to take a look,
the thing had time to run away. There was garden around and the
thing had time to go hide in the garden. Each time he returned inside,
a thing there was beating up the dogs again, a fight going on. *So* one
time my father said he is going to find out who is boss.

A resultative sentence can encode a variety of semantic functions and has
the form in (19).

(19) resultative sentence = (resultative sentence conjunction) sentence
nucleus

The resultative sentence conjunctions that can connect a resultative sentence to the previous context include *kon sa, eben, so, alò,* and possibly others.

Causal

A causal relationship between sentences is expressed by means of the
causal sentence conjunction *paskè* 'because' or one of its variant forms such
as *paski, piski, pas, pis.* Often a word borrowed from English—*bikòz*—is

34 David B. Frank

used. Some speakers of Creole prefer to use a mixture of the two: *bikòzki*. A causal relationship is similar to a resultative relationship except that the order is reversed.[5] At least two different semantic relationships are expressed by means of a causal sentence, viz, result-reason and conclusion-grounds. Examples (20) and (21) are of causal sentences.

(20) *sé mèyè ou wété andidan-an.* **paski** *si ou sòt an dèwò, ou kay tonbé*

It is better for you to remain inside. *Because* if you go outside, you will fall.

(21) *m'a vlé ou janbé chimen-an. sé lè ou ka janbé chimen-an délè motoka ka vini èvèk yo sa kwazé'w*

I don't want you to cross the road. It is when you cross the road sometimes cars come and they crush you.

In (21) the causal sentence conjunction is implicit but not expressed in the second sentence. Where it is expressed, as in (20), it might be better to gloss the conjunction in English *for*, since we usually think of *because* as only working within a sentence marking a subordinate clause. In St. Lucian French Creole, it can be used either as a subordinating conjunction within a sentence, or it can be used as a sentence conjunction.

In (20) and (21) the semantic relation is that of conclusion-grounds. In (22), the relationship is result-reason.

(22) *lè zòt mété abiman sala, dépi zòt ka maché, zòt onkouwajé sé ti bway-la pou vini asou zòt.* **bikòzki** *sé pa abiman zòt sèlman ka fè sé ti bway-la dakò pou yo kwiyé zòt, bikòzki yo ka wè zòt abiyé mannyè zòt abiyé*

When you put on those clothes, once you are out walking, you encourage the boys to come after you. *For* it is your clothes alone that make the boys want to call you, because they can see you are dressing the way you are dressing.

The structure of a causal sentence is expressed in the formula in (23).

(23) causal sentence = (causal sentence conjunction) sentence nucleus

---

[5] Halliday and Hasan (1976, chapter 5) use "causal" for what I, in following Quirk et al. (1972), call "resultative." My "causal" corresponds to their "reversed causal." It is just a matter of perspective.

In conclusion, there are some types of sentences in St. Lucian French Creole that are dependent and obviously require analysis in terms of a larger context. Additive, sequential, contrastive, resultative, and causal sentences are five main types. These sentence types consist of an additive, sequential, contrastive, resultative, or causal sentence conjunction together with a sentence nucleus. The study of these five kinds of sentence conjunctions helps show how logical relations are expressed through the grammar of St. Lucian French Creole and how sentences are connected in discourse.

References

Beekman, John, John Callow, and Michael Kopesec. 1981. The semantic structure of written communication. 5th ed. Dallas: Summer Institute of Linguistics.

Halliday, Michael A. K. and Ruqaiya Hasan. 1976. Cohesion in English. London: Longman.

Quirk, Randolf, Sidney Greenbaum, Geoffrey Leech, and Jan Svartvik. 1972. A grammar of contemporary English. London: Longman.

Waterhouse, Viola. 1963. Independent and dependent sentences. IJAL 29:45–54.

Connectives and Clause Combining in Banggi

Michael E. Boutin

An important aspect of textual cohesion is the relationship between the clauses in a text. At the level of clause combinations, rhetorical relations may or may not be overtly marked. This article is concerned with a small set of rhetorical relations in Banggi. It examines the types of signals used to indicate these rhetorical relations when they are not overtly marked.

The discussion begins with intraclausal morphosyntax in Banggi (§1). This is followed by an overview of clause combinations from the syntactic point of view (§2). I then examine some rhetorical relations at the level of clause combinations in order to see not only how these relationships are signalled in the morphosyntax, but also the discourse function of the clauses (§3).

1. Intraclausal morphosyntax

Banggi is a North-western Austronesian language spoken by approximately 1,400 people on the islands of Banggi and Balambangan in the Kudat District of Sabah, Malaysia.[1]

---

[1] The information for this article was collected on Banggi Island between January 1983 and October 1989.

38 Michael E. Boutin

Banggi is a Philippine-type language, which are known for their voice (or verbal focus) systems. Each clause contains one nominal which is formally marked as a grammatically prominent syntactic constituent. This marking occurs in the form of voice-marking affixes on the verb (Kroeger 1989:1).

The nominal which is selected for grammatical prominence has been called by various names: subject (Blake 1916; Bloomfield 1917; McKaughan 1973), topic (McKaughan 1958; Naylor 1975), focused noun (Thomas 1958), focused-complement (Pike 1963:217), Prominence-1 (Dik 1981:89), pivot (Foley and Van Valin 1984), and trigger (Wouk 1986:136).

We are not concerned with the syntactic status of the prominent nominal, which, for the purpose of this article, can be equated with subject. (For a discussion of the role of subject in Philippine-type languages, cf. Bell (1976, 1983) and Schachter (1976, 1977). For a discussion of the terminological history surrounding the voice system in Philippine languages, cf. French (1988).

Gil (1984) provides evidence that Tagalog is a patient-prominent language. Gil (1982) and Starosta, Pawley, and Reid (1982) argue that patient-prominence is characteristic of the Austronesian language family. Recently attempts have been made to characterize Philippine languages as ergative on the basis of the high frequency of patients occurring as the prominent nominal (Payne 1982; Gerdts 1988; De Guzman 1988).

Although Banggi is a Philippine-type language in the sense that it has a voice system like other Philippine-type languages, Banggi is not patient-prominent, but is instead an actor-prominent language like Ida'an, another Austronesian language spoken in Sabah (Moody 1989:23). The data for this article is taken from texts which have been recorded and transcribed. This text corpus contains 472 clauses. Overall text frequency is given in the table in (1).

(1)   Overall frequency of clauses

Nonverbal	30	(6%)					
Verbal	442	(94%)					
			State	69	(16%)	1 Arg	231	(52%)
			Event	373	(84%)	2 Arg	211	(48%)
		—		—			—
Total	472	(100%)	442 (100%)			442 (100%)
					2 Arg Subj = Act	189	(90%)
					2 Arg Subj = Und	22	(10%)
						—
					Total	211	(100%)

The data base which was used contains 30 nonverbal clauses and 442 verbal clauses. The verbal clauses are divided into states (69) and events

Connectives and Clause Combining in Banggi

(373). Stative verbs, like events, can have one or two core arguments (Arg). There were 211 two-argument verbs in the corpus, of which 189 (90%) have actor (Act) as subject. The other ten percent have a nonactor subject which I refer to as undergoer (Und).

The actor is the person or thing that performs, instigates, or controls the state or action expressed by the predicate. The undergoer is the person or thing affected by the state or action expressed by the predicate (Foley and Van Valin 1984:29). Actor and undergoer are the two core arguments in a clause.

The core arguments are not marked for case except for nominals that refer to humans. Prepositions mark the noncore or oblique arguments in a clause. Nonsubject actors which are pronouns are marked for genitive case. Word order is used to distinguish between the core arguments with subject occurring before other nominal arguments.

The subject nominal may be marked by a special particle introducing the NP, or by nominative case pronouns (cf. §2.4), or by word order. The voice system marks a special syntactic relationship between the predicate of a clause and the subject.

The verb is usually affixed, indicating both the situation type (state, achievement, activity, or accomplishment) and the semantic role of the referent encoded by the subject. Banggi uses a system of verbal semantics and a system of verbal affixes to distinguish verbal situations.

1.1 Stative verbs

States are static situations which are ongoing. The stative verb class marker is m-. The prefix *kV*- marks nonvolitional stative verbs when affixed to adjective roots and some perception verbs. Possessive and existential verbs are also stative. (2) illustrates three different stative verbs: existential, an adjective root prefixed with *kV*-, and an adjective root affixed with *m*-. (3) illustrates two stative verbs.[2]

(2) *nd-ara*[3] *ke-doot* *m-pia*
    not-EXIST NVˆST-bad ST-good
    (He) is not bad, (but) good.

---

[2] Abbreviations used in this article are: ACC, accomplishment verb; ACH, achievement verb; ACT, actor; ACY, activity verb; DEF, definite; EXIST, existential stative verb; NS, nonsubject; NV, nonvolitional; PAST, past tense; PFT, perfect; POS, possessive stative verb; ST, stative verb; SUBJ, subject; UND, undergoer; *, part of the stem, where the stem has been divided by an infix. The subject is in italic in the English translations.

[3] Orthographic convention: *ng* = /n/ ' = /ʔ/

40 Michael E. Boutin

(3) *ou kibunggakng **si** **reida** ki-ara sinsɪkng kulunggaadn i laum*
I surprised SUBJ Reida POS-has ring payment NS Laum
I am surprised *Reida* has a ring (which is) Laum's payment (for taking a second wife).

1.2 Achievement verbs

Achievements are events which are initial-endpoint oriented. They refer to nonvolitional changes of state which a patient experiences or undergoes. (4) and (5) illustrate achievement verbs.

(4) *n-dabu'* ***ou** dii gimbatadn dioo*
PAST^ACH-fall[4] I at dock yonder
I fell at the dock over yonder.

(5) *bakng nda' biriadn t-um-uhal*
if not given *-ACH-thin
If (she) is not given (it), (she) will become thin.

1.3 Activity verbs

Activities are events which involve a volitional actor and which often have no clear endpoint. Activity verbs are activity-oriented. (6) and (7) illustrate activity verbs.

(6) *peg-luas **ku** aludn^aludn s-i-m-elehei ou dii bal*
when-exit I road *-PAST-ACY-go^up I in house
When I went out on the road, I went up into the house.

(7) ***odu'** t-em-eis kei*
grandmother *-ACY-cry also
Grandmothers cry also.

---

[4] For the purpose of this article, some verbs are simply glossed as (past). For a discussion of the function of these affixes see Boutin 1989.

Connectives and Clause Combining in Banggi 41

1.4 Accomplishment verbs

Accomplishment verbs are events which refer to a single change of state that is brought about by a volitional actor. Clauses with these verbs have both core arguments actor and undergoer, either of which can be the subject. Accomplishment verbs are marked by *N-* when the actor is subject. (8) illustrates an accomplishment verb with an actor as subject.

(8)   *N-opuk[5]*   *sia   odu^odu*
      ACC-shoot^blowgun   he   every^day
      He shoots a blowgun every day.

Accomplishment verbs are marked by either a suffix *-Vdn* or an infix when the undergoer is subject. (9) illustrates the same verb as in (8) only with an undergoer as subject.

(9)   *ina na supuh-adn[6]*   ***tupi***
      that DEF shoot^blowgun-UND^SUBJ squirrel
      Squirrels are what you shoot with a blowgun.

The different types of events (achievements, activities, and accomplishments) will usually not be illustrated in the examples that follow except in the case of accomplishment verbs whose subject is an undergoer (i.e., a nonactor).

2. Clause combinations from the view of syntax

This section provides an overview of clause combinations which are syntactically possible in Banggi. Following Lehmann (1988), I view types of clause combinations as being organized along a continuum. In this section I present the focal points on the syntactic continuum. The presentation is based on prototype theory as described in Lakoff (1987). According to Lakoff (1987:17), every category has both central and noncentral members. Thus, there can be good and bad examples of a category. The examples presented in this section are good examples in the sense that they highlight the focal points on the syntactic continuum.

Following (Lehmann 1988:182), a clause is defined as any syntagma containing one predication. A predication is usually encoded as a verb and

---

[5] *N-opuk* = *N-sopuk*
[6] *supuh-adn* = *sopuk-Vdn*

42   Michael E. Boutin

its arguments, i.e., verbal clause, but it occasionally consists of two NPs in
an equational relationship (nonverbal clause) in (1).

2.1 Paratactic clause combinations

The loosest type of syntactic linkage in Banggi involves the linking of
clauses which have equivalent syntactic status. This type of clause combination is usually referred to as coordination (Dik 1972:25) or parataxis
(Halliday and Hasan 1976:222). Clauses joined by coordination function in
the same way as an equivalent simple clause (p. 234).

The neutral coordinate conjunction in Banggi is *ma'* 'and' which can occur between phrases or clauses. In (10), *ma'* is a connective between two
noun phrases (*eihi dua ma' i Meikul*) and also between two clauses
(...*Meikul, ma' hina...*).

(10)   *odu hina   kira^kira puhul dua   belas inuhat   **eihi** bali*
       day   earlier   about   time   twelve   -   measured we   house

       ***eihi dua** ma' i   meikul   ma' hina   **seilan** mulei igahut*
       we   two   with NS Michael   and earlier Seilan   begin carried

       pekahas bali   ngia
       poles   house   his
       Earlier today about 12 o'clock, the *two of us*, Michael and I, *we*
       measured the house, and earlier *Seilan* began to carry poles for the
       house.

The linguistic units in a coordinate construction are bound together by
means of a linking device. The linking device can be a coordinator like *ma'*
or it can consist in mere juxtaposition of the coordinated members. As Dik
(1972:32) points out, "Coordination does not require coordinators, but coordinators presuppose coordination" (cf. Lehmann 1988:182 on parataxis).
Haiman (1983:788) claims that the conceptual distance between clauses with
coordinators is greater than that between clauses which are simply juxtaposed (cf. Longacre 1985:239).

Asyndetic coordination, i.e., coordination without any explicit conjunctive, is quite common in Banggi. Asyndetic coordination of clauses is illustrated in (11).

(11)   *si   tagi   mudukng rigiodu   Ø   manas kupi' susu   Ø pinum*
       SUBJ Tagi   get^up   morning   heat coffee milk   give^drink

Connectives and Clause Combining in Banggi

> *Tual ma' i   laum*
> Tual and NS Laum
> *Tagi* gets up in the morning, heats coffee with milk, and gives it to
> Tual and Laum.

The clauses in (11) involve coreference between a noun phrase and a
zero pronoun. In Banggi, an overt pronoun can (but usually does not) occur
in cases of coreference when clauses are coordinated. Lehmann (1978:194)
points out that coordination accompanied by ellipsis is especially common in
SVO languages. An overview of word order for the corpus is given in the
table in (12).

(12)   Word order for verbal clauses

SV	136	(31%)
VS	65	(15%)
S elided/∅	241	(54%)
Total	442	(100%)

Due to the large number of clauses with elided or zero subjects, it is difficult to say anything definitive about word order without making reference
to discourse. However, SV does appear to be the preferred word order in
Banggi.

Mithun (1988:339) provides evidence that coordinating conjunctions are
absent in many languages and are often derived from a word originally
meaning 'with'. Besides having a coordinating function, *ma'* also functions
as an instrumental preposition as in (13).

(13)   **sia** *limidik ma' badi'   ku*
        he   slash   with machete my
        He slashes (brush) with my machete.

There are other paratactic connectors in Banggi but clauses linked by *ma'*
are the prototypical examples of parataxis.

2.2 Complement clause combinations

A complement is a clause which has a nominal function in another
clause. In Banggi, complements are sentential expansions which function as
a core argument of matrix verbs. McCawley (1988:115) defines a comple-
mentizer as an element that marks a constituent as a complement. There are
no complementizers in Banggi.

44   Michael E. Boutin

The first type of complement involves the deletion of the subject of the complement clause when it is coreferential with the subject of the matrix clause. This is illustrated in (14).

(14)   *Nd-ou   mingin   ngirubm   saa   toyuk   ou   pa*
       not-I   want   look^for   spouse   small   I   yet
       I did not want to look for a husband, (because) I was still young.

In (14), the subject of the complement verb *ngirubm* 'look for' is deleted because it is coreferential with the subject of the matrix verb *mingin* 'want'. Thus,the subject of the complement is controlled by the matrix subject (cf. Comrie 1984:450). The deletion of coreferential complement subjects is obligatory in Banggi.

The second type of complement clause occurs when the subject of the complement clause is raised to the object position of the matrix clause. This is illustrated in (15).

(15)   **sia**   *mingin   diaadn   ngirubm   saa*
       he   want   me   look^for   spouse
       He wants me to look for a husband.

In (15), *sia* 'he' is the subject of the matrix clause and *diaadn* 'me' is the object. The raised argument (*diaadn*) is semantically an argument of the complement clause but syntactically a part of the matrix clause (cf. Noonan 1985:69). The subject of the complement is coreferential with the matrix object, thus, the object of the matrix clause controls the deletion of the complement subject (cf. Comrie 1984:450).

The syntactic constructions described in (14) and (15) should be compared with the auxilary verb construction in (16).

(16)   **sia**   *mulai   ngirubm   saa*
       he   begin   look^for   spouse
       He began to look for a wife.

In (16) *mulai* 'begin' is an auxiliary verb marking inceptive viewpoint aspect (Boutin 1989:9). That auxiliaries are different from matrix verbs with complements is shown in (17) since raising cannot occur with auxiliary verbs.

(17)   ***sia** mulai   diaadn   ngirubm   saa*
       he   begin   me   look^for   spouse
       **He* began me looking for a wife.

Connectives and Clause Combining in Banggi

From the syntactic point of view, paratactic clauses connected with *ma'* 'and', e.g., (10), and complement constructions like those described in (14) and (15), represent the two extreme types of clause combinations at either end of the clause combination continuum. Paratactic clauses connected by *ma'* are maximally separate, while matrix clauses and their complements are minimally separate, since complements function as core arguments of the matrix clause predicate (cf. Lehmann 1988:218). Haiman (1983:799) points out that the grammatical separateness of a clause corresponds to the conceptual independence of the proposition expressed by that clause. The syntactic clause combinations described in §§2.3 and 2.4 below represent focal points on the continuum between the two extremes.

2.3 Serial verb clause combinations

Serial verb constructions contain two or more predicates sharing a common core argument (Foley and Van Valin 1984:189). The rhetorical relation motion-purpose is realized by serial verbs in Banggi. (18) and (19) illustrate serial verbs.

(18) *ngundakng mapit natak dii diaadn dii*
     almost   stop^by leave to me   there
     (*He*) almost stopped by, to leave me (some) there.

Serial verbs only occur when the subject of the satellite clause is the same as the subject of the nuclear clause. The terms nuclear and satellite are taken from Matthiessen and Thompson (1988:289) where they are used to describe different types of rhetorical relations between parts of a text. In (18), the subject of both the nuclear and the satellite clauses is the actor which is elided in the nuclear clause and deleted under coreference in the satellite clause. Serial constructions are unlike complements in that the satellite clause does not have a nominal function in the nuclear clause. Aissen (1984:565ff) discusses the possible syntactic relations between verbs of motion and satellite clauses in motion-purpose constructions in Tzotzil. In Banggi, the subject of the motion verb controls the subject of the satellite purpose clause.

Serial verbs do not have to be contiguous as is shown in the serial verb construction in (19).

(19) *mili'   ou kindii bali   raya   nginum beig gulu*
     returned I to   house community   drink   water first
     I returned to the community center to drink water first.

46   Michael E. Boutin

In (19), the subject of both the nuclear and the satellite clauses is 'I'
which is deleted under coreference in the satellite clause.

4 Reduced satellite constructions

The clause combinations discussed in this section involve clauses which
stand in a nuclear-satellite relationship to each other and do not share core
arguments. The satellite clause is reduced, but it is not part of the nuclear
clause.

Temporal clauses are used to exemplify reduced satellite clauses. From
the syntactic point of view, temporal clauses are reduced clauses which have
been desententialized (cf. Lehmann 1988:193). Temporal clauses usually
precede their nuclear clauses as illustrated in (20).

(20)   *atakng* **ku** *mpanu* **gimbatadn** *irumbak*   *na*
        while   I   walk   dock   collapsed   PFT
        While *I* was walking, the *dock* collapsed.

In Banggi, nominals may appear in one of three cases: nominative, accusative, or genitive. (21)–(24) illustrate these three cases using first-person
singular pronouns (*ou* 'I', *diaadn* 'me', and *ku* 'my').

(21)   **ou** *imori*   *ngia*   *siidn*
        I   gave   her   money
        I gave her money.

(22)   **sia** *imori*   *diaadn* *siidn*   *ku*
        she   gave   me   money   my
        She gave me my money.

(23)   **siidn**   *bineiri*   *ku*   *dii* *ngia*
        money   wasˆgiven   I   to   her
        Money was given to her by me.

(24)   **ou**   *bineiri-adn*   *ngia*   *siidn*
        I   wasˆgiven-UNDˆSUBJ   her   money
        I was given money by her.

In nuclear clauses, the first-person singular nominative pronoun is *ou* 'I'.
In (21), the actor is subject while in (24) an undergoer is subject, but in both
cases the subject pronoun is the same, i.e., nominative case. In (22), *diaadn*
'me' is a nonsubject core argument which occurs in accusative case, while

Connectives and Clause Combining in Banggi   47

ku 'my' is a genitive pronoun modifying *siidn* 'money'. In (23), an undergoer is subject and the actor (*ku* 'I') occurs in the genitive case. Nonsubject actor pronouns always occur in the genitive case.

In temporal clauses such as that found in (20), the subject occurs in the genitive case (*ku* 'I'). Lehmann (1988:196) points out that the reduction of the subject to genitive case is common in desententialized clauses.

The voice-marking affixes on the verb are the same in desententialized clauses as in independent nuclear clauses. Compare the verb *mpanu* 'walk' in the desententialized clause in (20) with the same verb in the independent clause in (25).

(25) *ou mpanu dii gimbatadn hina*
     I   walk   on   dock   earlier
     I walked on the dock earlier.

The verb is the same in both (20) and (25). In both clauses the actor is the subject; however, in (25) the subject is in the nominative case while in (20) it is in the genitive case. It is this reduction of the subject to genitive case which distinguishes reduced satellite clauses syntactically from other types of clause combinations.

2.5 Syntactic clause combination summary

The focal points on the syntactic continuum of clause combination strategies which have been described in §2 are summarized in (26).

(26) Focal points on clause combining continuum

    maximal   minimal
    $\longleftarrow$———————— separateness ————————$\longrightarrow$

paratactic	reduced	serial	complement
clauses	satellite	verb	clauses
	clauses	clauses	

The four clause combination strategies described above are the basic syntactic mechanisms available in Banggi. Other clause combinations are variations of these strategies. For example, juxtaposition of two clauses without an overt connector is a variation of the paratactic strategy from the syntactic point of view. This is illustrated in (27) where the first clause is a consequence and the second a condition.

(27) *si   laum nggerampus diaadn **kumut** **ku** mpanggar obu*
     SUBJ Laum mad   me   clothes my stiff   smell

48 Michael E. Boutin

> *pasakng*
> urine
> *Laum* would be mad at me, (if) *my clothes* were stiff and smelled like
> urine.

Pronominal subjects in conditional clauses are not reduced to genitive case. The subject of the conditional clause in (27) is nonhuman. Only pronouns and nominals referring to humans are marked for case (cf. §1). In (28), the subject of the conditional clause occurs in the nominative case.

(28) *bakng* **ou** *nggerampus diha nd-ou mori diha*
if I mad you not-I give you
If *I* was mad at you, *I* would not give (it) to you.

There are two types of relative clause constructions in Banggi. One type uses the complement clause-combining strategy, the other type uses the reduced satellite clause-combining strategy. Both types of relative clauses follow their antecedent (Comrie 1981, head noun; Keenan 1985, domain noun) which is common in SVO languages (Lehmann 1978:175).

One difference between the two types of relative clauses is the relationship between the head noun and the subject of the relative clause. Comrie (1981:140) states that the encoding of the role of the head noun in the relative clause is very important typologically.

If the head noun is the subject of the relative clause, then no relative clause marker, i.e., relative pronoun, occurs. In which case, the noun which is relativized is common to both the matrix clause and the relative clause (cf. Lehmann 1978:175). That is, the matrix clause and the relative clause share a core argument. This is illustrated in (29) where the subject (*oid* 'boat') of the matrix clause is relativized and in (30) where the nonsubject core argument (*dagikng* 'meat') of the matrix clause is relativized.

(29) *mi-gia* **oid** *b-in-uat* *ngia*
ST-big boat *-PAST^UND^SUBJ-make him
The [*boat* he made] was big.

(30) **sia** *igapi* **dagikng** *in-aap* *ngia*
he cooked meat PAST^UND^SUBJ-get him
He cooked [the *meat* he got].

In (29) and (30), the subject of the relative clause is an undergoer. The subject of the relative clause may also be an actor as illustrated in (31) and (32).

Connectives and Clause Combining in Banggi 49

(31) **lama** *pandi* *uubm* *bonggi* *kaap* *miaa'*
people know language Banggi may follow
[*People* (who) know the Banggi language] may follow.

(32) **sia** *mori* **lama** *ki-ladu*
she give people POS-sickness
She gives (it) to [*people* (who) are sick].

In (29) and (31), the head and relative clause are a subject complement
while in (30) and (32), they are an object complement. Thus, all four of the
relative clauses described so far are a variation of the complement clause-
combining strategy.

Banggi also has a relative-pronoun strategy for forming relative clauses.
The relative pronoun occurs in clause-initial position. This strategy destroys
the basic SVO order since the relative pronoun is moved to clause-initial
position. The relative pronoun encodes the head noun and it is not the subject of the relative clause (cf. Comrie 1981:142). In the nonrelative-pronoun
strategy, e.g., (29)–(32), the basic SVO order is retained. The relative-
pronoun strategy for forming relative clauses is illustrated in (33).

(33) *kiara* **barabm** **medoot** *nuan* **ngia** *ngondi'*
EXIST many things which he throw^away
There are *many things* [which *he* throws away].

The relative pronoun used in (33) is *nuan* which is immediately preceded
by the head. The subject of the relative clause is a reduced argument in the
genitive case.

In the nonrelative-pronoun strategy, the subject of the relative clause can
be either an undergoer, e.g., (29) and (30), or an actor, e.g., (31) and (32). In
the relative-pronoun strategy, the reduced subject of the relative clause is
always the logical subject of the verb (which is the actor in a transitive
predication, e.g., (33).

There is a correlation between relative-clause strategy and clause combining strategy. Relative clauses which do not have a relative pronoun, share
a core argument with the matrix clause, i.e., the head noun is part of both the
matrix and the relative clause. Thus, they are an example of complement
clause combining. Relative clauses which do have a relative pronoun, do not
share a core argument with the matrix clause. Thus, they are another instance of reduced satellite clauses.

Relative clauses which are formed via the relative-pronoun strategy always select the logical subject as subject. Temporal clauses like that described in (20) also always select the logical subject as subject. Thus, in desententialized clauses, the subject is always the logical subject.

50   Michael E. Boutin

One of the functions of desententialized clauses is to make (or keep) the actor as the subject. As mentioned in §1, Banggi is an actor-prominent language. Unmarked linguistic attention flow in a two-argument clause is from actor to undergoer. This unmarked linguistic attention flow and unmarked word order mirror the natural attention flow from source to goal (cf. DeLancey 1981:633).

3. Discourse view of clause combinations

Matthiessen and Thompson (1988:286) claim that the grammar of clause combining reflects discourse organization, and that all text can be described in terms of rhetorical relations (p. 289). In this section, I examine some rhetorical relations between clauses in terms of their morphosyntactic signals and their discourse functions.

Rhetorical relations are relations which relate propositions (the semantic counterpart of clauses) to each other. Matthiessen and Thompson (1988) state that there are two types of relations: nucleus-satellite relations and list relations. Beekman and Callow (1979:54) make a similar distinction between support relations and addition relations (cf. also Larson 1984:275 for use of the terms support and addition). Matthiessen and Thompson claim that the distinction between listing and nucleus-satellite relations is paralleled by the grammatical distinction between parataxis, e.g., coordination and apposition, and hypotaxis (1988:300), and that nucleus-satellite relations are often, but not always, coded as hypotaxis (p. 308). Beekman and Callow (1979:54) refer to this parallel relationship between types of semantic relationships and grammatical structure, and they add that skewing can and often does occur between semantic relationships and grammatical forms.

Jordon (1988:278) claims that there is general consensus regarding the nature of textual cohesion and he summarizes this consensus as follows: 1) text is organized in terms of rhetorical relations; 2) relations are essentially binary and apply at all levels of text; 3) textual complexity results from complicated combinations of relations; 4) various lengths of text are related; and 5) relations can be signalled or unsignalled.

3.1 Enhancing relations

The rhetorical relations I will examine in this section are two enhancing relations: purpose and condition (Matthiessen and Thompson 1988:297). "Enhancing relations are used when units are circumstantially related to one another" (p. 298).

Matthiessen and Thompson suggest there is a relationship between clause combining and rhetorical relations (p. 301). Specifically, they hypothesize

Connectives and Clause Combining in Banggi 51

that clause combining of the enhancing hypotactic kind is a grammaticalization of enhancing rhetorical relations.

Enhancing hypotaxis refers to hypotactic clause combining involving circumstantial relations. One clause enhances another clause circumstantially (Matthiessen and Thompson 1988:283–84). Enhancing hypotaxis involves clauses which are interdependent and stand in a kind of head-dependent relation to one another at some level, but one is not part of the other.

Purpose. In a purpose relation, the satellite clause provides a purpose for which the action (motion) in the nuclear clause is undertaken (Matthiessen and Thompson 1988:296). As discussed in §2.3, motion-purpose is realized by serial verbs in Banggi (cf. (18) and (19)). These purpose clauses are reduced clauses in two ways. First of all, the subject is deleted under coreference with the matrix subject. Secondly, tense oppositions are neutralized in that past tense never occurs (cf. Haiman and Thompson 1984:512–13; Lehmann 1988:195). However, there is a semantic explanation for the lack of a past tense. Purpose clauses express a motivating event which must be unrealized at the time of the nuclear event (Thompson and Longacre 1985:185).

There are twenty-one motion-purpose clause combinations in the corpus examined. In each case the following always occur: 1) the motion clause precedes the purpose clause; 2) the subject of the purpose clause is deleted under coreference with the subject of the motion clause; and 3) the purpose clause verb is nonpast tense.

The predicate of the motion clause is usually an activity verb (14 of 21), but can also be an accomplishment verb (7 of 21) with an object (2 of the 7 accomplishment verbs). Serial verbs do not have to be contiguous (cf. §2.3) but the motion clause must be contiguous with the purpose clauses. Example (34) illustrates a motion-purpose clause combination in which the verb of the motion clause takes an object.

(34)   *ou*   nda' bas   ngai   lama   nggesaa
      I   not   already take   person   marry
      I have never taken anyone to marry.

Mann and Thompson (1987:64) claim that the purpose relation requires a constraint upon the satellite clause whereby the situation in the satellite clause is unrealized. This situation is unrealized with respect to the deictic center. The unmarked center for temporal deixis is time of utterance. In narrative, however, the deictic center is usually the time of the last main event presented in the discourse (cf. Boutin 1989:12). Thus, with respect to time of utterance, purpose clauses are sometimes already realized, but with respect to the shifted deictic center, they are unrealized. This is illustrated in (35)

52   Michael E. Boutin

where the purpose clause was known to be realized at the time of utterance, but unrealized with respect to the shifted deictic center.

(35) **ihi dua** *igbalik^balik*   *nggahut karukng*
       we   two   keep^going^back   carry   gunny^sack
       We two kept going back and carrying the gunny sacks.

Malay uses an overt connector to mark purpose clauses. The connector *supaya* 'so that' is borrowed from Malay and only occurred once in the corpus. (I have heard it many times and probably use it much more frequently than native Banggi speakers due to the influence of English and Malay on my Banggi. I expected to find several examples in the corpus.) Most speakers use the Malay form *supaya* but some speakers say *subai*. The one instance of this connective found in the corpus is illustrated in (36).

(36) *nda'   mou'   ngai   sala'   subai   kiid diaadn*
       not   want   take   mistake so^that   see   me
       (*He*) did not want to make a mistake (with another woman), (what he wanted was) to see me.

Although *subai* (Malay *supaya*) marks purpose clauses in Malay, it has a contrastive function in (36). In (36), the *ngai sala'* is an object complement of the verb *mou'*. The clause introduced by subai contrasts with the matrix verb *mou'* and cannot be interpreted as a purpose for 'making a mistake'. Thus, the single use of the overt connector *subai* in the corpus does not introduce a purpose clause.

Malay uses an overt connector to mark reason clauses. The connector *pasal* is a borrowing of Malay *fasal* 'reason'. *pasal* occurs only three times in the corpus. Twice it introduces reason clauses and once it introduces a purpose clause. The use of pasal to introduce a purpose clause is illustrated in (37).

(37) *nggit nguduaa kibori berahat pasal   nd-ara   onu^onu*
       bring pray   ask   blessing so^that not-EXIST nothing
       (*He*) got (us) to pray (and) ask for a blessing so that *nothing* will happen.

Many languages use the same morphology for purpose and reason clauses (Thompson and Longacre 1985:185). Purpose clauses describe a situation which is not realized, while reason clauses describe a situation which may be realized. (38) illustrates a reason clause introduced by *pasal* 'because'.

Connectives and Clause Combining in Banggi

(38) *pasal* **sia** *nda' ketaadn mudapadn igundas na mili'*
because he not hold^out hungry quickly PFT returned
Because *he* could not hold out (and) was hungry, (*he*) quickly returned.

Since the same connector is used to signal both purpose and reason, the unrealized/realized status of the purpose/reason must be signalled somehow. Although (37) and (38) differ with respect to clause order and the tense of the nuclear clause verb, it is primarily the semantics of the satellite verb that signals whether the satellite clause is unrealized or realized. This can be seen in (39) where the satellite verb (*kiara*) is realized.

(39) *nggit nguduaa kibori berahat pasal* **kiara** **kususaadn**
bring pray ask blessing because EXIST difficulty
(*He*) got (us) to pray (and) ask for a blessing because there were *difficulties*.

Reason clauses, like purpose clauses, are not always explicitly marked with an overt connective. In (14), the postposed clause *toyuk ou pa* 'I was still young' is an example of a reason clause which is not explicitly marked.

There is a good grammatical explanation why Banggi would borrow *supaya* 'so that' to mark some purpose clauses. Serial verb constructions only occur when the subject of the satellite clause is coreferential with the subject of the nuclear clause. When the subjects are not coreferential, the connector *supaya* is used to signal purpose clauses. Although this is not born out in the corpus examined, it does appear to be the case. (40) illustrates a purpose clause introduced by *supaya*.

(40) **sia** *mapit supaya* **ou** *nda' mutumang*
he stop^by so^that I not leave^behind
He will stop by so that *I* will not be left behind.

Condition. In a condition relation, the satellite clause presents a hypothetical, future, or otherwise unrealized situation which must be realized for the situation in the nuclear clause to be realized (Mann and Thompson 1987:65).

The condition relation occurs fifteen times in the corpus examined. The verb in conditional clauses is never marked for past tense and Thus, nonfinite. The connector *bakng* 'if' is used to introduce most (60%) of the condition satellite clauses. The table in (41) provides an overview of condition relations in the corpus.

54 Michael E. Boutin

(41) Condition relations in corpus

Connector 9 (60%)		No Connector 6 (40%)	
Preposed	Postposed	Preposed	Postposed
9 (1.00)	---	3 (50%)	3 (50%)

The figures in (41) suggest that there is a correlation between the presence of the connector *bakng* and preposed conditional clauses, since *bakng* only occurs in preposed conditional clauses in the corpus. Other data outside of this corpus, however, provide evidence that *bakng* can occur in postposed conditional clauses. The text segment in (42) illustrates preposed conditional clauses which are introduced by *bakng* ((42a) and (42b)), and a preposed conditional clause which has no overt connective. The text is about Banggi marriage customs in the old days.

(42) a. *poro' susuad bonggi hai bakng **libudn** nggulu timiligud*
    tell   say   Banggi also if   woman   first   turn^over

    libudn *nggulu mati*
    woman   first   die

   b. *bakng **lahi** nggulu timiligud **lahi** nggulu mati*
    if   men   first   turn^over men first   die

   c. ***salakng** nda' kaap puda-adn kutuladn leid*
    resin^fuel not   may   extinguish-UND^SUBJ three^days long

   d. *nda' totog nggesaa nda' bulei pudaadn **salakng***
    not sure marry   not may extinguish resin^fuel

The Banggi also say, if the *woman* turns over first, the *woman* will die first. If the *man* turns over first, the *man* will die first. The *light* cannot be extinguished for three days. (If) the marriage is not consummated, the *light* cannot be extinguished.

Conditionals are generally hypothetical (Haiman 1978:581) and behave like sentence topics. Hypothetical conditionals are illustrated in (5), (28), (42a), and (42b). In each case, they function as sentence level topics.

The lack of an overt connective in (42d), however, makes the rhetorical relationship somewhat ambiguous. The preposed satellite clause in (42d) might also be interpreted as a temporal clause. Thompson and Longacre (1985:193) point out that in Indonesian, there is no distinction between IF-clauses and WHEN-clauses. This is not the case in Banggi. Temporal

Connectives and Clause Combining in Banggi

clauses (or WHEN-clauses) are reduced satellite constructions in that pronominal subjects of these clauses occur in the genitive case, e.g., (20); cf. §2.4. On the other hand, conditional clauses (or IF-clauses) are not reduced satellite constructions (in the sense described in §2.4) in that pronominal subjects of these clauses occur in the nominative case, e.g., (28).

One argument for a temporal analysis of (42d) is that temporal satellite clauses usually precede their nuclear clauses, e.g., (6) and (20). The same argument could be used for the conditional analysis since conditional clauses are preposed eighty percent (12 of 15; cf. (41)) of the time. The strongest argument against a temporal analysis is that temporal satellite clauses are always formally marked either by an overt connective such as *atakng* 'while', e.g., (20), or by an affix such as *peg-* 'when', e.g., (6). Since (42d) lacks a formal marker, it would have to be an exception if the temporal analysis was correct. On the other hand, conditional clauses can lack overt connectives, e.g,. (43); cf. (41), and causal relationships frequently lack overt connectives, e.g., (14), (18), (19), (27), (34), and (35). (43) illustrates a postposed conditional clause which lacks an overt connective.

(43)   *mati   nda'   biriadn*
        die   not   given
        (*She*) will die, (if *she*) is not given it.

Because temporal clauses require formal markers and conditional and causal clauses do not, (42d) is analyzed as a conditional clause. Having dismissed the possibility of (42d) being temporal due to the lack of formal marking, however, another problem arises. How does one know that (42d) or (43) for that matter, involve conditional relations and not some other rhetorical relation? Two corollary questions are: why are some connectives sometimes explicit and sometimes implicit?; and why are satellite clauses sometimes preposed and other times postposed with respect to the nuclear clause? In §3.2 I will try to answer these three questions.

3.2 Functional explanations

In this section, I will try to answer the questions posed above by examining the data in terms of some of the explanations offered in the literature.

Thus far I have shown that in Banggi there is a relationship between some rhetorical relations and morphosyntax. Specifically, purpose relations are realized as serial verbs when the subject of the nuclear and satellite clauses are coreferential. The Malay connective *supaya* 'so that' has been borrowed in order to link purpose clauses to nuclear clauses when the subjects are not coreferential. Temporal relations (simultaneity and sequence) are realized as reduced satellite clauses with pronominal subjects in the

56   Michael E. Boutin

genitive case.[7] Conditional clauses are not as reduced in that the subject occurs in the nominative case, but are reduced in that the conditional clause verb is nonfinite with respect to tense. As Lehmann (1988:193) points out, desententialization or reduction is a matter of degrees.

The relationships between rhetorical relations and morphosyntax which I have described thus far have been accounted for in sentence-level terms. Matthiessen and Thompson (1988:275) suggest that it is not possible to characterize clause combinations in strictly sentence-level terms. In order to answer the questions posed at the end of the previous section, I will examine discourse factors which might provide functional explanations.

Ramsey (1987:383) claims that in English, preposed conditional clauses perform a different job in discourse than do postposed ones. Specifically, she states that preposed conditional clauses are thematically associated to the preceding discourse as well as to the nuclear clause. On the other hand, postposed conditional clauses are only related to their nuclear clauses (p. 385).

To try and assess the different functional distribution of preposed and postposed conditional clauses, I measured the referential distance, which is the number of clauses between the subject of the conditional clause and the closest previous reference to that same NP (cf. Ramsey 1987:387). The table in (44) shows the results of measurements of referential distance. Following Givón (1983:13), referential indefinite subjects are assigned a value of 20. All 10 instances of referential indefinite subjects occurred in three hypothetical texts which described old marriage customs, death customs, and giving directions. Two syntactic coding devices were used for these indefinite subjects: zero anaphora (5 of 10) and referential indefinite NPs (5 of 10).

(44)   Referential distance for subjects

Preposed Clauses   Postposed Clauses

Nbr of clauses	% to total nbr of clauses	Referential distance	% to total nbr of clauses	Nbr of clauses
3	25	1	33	1
		2	33	1
9	75	20	33	1
12	100		100	3

---

[7] The developmental marker *nubu'* 'and then' which is used in narrative discourse is not discussed in this article. It has a different sort of temporal function than what is being described here. Banggi *nubu'* indicates progression or continuity in a narrative (cf. *dadi'* in Coastal Kadazan (Miller and Miller 1989:28) and *kat* in Ida'an (Moody 1989:20); also cf. Levinsohn 1987:83ff.).

Connectives and Clause Combining in Banggi

Ramsey (1987:388) also suggests measuring the scope, which she defines as the number of clauses to the left of the conditional clause that are needed in order to understand the whole conditional clause. I tried to do this, but eventually gave it up as too subjective an exercise.

The Banggi data in (44) support Ramsey's conclusion that postposed clauses have a higher referential continuity with the nuclear clause than preposed clauses (p. 402). It does not, however, support her hypothesis that postposed clauses are only related to their nuclear clauses (p. 385; cf. the explicitness of connective in §3.2).

Returning to the problem of determining rhetorical relationships when there are no overt connectives, it is helpful to compare (27) (repeated here as (45)) and (46).

(45)   *si*   *laum*   nggerampus *diaadn* **kumut ku**   mpanggar   obu
        SUBJ   Laum   mad   me   clothes my   stiff   smell

          pasakng
          urine
          Laum would be mad at me, (if) *my clothes* were stiff and smelt like urine.

(46)   *si*   *ama'*   *munu'*   *diaadn*   *nd-ou* mou   *dii*   *laum*
        SUBJ   father   fought   me   not-I   want   at   Laum
        My father got angry with me, (because) *I* did not want Laum.

Syntactically (45) and (46) are very similar. But they have different rhetorical relations. (45) illustrates a condition relation, while (46) illustrates a reason relation. The difference in rhetorical relation is due to the fact that the satellite clause is unrealized in (45), but realized in (46). Purpose and condition share the same constraint on the satellite clause, i.e., the satellite clause must be unrealized (cf. Mann and Thompson 1987:64–65). Thus, purpose and condition are distinguished from reason on a semantic basis (unrealized versus realized situation), while purpose is distinguished from condition on a morphosyntactic basis, i.e., purpose clauses, but not condition clauses, are realized as serial verbs or with a borrowed connector.

In both (45) and (46), the preceding context indicates whether the satellite clause is realized or not. In the text in which (45) occurs, the speaker is stating a negative opinion about people who do not bathe regularly. The immediately preceding context is shown in (47).

(47)   *nda' na*   *puduli'* *tapi'*   *diaadn*   *nd-ou*   *ketaadn*   nga   rua
        not   PFT   care   but   me   not-I   hold⌐out   that   way
        (*They*) do not care, but as for me, *I* cannot stand that.

58   Michael E. Boutin

In (47), the speaker states that she cannot stand being a certain way, and then in (45), she states what would happen if she were that way.

In the text in which (46) occurs, the speaker is talking about how she did not want to marry her husband. The immediately preceding context is shown in (48).

(48)   *si   laum* ngupadn diaadn *ou*   nda' mou'
        SUBJ Laum bait   me   I   not   want
        Laum baited me. *I* did not want (him).

In (48), the speaker states that she did not want to marry her husband, and then in (46), she adds that her father got angry with her because she did not want to marry her husband. She states elsewhere in the text that her father made her marry her husband.

Explicitness of connective. I have shown how the rhetorical relations condition, purpose, and reason are distinguished in Banggi when they are not overtly marked (cf. §3.2). I now offer some explanations for the occurrence or lack of occurrence of overt connectors.

General points which have been made concerning the explicitness of connectors include the following: "The presence or absence of a connective device between two clauses has nothing to do with parataxis vs. hypotaxis, but is exclusively a question of syndesis" (Lehmann 1988:210). "Probably the very absence of conjunction in sentences that employ juxtaposition necessitates a tighter unity-which is signaled by phonological and lexical means" (Longacre 1985:239). "The relationship between small chunks of text immediately following each other is sufficiently clear from the mere adjacency. Large passages need explicit linking in order to form a cohesive text" (Lehmann 1988:211). Logical connectors are less frequent in spoken than written languages (Brown and Yule 1983:16). People often leave out connectors, because they feel the connectors can easily be inferred by the listener or reader (Schank and Abelson 1977:22–23). In unplanned discourse, relations between propositions are more likely to be left implicit and determined by context than in planned discourse (Ochs 1979:66). Relations between propositions may be signalled by connectives of various syntactic categories (conjunctions, adverbs, and particles) (van Dijk 1977:45).

The following summarizes the points above in terms of the Banggi data in question: Banggi society is preliterate; the corpus examined consists of unplanned spoken texts; the rhetorical relation under consideration here is condition, which may or may not be explicitly marked.

The first step in determining whether a connective will be made explicit or left implicit, involves examining the morphosyntactic constraints on the distribution of the connective. The use of Malay *supaya* 'so that' in purpose

Connectives and Clause Combining in Banggi

clauses whose subject is different from the nuclear clause, is an example of a morphosyntactic constraint (cf. "Purpose" in §3.1).

As mentioned under Condition in §3.1, *bakng* 'if' only occurs in preposed clauses in the corpus. The examples in (49) and (50) illustrate postposed conditional clauses which were taken from a working dictionary. These clauses were produced by native speakers in conversation and not elicited.

(49) *kaap nilu' kulubutadn bakng nd-ara   buaidn*
      can   spear squid   if   not-EXIST moon
      (*You*) can spear squid, if there is no moon.

(50) *nda' kaap **sia** deirdn na   bakng nd-ara   kuli'*
      not   can   he   himself DEF if   not-EXIST worker
      He cannot (do it) himself, if there are no workers.

The postposed conditional clauses in (49) and (50) only relate to their nuclear clauses. This appears to be the case whenever the connector *bakng* occurs in postposed clauses. Thus, the absence or presence of an explicit conditional marker in postposed clauses is related to the scope of the conditional clause. Postposed conditional clauses which have an explicit connector are only related to their nuclear clause, while those without an explicit connector have a broader scope. This is a qualified version of Ramsey's hypothesis (Ramsey 1987:385; cf. §3.2).

Having dealt with the explicitness or lack thereof in postposed conditional clauses, I turn now to preposed clauses. As shown in the table in (41), preposed clauses are usually (75 percent) marked with explicit connectives. In the corpus, nine of the twelve preposed clauses contain the connector *bakng*.

Lehmann (1988:211) claims that the explicitness of the linking device is related to the size of the entities being linked. More specifically, large passages need explicit linking and small adjacent chunks (presumably clauses) do not.

I assume that discourse is structured, and that clauses combine into larger thematic units which I will call paragraphs (cf. Givón 1983:7). "A paragraph is roughly defined as a grouping of sentences that is bound by discontinuities in temporal or locational setting or by changes in participant interaction" (Dooley 1986:48). Relationships between sentences within a paragraph tend to be causal (p. 66).

All fifteen of the conditional clauses in the corpus are linked to other clauses within the same paragraph, and usually to a clause in the preceding sentence (14 of 15). That is, conditional clauses are not used to link paragraphs, but rather they form a cohesive device within paragraphs.

60   Michael E. Boutin

The explicitness of conditional linkage in Banggi preposed clauses is not related to the size or distance (scope) of the entities being linked. The crucial factor appears to be the nature of the link between the conditional sentence and the preceding sentence. When the conditional clause is contrastive with the preceding independent clause, there is a high degree of lexical cohesion between the two adjacent clauses. Two of the three preposed clauses which lack overt connectors are contrastive restatements of the previous independent clause. This is illustrated in (51) where the preposed conditional clause in (51b) is a contrastive restatement of the independent clause in (51a).

(51)   a. *iniaan*   *dii*   *kimidiadn*   *lumuas*
          afterbirth at   afterward   come^out

       b. *nda' lumuas*   *iniaan*   *kiara metandadn*
          not come^out   afterbirth   EXIST stuck
       The *afterbirth* comes out afterward. (If) the *afterbirth* does not come out, (it) is stuck.

The conditional clause in (51b) is a satellite clause in relation to the nuclear clause which follows, but it is in a contrastive relationship to the independent clause (51a) which precedes it.

The other preposed conditional, which lacks an overt connector, occurs in a sentence in which the nuclear clause is a restatement of the previous independent clause. This was illustrated in (42c) and (42d) which are repeated here as (52a) and (52b).

(52)   a. *salakng*   *nda' kaap* *puda-adn*   *kutuladn*   *leid*
          resin^fuel not   may   extinguish-UND^SUBJ   three^days long

       b. *nda' totog nggesaa nda' bulei pudaadn*   *salakng*
          not   sure   marry   not may   extinguish resin^fuel
       The *light* cannot be extinguished for three days. (If) the marriage is not consummated, the *light* cannot be extinguished.

The nuclear clause in (52b) is a restatement of the independent clause in (52a).

The conditional sentences illustrated in (43) and (5) occur in the same text. The conditional clause in (5) is a restatement of the conditional clause, and not the nuclear clause in (43). In the text, there is an intervening sentence between (43) and (5), with (5) being linked to the sentence which precedes it: the intervening sentence.

Connectives and Clause Combining in Banggi 61

Thus, the explicitness of the conditional marker in postposed clauses is related to the scope of the conditional clause, but in preposed clauses it appears to be related to whether the conditional clause is contrastive with the preceding independent clause.

Clause order. I have shown how certain rhetorical relations are distinguished when they are not overtly marked and why these relations are sometimes made explicit and other times left implicit (cf. §3.2). I now turn to the question of why conditional clauses are sometimes preposed and other times postposed with respect to the nuclear clause.

The following factors may influence the syntactic order of clauses: (1) the unmarked syntactic order of the clause complex; (2) the order of events; and (3) given versus new information constraints (Prideaux 1988:310).

Texts are normally organized with temporal structure in mind. Events are usually given in the natural sequence in which they occur (Givón 1983:8). The natural or unmarked order in a condition relation is for the satellite condition to precede the nuclear consequence, because the consequence depends upon the realization of the condition. Thus, postposed conditional clauses are marked or nonnormal. This is confirmed by the data in the corpus in that eighty percent (12 of 15) conditional clauses are preposed (cf. the table in (41)).

Only one of the fifteen condition relations contained strictly given information in the nuclear clause. This was illustrated in (52b). The satellite conditional clauses contained strictly given information in six of the fifteen examples.

There appears to be no correlation between information structure and clause order. The natural order of events accounts for the tendency for preposed conditional clauses. Lehmann (1978:196) points out that it is fairly universal for conditional clauses to precede nuclear clauses.

There are two types of postposed conditional clauses. The first type was illustrated in (49) and (50) where the conditional clause only relates to the nuclear clause which precedes it. This type is explicitly marked by *bakng*. The function of these conditional clauses is to comment on the nuclear clause which precedes it (cf. Chafe 1984:448).

The second type of postposed conditional clause occurs in texts when the speaker wants to highlight the consequence. These conditional clauses are marked in several ways: 1) there is no overt connective linking the conditional satellite clause with the nuclear consequence clause; 2) the events are not in their natural order; and 3) the consequence is highlighted with respect to the condition. A postposed conditional clause of this type is illustrated in (53c), where the consequence is highlighted by fronting it.

62 Michael E. Boutin

(53) a. ***ou*** *kibunggakng* *si* ***reida*** *kiara* *sinsikng* *kulunggaadn*
I surprised SUBJ Reida has ring payment

        i   *laum*
        NS Laum

b. *kulunggaadn* *i* *laum* *ma'* *ny* *ombok*
payment NS Laum with NS Ombok

c. *mati* *nda'* *biriadn*
die not given

I am surprised *Reida* has a ring (which is) Laum's payment (for taking a second wife). It is Laum's fine for taking Ombok as a second wife. (*She*) will die, (if *she*) is not given it.

The speaker of (53) is the first wife and the mother of Reida. She is concerned that her daughter would die if the fine is not paid. Thus, the consequence is highlighted by fronting it.

In conclusion, this article has presented an overview of the syntactic clause-combining strategies in Banggi. Clause combining is described in terms of a continuum. What are traditionally called subordinate clauses are divided into two major groups in Banggi. Conditional and other causal satellite clauses are more 'paratactic'-like than temporal clauses which are more 'complement'-like. This is seen in the difference in the degree of reduction of temporal clauses as opposed to conditional clauses.

Rhetorical relations are signaled in the morphosyntax, either by explicit connectives, or by clause-combining strategy, for example serial verbs, or by contextual clues, for example other clauses accounting for the realized versus unrealized status of the clause in question.

The explicitness of conditional connectors is related to the function of the conditional clause in the discourse. The general constraint on clause ordering of conditionals is the natural order of events in the real world. Exceptions are related to the function of the conditional clause, sometimes to qualify the preceding nuclear clause—those marked by *bakng*—and other times to downgrade the condition as opposed to the preceding highlighted consequence—those not marked by *bakng*.

References

Aissen, Judith L. 1984. Control and command in Tzotzil purpose clauses. Proceedings of the Tenth Annual Meeting of the Berkeley Linguistic Society 10:559–64.

Beekman, John and John Callow. 1979. The semantic structure of written communication. Prepublication draft. Dallas: Summer Institute of Linguistics.

Bell, Sarah J. 1976. Cebuano subjects in two frameworks. Bloomington: Indiana University Linguistics Club.

———. 1983. Advancements and ascensions in Cebuano. In David M. Perlmutter (ed.), Studies in relational grammar 1:143–218. Chicago: University of Chicago Press.

Blake, Frank R. 1916. The Tagalog verb. Journal of the American Oriental Society 36:396–414.

Bloomfield, Leonard. 1917. Tagalog texts with grammatical analysis. University of Illinois Studies in Language and Literature 3(3). Urbana: University of Illinois.

Boutin, Michael E. 1991. Aspect and temporal reference in Banggi. In Stephen H. Levinsohn (ed.), Thematic continuity and development in languages of Sabah, 7–28. Pacific Linguistics C118. Canberra: Australian National University.

Brown, Gillian and George Yule. 1983. Discourse analysis. Cambridge: Cambridge University Press.

Chafe, Wallace. 1984. How people use adverbial clauses. Proceedings of the Tenth Annual Meeting of the Berkeley Linguistic Society 10:437–49.

Comrie, Bernard. 1981. Language universals and linguistic typology. Chicago: University of Chicago Press.

———. 1984. Subject and object control: Syntax, semantics, pragmatics. Proceedings of the Tenth Annual Meeting of the Berkeley Linguistic Society 10:450–64.

De Guzman, Videa P. 1988. Ergative analysis for Philippine languages: An analysis. In Richard McGinn (ed.), Studies in Austronesian linguistics, 323–45. Ohio University Monographs in International Studies, Southeast Asia Series 76.

DeLancey, Scott. 1981. An interpretation of split ergativity and related patterns. Language 57(3):626–57.

Dik, Simon. 1972. Coordination. Amsterdam: North-Holland.

———. 1981. Functional grammar. North-Holland Linguistic Series 37. Amsterdam: North-Holland.

Dooley, Robert A. 1986. Sentence-initial elements in Brazilian Guarani. In Joseph E. Grimes (ed.), Sentence inital devices, 45–69. Dallas: Summer Institute of Linguistics.

Foley, William A. and Robert D. Van Valin. 1984. Functional syntax and universal grammar. Cambridge Studies in Linguistics 38. Cambridge: Cambridge University Press.

French, Koleen Matsuda. 1988. The focus system in Philippine languages: An historical overview. Philippine Journal of Linguistics 19(1):1–27.

Gerdts, Donna B. 1988. Antipassive and causatives in Ilokano: Evidence for an ergative analysis. In Richard McGinn (ed.), Studies in Austronesian linguistics, 295–321. Ohio University Monographs in International Studies, Southeast Asia Series 76.

Gil, D. 1982. Quantifier scope and patient prominence. Some data from Batak, Buginese, and Tagalog. UCLA Working Papers in Semantics 1.

————. 1984. On the notion of "direct object" in patient prominent languages. In Frank Plank (ed.), Objects: Towards a theory of grammatical relations, 87–108. London: Academic Press.

Givón, Talmy. 1983. Topic continuity in discourse: An introduction. In Talmy Givón (ed.), Topic continuity in discourse: A quantitative cross-language study, 1–41. Amsterdam: John Benjamins.

Haiman, John. 1978. Conditionals are topics. Language 54(3):564–89.

————. 1983. Iconic and economic motivation. Language 59(4):781–819.

———— and Sandra A. Thompson. 1984. "Subordination" in universal grammar. Proceedings of the Tenth Annual Meeting of the Berkeley Linguistic Society 10:510–23.

———— and ————, eds. 1988. Clause combining in grammar and discourse. Amsterdam: John Benjamins.

Halliday, Michael A. K. and Ruqaiya Hasan. 1976. Cohesion in English. London: Longman.

Jordon, Michael P. 1988. Relational propositions within the clause. The Fourteenth LACUS Forum 1987, 278–88.

Keenan, Edward L. 1985. Relative clauses. In Shopen, 2:141–70.

Kroeger, Paul R. 1989. The Morpho-syntax of voice in Kimaragang. Unpublished ms.

Lakoff, George. 1987. Women, fire, and dangerous things: What categories reveal about the mind. Chicago: University of Chicago Press.

Larson, Mildred L. 1984. Meaning-based translation: A guide to cross-language equivalence. Lanham: University Press of America.

Lehmann, Christian. 1988. Towards a typology of clause linkage. In Haiman and Thompson, 181–225.

Lehmann, Winfred P. 1978. English: A characteristic SVO language. In Winfred P. Lehmann (ed.), Syntactic typology, 169–222. Austin: University of Texas.

Levinsohn, Stephen H. 1987. Textual connections in Acts. Atlanta: Scholars Press.

Longacre, Robert E. 1985. Sentences as combinations of clauses. In Shopen, 2:235–86.

Mann, William C. and Sandra A. Thompson. 1987. Rhetorical structure theory: A theory of text organization. Reprinted from The structure of discourse. Marina del Rey: Information Science Institute.

Matthiessen, Christian and Sandra A. Thompson. 1988. The structure of discourse and 'subordination'. In Haiman and Thompson, 275–329.

McCawley, James D. 1988. The syntactic phenomena of English. Chicago: University of Chicago Press.

McKaughan, Howard P. 1958. The inflection and syntax of Maranao verbs. Manila: Bureau of Printing.

———. 1973. Subject versus topic. In Andrew B. Bonzalez (ed.), Parangal kay Cecilio Lopez, FSC, 206–13. Quezon City: Linguistic Society of the Philippines.

Miller, John and Carolyn Miller. 1991. Thematic continuity and development in Coastal Kadazan narratives. In Stephen H. Levinsohn (ed.), Thematic continuity and development in languages of Sabah, 105–35. Pacific Linguistics C118. Canberra: Australian National University.

Mithun, Marianne. 1988. The grammaticization of coordination. In Haiman and Thompson, 331–59.

Moody, David C. 1991. Continuity and development in Ida'an narrative discourse. In Stephen H. Levinsohn (ed.), Thematic continuity and development in languages of Sabah, 137–62. Pacific Linguistics C118. Canberra: Australian National University.

Naylor, Paz Buenaventura. 1975. Topic, focus, and emphasis in the Tagalog verbal clause. Oceanic Linguistics 14(1):12–79.

Noonan, Michael. 1985. Complementation. In Shopen, 2:42–140.

Ochs Elinor. 1979. Planned and unplanned discourse. In Talmy Givón (ed.), Syntax and semantics, 12: Discourse and syntax, 51–80. New York: Academic Press.

Payne, Thomas E. 1982. Role and reference related subject properties and ergativity in Yup'ik Eskimo and Tagalog. Studies in Language 6:75–106.

Pike, Kenneth L. 1963. A syntactic paradigm. Language 39(2):216–30.

Prideaux, Gary D. 1988. Discourse influences on the syntax of ordered events: Evidence from texts. The Fourteenth LACUS Forum 1987, 309–17.

Ramsey, Violeta. 1987. The functional distribution of preposed and postposed "if" and "when" clauses in written discourse. In Russell S. Tomlin (ed.), Coherence and grounding in discourse, 383–408. Amsterdam: John Benjamins.

Schachter, Paul. 1976. The subject in Philippine languages: Topic, actor, actor-topic, or none of the above. In Charles N. Li (ed.), Subject and topic, 491–518. New York: Academic Press.

—————. 1977. Reference-related and role-related properties of subjects. In Peter Cole and Jerrold M. Sadock (eds.), Grammatical relations, 279–306. New York: Academic Press.

Schank, Roger and Robert Abelson. 1977. Scripts, plans, goals, and understanding: An inquiry into human knowledge structures. Hillsdale, N.J.: Lawrence Erlbaum Associates.

Shopen, Timothy, ed. 1985. Language typology and syntactic description. 2 vols. Cambridge: Cambridge University Press.

Starosta, Stanley, Andrew K. Pawley, and Lawrence A. Reid. 1982. The evolution of focus in Austronesian. Papers from the Third International Conference on Austronesian Linguistics, 2. In Amran Halim, Lois Carrington, and S. A. Wurm (eds.), Tracking the travellers, 145–70. Pacific Linguistics Series C75.

Thomas, David D. 1958. Mansaka sentence and sub-sentence structures. Philippine Social Sciences and Humanities Review 23:330–58.

Thompson, Sandra A. and Robert E. Longacre. 1985. Adverbial clauses. In Shopen, 2:171–234.

van Dijk, Teun A. 1977. Text and context: Explorations in the semantics and pragmatics of discourse. London: Longman.

Wouk, Fay. 1986. Transitivity in Proto-Malayo-Polynesian and Proto-Austronesian. In Paul Geraghty, Lois Carrington, and S. A. Wurm (eds.), FOCAL I: Papers from the Fourth International Conference on Austronesian Linguisics, 133–58. Pacific Linguistics Series C93.

A Look at Two Ifè Connectives

Marquita Klaver

In Ifè, the connectives *bí* and *kíbí* can both be used to introduce subordinate clauses and they can both be glossed as when in clauses which give the circumstance for the event in the main clause, as shown in (1) and (2).

(1) *kíbí   ň   lɔ   nádzà   á   ň   ra   tìmátì*
     when 1s go to^market DEF[1] 1s^REAL buy tomato
     When I went to market, I bought tomatoes.

(2) *bí   ň   lɔ   nádzà   màa   ra   tìmátì*
     when 1s go to^market 1s^PRED buy tomato
     When I go to market, I will buy tomatoes.

This article attempts to define the difference in meaning between *bí* and *kíbí* and to predict when each one will be used in circumstance clauses.

A second but related problem is that some clauses introduced by *kíbí* have a clause-final definite particle *é/á*, while other *kíbí* clauses do not have this particle. bí clauses rarely have a definite particle[2] marking the clause; however, a word or phrase within the clause may have a definite particle.

---

[1] Abbreviations: DEF, definite particle; DEM, demonstrative; EMPH, emphatic; HAB, habitual aspect; INC, incompletive aspect; NEG, negative; p, plural; PRED, predictive mood; REAL, realis mood; s, singular; SUBJ, subjunctive mood; 1 2 3, first, second, and third person.

[2] The definite particle in Ifè is a clitic, either *é* or *á* depending on the phonological environment. It marks known information and can be used at the word, phrase, or clause level.

68   Marquita Klaver

Two clues were found to the possible solution of when the different connectives are used. One clue is that *bí* introduces conditional as well as circumstantial clauses, while *kíbí* never occurs in conditionals. The second clue
is that bilingual speakers consistently gloss bí as 'if'. On reflection, it is apparent that 'when' in English has two different uses: (1) for unrealized circumstances ('when I go to the store next week') and (2) for already realized
events ('when I went to town yesterday'). From these clues, the following
hypothesis was developed about the connectives *bí* and *kíbí*:

> *bí* circumstance clauses will refer to unrealized events.
> *kíbí* circumstance clauses will refer to realized events.

1. Circumstance clauses

A look at data from Ifè texts confirms this hypothesis. Examples (3) and
(4) are from a narrative text. In both, the circumstance clause is introduced
by *kíbí*. From the perspective of the speaker, both the main clause and the
subordinate clause events have already been realized. The main clauses in
both examples are in realis mood.

(3) *kíbí   ilè   má   á   kètógbe   fúḍá*
     when earth beˆlight DEF Ketogbe comeˆout
     At daybreak, Ketogbe came out (of her house).

(4) *kíbí   à   lɔ náàkpáré é   à   rè̃   náàŋíri-ilú   é*
     when 3p go toˆAkpare DEF 3pˆREAL walk throughout-village DEF
     When they went to Akpare, they walked all through the village.

Example (5) is from a folktale narrative. The *bí* clause contains a circumstance which is as yet unrealized at the time the speaker in the story makes this
statement. The verb of the main clause is in the subjunctive mood (irrealis).

(5) *bí   ó   kó   ɔḍɔ́ méɛta ná   àŋa   kó   sè̃   wá*
     when 3s complete year three already 3pˆEMPH SUBJ repeat come

     kpaḍé bè   é
     meet   there DEF
     When three years would have been completed, they would return and
     meet there.

A Look at Two Ifè Connectives 69

Example (6) is part of a procedural text about preparing a cornfield. The text is referring to a hypothetical situation: 'Supposing that you want to make a cornfield, these are the things you must do.' This example is one of the steps in clearing the field.

(6)   *bí*   *à*   *gbẽ*   *nà*   *tanã́*   *gú*   *oko*   *ế*
       when   3p   be^dry   2s^HAB set^fire   burn   field   DEF
       When they (brush) are dry, you burn the field.

The speaker is not referring to any specific instance of brush drying and a field being burnt, but is stating a general truth about brush being dry before burning a field. In this instance, the habitual aspect has the force of an imperative and is irrealis.

In all of the examples given thus far, a *kíbí* circumstance clause is subordinated to a main clause with a verb in realis mood, while *bí* circumstance clauses have main clause verbs in irrealis mood. This seems to substantiate the realized and unrealized nature of *kíbí* and *bí,* respectively. Also, it is grammatically unacceptable to use a *kíbí* circumstance clause with an irrealis main clause, as in (7).

(7)   **kíbí*   *ǹ*   *lɔ*   *nádzà*   *á*   *màa*   *ra*   *tìmátì*
       when   1s   go   to^market   DEF   1s^PRED   buy   tomato
       *When I went to market, I will buy tomatoes.

It is also unacceptable to use a *bí* circumstance clause when the main clause verb is in realis mood as shown in (8).

(8)   **bí*   *ǹ*   *lɔ*   *nádzà*   *ǹ*   *ra*   *tìmátì*
       when   1s   go   to^market   1s^REAL   buy   tomato
       *When I go to market, I bought tomatoes.

The Ifè verb system is marked for mood and aspect, but not for tense. The realis mood is marked by Ø, as is the perfective aspect. An example of this is the main clause in (4). Irrealis moods and imperfective aspects are marked by either preverbal particles, as in the main clause of (5), or by change in subject pronoun, as in the main clause of (6). It is to be noted that circumstance clauses, whether introduced by *bí* or *kíbí* also have Ø marking for mood, so they could be considered to be either realis mood or unmarked for mood. As for aspect, both types of circumstance clause can be marked for imperfective aspect as in (9) and (10).

70 Marquita Klaver

(9) *kíbí   à   wà   seé   ɛ́   ɔ̀nyà-kà̰   wà   tsí   wà   kɛ́ɛ   tsí*
   when 3p INC pick^it DEF person-one exist and INC take^it and

   wà   ń   dzɛ   géni
   INC it eat only
   While they were picking (fruit), one person was just taking them and
   eating them.

(10) *bí   ó   wà   wó   à   náa   wo   bɔ̀lú   ɔma   mέὲdzì*
    when 3s INC bubble 3p HAB unwrap bouillion^cube child two

    si   ńnὲ
    put in^it
    When it is boiling, you unwrap two bouillion cubes and put them in.

In the data examined thus far, all *kíbí* clauses have been marked by the
definite particle *ɛ́/á*, while none of the *bí* clauses have been. This makes
sense if one considers a realized event to be like a definite referent, and an
unrealized event to be a nonspecific referent.

2. Other types of subordinate clauses

After confirming the initial hypothesis, the investigation was continued to
find the role of *bí* and *kíbí* in other types of subordinate clauses. The original
hypothesis was expanded to propose that *bí* clauses of all types will always
be unrealized in nature, while *kíbí* clauses will always be realized.

Another type of subordinate clause in which *bí* occurs is the if clause of
a conditional sentence. Conditional sentences are always unrealized and in
Ifè will always have a main clause verb in irrealis mood. Example (11) is
from a folktale narrative. The lizard in the story is speaking to the man, using indirect speech.

(11) *bí   ó   kpa   òŋu   kpáà   ìnà-ɛnɛ   yὲé   nákó   kú*
    if 3s kill 3s^EMPH SO   mother-of^person that^one PRED die
    If he (man) kills him (lizard), that one's mother will die.

This is a conditional of the predictive type, according to the classification
by Thompson and Longacre (1985).

Example (12) is a habitual or generic conditional. It is the closing sentence of the text mentioned earlier on how to make a cornfield, and states a
general truth. Note the use of the habitual aspect in the main clause.

A Look at Two Ifɛ̀ Connectives

(12) *bí ò kò máa tse àŋa kpó náa rá*
if 2s NEG know^how do 3p^EMPH all HAB die
If you don't know how to do it, all will perish.

kíbí, on the other hand, is used in subordinate clauses to state the grounds for an assertion in the main clause, as in (13), or the reason for a result, as in (14). Example (13) is from a folktale in which a father and his children have been working hard in the fields. The father makes the following proposal:

(13) *kíbí ó ká àŋa béè ó wà ní ɛnɛ*
since 3s tire 3p^EMPH like^that 3s^REAL exist that person

        kṹnukṹ kó wè
        each^one SUBJ bathe
Since we are so tired, let's all bathe (in the river).

In (14), the reason (subordinate) clause is introduced by *kíbí* and follows the result (main) clause. In Ifɛ̀, clauses with a reason-result relationship can have the order reason-result or result-reason.

(14) *àwa kpó àa kí yàà kíbí ɛnɛ ŋè wáa*
1p^EMPH all 1p^REAL greet astonishment how person DEM INGR

        tsole bè
        steal like^that
We were all astonished how someone had stolen like that.

In both (13) and (14) the event in the *kíbí* clause is already realized from the point of view of the speaker, that is the father and the narrator, respectively. The main clause verb in both is realis mood.

3. Complement clauses

Both *bí* and *kíbí* can also be used as complementizers. The use of both connectives is limited to certain complement taking verbs of perception and cognition, such as 'know' and 'see', as in (15), (16), and (17).

(15) *kò ma bí kó tse ńɖi-ìsìkéké é*
NEG know how SUBJ make place-of^sleeve DEF
She didn't know how to make the armholes.

(16) àa nákó rí bí à náa malé   fáà
1p PRED see how 3p HAB build^house query
We will see how one builds a house.

(17) maḍé ɛ́ rí kíbí ó   dzokó si ɛ́
child DEF see how 3s^REAL sit^down place DEF
The child saw how he was sitting there.

In these sentences, the *bí* clauses themselves are marked for irrealis mood, with the habitual in (16) having the force of irrealis, while in (17), the *kíbí* clause is realis mood.

kíbí can also be used in a subordinate clause of comparison, as in (18).

(18) síso ɛ́   wà   kíbí àḍùbá oḍé
fruit DEF exist like papaya little
The fruit is a little like papaya.

In this type of construction, the verb in the *kíbí* clause is ellipsed: 'The fruit is a little like papaya (is)'. A known concept in the *kíbí* clause is being used to define more clearly an unknown or poorly understood concept in the main clause. The known item, like a realis event, is something that the speaker is sure of.

In conclusion, the difference between the use of *bí* and *kíbí* in all types of clauses is dependent on the distinction between realized and unrealized events from the speaker's point of view. This is consistent with the language as a whole. Ifè is a heavily verb-oriented language and the major tense/mood/aspect distinction in the verb system is that of realis versus irrealis moods.

The obligatory use of the definite particle to mark *kíbí* clauses seems to be limited to clauses of the circumstance type. The language is making a distinction between subordinate clauses which give background information about the event in the main clause and those which have a logical relation to the main clause event, such as the reason for a result or the grounds for an assertion.

Reference

Thompson, Sandra and Robert E. Longacre. 1985. Adverbial clauses. In Timothy Shopen (ed.), Language typology and syntatic description 2:171–234. Cambridge: Cambridge University Press.

A Pragmatic Analysis of a Failed Cross-Cultural Communication

Barbara J. Sayers

1. Introduction: An aboriginal-white encounter

"He didn't listen to me. He kept butting in on me with that word of his. He didn't listen to me right through to the end. He didn't listen to me. That (man) butted in on me. That young fellow butted in on me. He is not an important man, one trained to listen. An important man listens to (a person's) talk. This young man butted in on me with his ignorance" (text, lines 35–44).[1]

The context of these remarks is an account by an Australian aboriginal man of his encounter with a white (nonaboriginal) Social Security officer. The anger expressed by this aboriginal speaker was obvious to Geytenbeek, the supplier of the text, who reports that this speaker was usually calm and a known peacemaker. What caused this angry outburst about the young Social Security officer he was describing?

The problem is not so much a matter of understanding the words actually used as it was the different meaning conveyed because of the different world

---

[1] The entire text of the letter of explanation is given in appendix 1 and a pragmatic analysis of the text in table form is given in appendix 2.

A somewhat shortened version of this article appeared in 1998 with the title *A Fair Go: Aboriginal Living and Learning in the Dominant Australian Culture*. Summer Institute of Linguistics Australian Aborigines and Linguistics 8.

74 Barbara J. Sayers

views and associated assumptions on which these words were based. The social and cultural background of the two men was radically different, so their unstated assumptions about the nature of things referred to were also very different. Levinson (1983:21) in one of his definitions of pragmatics says, "...understanding an utterance involves a great deal more than knowing the meaning of the words uttered and the grammatical relations between them. Above all, understanding an utterance involves making inferences that will connect what is said to what is mutually assumed or what has been said before."

The anthropologist Malinowski, as far back as 1935, recognized the importance of inferences in understanding utterances. He realized that the assumptions of the natives, as he called the Trobriand Islanders, were vastly different from his own and that he could not understand a text in their language without a detailed knowledge of their culture and society. He says (1935:4), "it is a long way from the mouth of the native informant to the mind of the English reader. But the value of the linguistic data is only in proportion to the ethnographer's own knowledge and his critical accuracy in drawing inferences." Furthermore he says, "that (language) stands in a definite relation to the life of the people who speak it and to their mental habits and attitudes. From this point of view it provides us with the most important documents illustrating types of human behavior other than linguistic" (p. 6).

Hasan (1985) recognizes the value of Malinowski's work and that too little attention has been paid to it. It was largely Malinowski's work that originally led Sayers to the study of world view, presupposition, and inference as she struggled to make sense of texts such as this one of Jack Horace and his encounter with the Social Security man. Without an understanding of the culture, particularly in relation to kinship with its all-pervasive influence in an Aboriginal community, Aborigines such as Horace will continue to be looked on as ignorant and unrealistic because they are perceived to be saying ridiculous things. The analysis of this text shows that Horace is no fool— rather he is an Aborigine whose assumptions are different from the average white Australian's. What he says is congruent with his understanding of how society functions.

This text which we are examining is one of a failed cross-cultural communication. The Aboriginal man, Jack Horace, is angry. His attempt to communicate in English to the English-speaking Social Security man had failed to achieve the result he desired. He reported to Geytenbeek on the event in his mother tongue, Nyangumarta, so that Geytenbeek could translate it into English for him to take back to the Social Security man the following day. It is this report that we are analyzing. What he actually said and how he

A Pragmatic Analysis of a Failed Cross-Cultural Communication   75

said it in English can only be a matter of conjecture, but regardless of what it was, the white man's responses evoked Horace's anger.

If we assume that when communicating each speaker gave "a guarantee of relevance" (Sperber and Wilson 1986), then we need to examine the assumptions behind each speaker's words, as well as the words themselves, to see why the communication failed. Obviously, the different social and cultural background of the speakers provided each of them with a very different set of presuppositions (or assumptions)—encyclopedic knowledge in Sperber and Wilson's terms—from which they spoke. These differences were not accessible to the hearers so the information which the speaker aimed to communicate did not have the intended effect. Instead, the conversation proceeded with each participant speaking past the other as each one was unable to process correctly the message he heard. Regardless of the processing effort exerted, it was impossible for either hearer to arrive at the intended message. And failure led to anger, at least on Horace's part.

Following an explanation of the immediate social situation at the Tjalku Wara Aboriginal community in §2, there is a detailed explanation of cultural issues in §§3 and 4 which have to be understood before the text can be examined. The text is then discussed in §5 in terms of structural linguistic features as well as pragmatic ones which relate to the anthropological information. This information makes clear what the presuppositions (implicatures) and implications are from Horace's perspective. For the sake of simplicity and to keep the focus on Horace, the white man's perspective is stated but not explained. Section 5 differs from the charted version in §6 since the main focus is kept on Horace's position. The charted analysis of the text keeps both the Social Security man's perspective and the resultant message separate from Horace's for each line of the text.

2. The immediate social setting of the encounter

Some time before the encounter analyzed here, Jack Horace, an elderly Aboriginal man of the Nyangumarta language group, gave Brian Geytenbeek, a linguist with the Summer Institute of Lingustics working in Nyangumarta, a report in glowing terms of the independent development of the Tjalku Wara community. This community had been established by a small number of recipients of Social Security benefits, specifically the Old Age and Invalid Pensions. These people wanted to be independent but close to the amenities of the town of Port Hedland, Western Australia.

This community was unique in that government grants for various projects were rejected by the Aborigines in favor of retaining their independence. Instead they paid for development out of their Social Security payments. These

76 Barbara J. Sayers

developments included a telephone service for emergencies, a windmill for water, fencing, and a vehicle to collect firewood. At the same time the Tjalku Wara people were traditional Aborigines. The old culture still meant much to them, and the related social custom was still observed (see §3).

All went well until some young Nyangumarta men descended on the community, finding it conveniently close to town for collecting their unemployment payments and for buying alcohol. While the residents of Tjalku Wara resented their behavior, they were unable to do anything about it. Traditional kinship responsibilities obligated them to provide food and shelter for these people who arrived drunk, having already spent their unemployment benefits on alcohol. At the same time the elderly people could not handle the drunken young men, nor did they have authority over them in relation to the money given by the Social Security men since they had not been involved in the giving or receiving of it.

In this way the elderly residents of Tjalku Wara became the victims of a reciprocal system of giving which had become one-sided. The transient drunkards never had anything to give, but expected to be provided for by their elderly relatives. Furthermore, their drunkenness led to fighting and vandalism and sometimes to physical injury to the residents. Added to this, once the food was gone everyone went hungry until the next pension day.

The white police were unable to help for two reasons. Firstly, the twenty-minute drive to the community meant that they rarely saw a fight, and secondly, none of the Aboriginal residents would give evidence in a white man's court, no matter how badly he or she had been treated.

The situation was threatening to destroy all that the Tjalku Wara residents had been working towards so successfully for several years. It was this situation that Jack Horace addressed at a two-day meeting of government officials and Aboriginal people. The aim of the meeting was to discuss issues facing Aborigines in this (the Pilbara) area of Western Australia.

Another factor that needs to be understood in interpreting the text is that, according to Geytenbeek, Jack Horace was aware of a system of "working for the dole" in some selected communities and wanted it for his community. This is the Community Development and Employment Program (C.D.E.P.) where the unemployment benefits are paid to the community in a lump sum, and the residents all have to do a prescribed amount of work to receive their part of it. Horace alluded to this but didn't mention it overtly.

3. Cultural background to the encounter

Traditionally, Aborigines have structured their society in accordance with kinship. They recognize a network of kin relationships that extends

A Pragmatic Analysis of a Failed Cross-Cultural Communication

throughout their whole group. This network provides a patterned structure for approved social interaction. Such behavior involves partiality: only certain people are in the right relationship with each other to have reciprocal rights and responsibilities. In this section we deal first with social structure and then with social process. Then we look at the outworking of kinship in economic affairs.

3.1 Social structure

In traditional Aboriginal communities everyone is related to everyone else. Aborigines classify particular groups of people under the terms used for close kin. For instance, using English terminology, an Aborigine refers to his/her mother and all her sisters as mother, and to father and his brothers as father. All these mothers' and fathers' children are his/her sisters and brothers. By contrast, he/she refers to mother's brothers as uncle and to father's sisters as aunt. Their children are his/her cousins. Similar patterning extends to the grandparents' and grandchildren's generations. Such classifications can be extended to cover not only the whole of any given Aboriginal group but to members of other Aboriginal communities, and indeed anyone else with whom the Aborigine has extended contact. While the details of classification differ between groups, for instance the Aranda eight-section system, the Nyangumarta four-section system, and the Pitjantjatjara alternate generations, such classificatory kinship systems are found Australia-wide. This is abundantly documented in the anthropological literature by writers such as Elkin (1974:84ff.) and the Berndts (1964:47ff.).

Because kinship patterning determines social behavior, everyone must be related in some way. A person coming into a strange group is usually allocated a kinship position. This may be done through some known intermediaries, or, as in the case of whites, by some other means. Sayers was assigned a kin relationship of daughter to two sisters who lived and worked near her. All other relationships were worked out from this one. The Berndts write about the role of kinship, showing the necessity for all in a community to be able to interact appropriately:

> ...Aboriginal Australia kinship is the articulating force for all social interaction. The kinship system of a particular tribe or language unit is in effect a shorthand statement about the network of interpersonal relations within that unit—a blueprint to guide its members. It does not reflect, except in ideal terms, the actuality of that situation; but it does provide a code of action which those members cannot ignore if they are to live in relative harmony with one another. And kinship, in this situation, pervades all aspects of social living. We cannot understand or appreciate traditional life in

78   Barbara J. Sayers

> Aboriginal Australia without knowing something, at least, of its so-
> cial organization and structure—of which kinship is the major inte-
> grating element or, to put it another way, the fine mesh which holds
> the society together. (1964:91)

Elkin (1974:142–43) puts it slightly differently and so brings out an additional point, that is, the rights and obligations of kinship. These features
arise from what he refers to as the "principle of reciprocity", a principle that
operates throughout Aboriginal society. By determining behavior, kinship
sets out the obligations, rights, and responsibilities of the individual in respect of, for instance, people classified as his/her father, mother, father-in-
law, grandparents. One has particular obligations and responsibilities towards certain of these individuals but does not have them towards others. As
Elkin puts it:

> The obligations of kinship govern a person's behavior from his
> earliest years to his death, and affect life in all its aspects: in con-
> versation, visiting and camping; at crises of life, namely, child-birth,
> initiation, marriage, sickness and death; and in quarrels and fights.
> (1974:144)

The responsibilities of kinship are important in the area of authority.
Meggitt (1965:249) points out that a man's authority in a given event depends on kinship status relative to the key person involved rather than on the
nature of the event as such, e.g., the relationship of the operator in a cir-
cumcision ceremony to the novice being circumcised. He puts it this way:

> ...the ascription of authority to particular men on particular
> occasions depended largely on considerations of kinship status and,
> by extension, of descent line and moiety affiliation. Thus, a man
> might lead a specific revenge expedition, or dispose of a certain
> woman in marriage, or direct actors in one circumcision ceremony,
> because of his genealogical connection with the person to whom the
> situation primarily referred—the deceased, the bride or the novice.
> On the next occasion of this sort, however, he might play only a
> minor role, being now in a different kinship category relative to the
> central figure.

An important feature of Aboriginal social structure that Meggitt
(1965:249) draws from this kind of situation is that it "militated against the
emergence of a class of permanent leaders of community enterprises, of men
who could regularly and legitimately direct group behavior in several fields
of action." In other words authority related to who you were in relation to
the event under consideration, not to an ascribed position of authority over a
broad range of similar events.

A Pragmatic Analysis of a Failed Cross-Cultural Communication 79

In Western society, also, kinship is important, but the number of those counted as kin is much more limited, and the range of behavior between kin shows considerable variation. Nevertheless, Aboriginal and Western society both recognize kin relationships and associated appropriate behavior. It is important, however, to recognize that in Western society there is an additional type of relationship which is also common. This is the one that we refer to as the business or professional relationship: for instance, that between employer and employee, doctor and patient, trader and customer. In this type of association kin relationship is, for the most part, irrelevant. This relationship depends on such things as the goal or purpose of the activity or on quantitative considerations. Further, unlike kin relationship, the business relationship can be terminated (Bain 1992, chapter 8). People who enter into such relationship behave towards one another in terms of that professional or business association. The significance of these different kinds of relationship is handled in §3.2.

Further to these observations, we note that in Western society authority is ascribed to many roles. A person in a particular role is given the right, when acting in that role, to perform certain ceremonies, such as a minister of religion who may marry or bury anyone regardless of the presence or absence of a kinship tie. Such a person may also have a position of prestige in a community because of that role.

3.2 Social process: Partiality versus impartiality

Social process, or social activity, can be regarded as relationship put into practice. Bain (1992, chapter 8) refers to social action undertaken between kin as interaction, and to social action resulting from business or professional relationship as transaction. We adopt that terminology here.

As shown above, Westerners practice both interaction and transaction. These types of social process are characterized by partial and impartial behavior, respectively. Furthermore, Bain (1992) points out:

> ...it is possible for the two forms of social process to co-exist in the one social event. In that case, for instance in a family business, interaction can put pressure on transaction, modifying its practical expression. Nevertheless, while a family business, or again an administrative agency, can accommodate some partiality towards kinsmen and friends, the impartiality of transaction must remain dominant if the business is to survive or if the administration is to remain acceptable and achieve its recognised objectives.

By contrast, in the Aboriginal social setting, kin relationship must control and partiality is culturally approved. Interaction accords with world view

80   Barbara J. Sayers

and, therefore, with acceptable social behavior. As a result, transaction has
no place at all. To put this another way, impartiality has no place in the
Aboriginal cultural repertoire since interaction permeates every aspect of the
Aboriginal social world. Such a wholesale use of interaction is as alien to
Westerners as impartiality is to Aborigines. This contrast between Aborigine
and Westerner is important for understanding the communication failure in
the text under discussion.

3.3 The outworking of kinship in economic affairs

We look now at traditional practice, specifically with reference to eco-
nomics and related affairs. As we have seen, Aboriginal social behavior is
patterned according to the network of kinship that extends throughout the
Aboriginal community. In order to understand the problem faced by Horace
we need to recognize that the traditional rights and obligations of Aboriginal
society are still important to the elderly residents of the Tjalku Wara community. This is so despite some evident accommodation to Western society.

Distribution of assets. In Aboriginal society, one way of expressing
kinship is through the distribution of material assets. Giving and receiving
occur only between appropriate kin, that is, where there is obligation to give
and right to receive, but equally it does not occur where those rights and
duties are absent. In other words, through giving and receiving material
things (which nowadays include money and alcohol) Aborigines express and
honor relationship. In this way they affirm their place in the Aboriginal
society within which they live. Under these circumstances, any refusal to
take up an obligation constitutes rejection or repudiation of relationship and
is contrary to culturally acceptable behavior and world view. Under-
standably, the individual is under immense pressure to conform (Bain 1992,
chapter 8). There is abundant evidence in support of this view both in the
literature and in our own experience (Elkin 1974:142–43; Albrecht 1974:37
and undated 13–14; Berndt and Berndt 1964:89).

In discussing gift exchanges that maintain relationship, Meggitt says
(1965:56) that most of them "were (and are) ceremonial or gift-exchanges
intended to meet kinship and ritual obligations. Although, in some situations,
rules specify the objects or services to be exchanged, the public act of giving
is usually the significant feature of the transaction." Meggitt gives a number
of specific social situations in which reciprocity is practiced, for example,
for a service such as to the operator in an initiation ceremony (see Meggitt
1965:82, 154, 158–59, 161, 226, 231, 267–68, 308, 315, 328).

A Pragmatic Analysis of a Failed Cross-Cultural Communication 81

In short, in traditional Aboriginal society individuals must take up their obligations. In this way they honor their relationships by maintaining acceptable interaction with kin. Culturally there is no alternative.

It should be noted that in many areas the influence of Western culture is strong. Nevertheless, in places where this has happened, Aborigines still hold firmly to the traditional rights and obligations of kinship.

Giving and receiving in daily living. Traditionally, Aboriginal people were hunters and gatherers. Each day they collected what was needed. Whatever was in hand was distributed according to traditional right, used straightaway until all was gone, and then more was collected. A side effect of this was that there was no cultural mechanism to handle surplus, since, even when there was an excessive amount to be distributed, the individual still did not have to give to everyone but only to those to whom kinship determined that there was an obligation. As a result, the system provided a means of limiting an individual's responsibility to give. By contrast, Westerners often use quantity as a means to limit the obligation to give and the right to receive. When this is the case, there is a place for surplus which is then handled by saving it for future use. This practice of giving and receiving, which is frequently related to quantity, is alien to traditional Aboriginal custom. In other words, for the Aborigine where there is obligation to give it is not culturally acceptable to limit the quantity given.

While reciprocity is meant to be two-way, it is commonly observed that Aboriginal giving becomes one-sided. This occurs, for instance, when certain individuals are perpetually in receipt of money such as Social Security payments, while others, for one reason or another, have little or nothing to give. In Australia, government Social Security payments are the right of all citizens, and the government controls the distribution of funds in accord with impartial bureaucratic practice. Aboriginal recipients, however, handle their benefits in accord with the traditional distribution of assets, that is, according to kinship.

Bain (1992, chapter 9) reports a typical case, that of one elderly Aboriginal woman at Aputula, Central Australia, who as an aged pensioner had a regular income source. On one occasion a young woman relative and her husband arrived by train to pay her a visit. These young people were heavy drinkers but the elderly woman was not. The visitors quickly spent all their money on liquor and then they both relied upon the woman for food. She was happy to fulfill her obligation and was able to do this by getting food on credit from the local store. It was not long, however, before she was in debt. In order to solve her problem, the elderly woman and her husband went out camping. As the husband was able to hunt, little was needed from the store so the woman was able to save her pension money and add to it from the sale of artifacts made

82   Barbara J. Sayers

while camping. By not being in the community, she was able to avoid the need to meet her obligations to her younger kin, and thus she avoided rejecting the mutual relationship. In two months she had saved enough to discharge her indebtedness, and in addition she purchased train tickets so that the young woman and her husband could return to their usual place of residence.

This one-sided giving was not questioned, for the receivers were known to be without funds at the time. In earlier days, when the whole community was dependent on hunting and foraging, situations such as this would not have arisen. Then reciprocal rights and obligations in giving and receiving provided a kind of insurance against bad fortune in hunting and foraging at any particular time.

As well as being associated in reciprocal giving and receiving, individuals cooperated in other ways. For instance, a giver, or the performer of a service, was seen to have a measure of authority over the recipient from whom he could rightly expect cooperation. The following two examples from Bain (1992, chapter 9) show the outworking of this authority in contemporary situations.

> The two Aboriginal storekeepers at Aputula had a tendency to provide goods to Aboriginal kin either free or at less than the correct price. Obviously the store suffered. However, at that time both men held considerable authority in camp. For instance, both were effective in breaking up drunken brawling among their relatives. Then one of the men tried to collect all the money due. Straight away he lost his authority among his kin, but the other man retained his. A few weeks later they both resigned from their jobs. As they explained to Bain they were unable to refuse the obligation to give to their kin. 'We can't say "No" to our relations', they said. '(It is) like having no relation.' This example shows the pressure on the men to conform with accepted practice. It also shows the wider connection with social behavior in camp, particularly in relation to authority.

> In another case, the elder brother of two sisters was a drinker. He used to ask them to buy liquor for him. The elder sister refused but the younger did as he asked. When a drunken quarrel flared, the younger sister was sometimes able to 'settle him down', but the man would not listen to the older sister. The younger sister attributed her ability to the provision of funds. It was the one who gave the money in expression of relationship who had the right to expect cooperation from the drunken brother.

Both of these examples show the relationship of kinship rights and obligations to authority. (For further examples see Albrecht 1974:38 and Bain 1992, chapter 9.)

A Pragmatic Analysis of a Failed Cross-Cultural Communication

4. Implications of the sociocultural context to the encounter

In the situation at Tjalku Wara the elderly residents had nothing to do with the arrangements between the young men and the Social Security department. Nevertheless, they were under pressure from the drunkards as a result of that arrangement because Tjalku Wara was a place for these kin to stay and when staying they demanded the residents food and damaged their property and also caused physical injury to the elderly people. One reason for this is that drunk Aboriginal men will not take no for an answer when they want something and will fight until they get it. What compounded the difficulty was the related fact that the source of supply of the money that provided the alcohol lay outside the Aboriginal community and, while these elderly people had a right to expect cooperation from the drinkers as the providers of food and shelter for them, they were unable to handle the young drunkards. They also knew that since they had not provided the funds for the purchase of alcohol, they should not have to deal with the problem the excessive drinking caused since they had no authority over the drinkers in relation to the supply of those funds. In other words, they had neither rights nor obligations in relation to the money because they simply were not involved in the giving or receiving of the funds in question.

On the other hand, the elderly Tjalku Wara residents thought the white Social Security men, who were actively involved in the fortnightly payment of checks had authority over the drinkers, if not as actual kin then as quasi-kin. This occurred since these traditionally oriented Aborigines did not recognize impartial bureaucratic relationships—transaction—which were severed once the business was completed. The only option Horace had was to recognize the derived kinship relationship, based on interaction between the Social Security men and the drinkers. In such a relationship, Horace expected them to use their authority to obtain cooperation from the drinkers. Traditionally some reciprocal obligation would have applied in such a relationship. As Horace said when talking about work and the control of the drunks (line 24), 'That is yours (job/responsibility/obligation)'.

5. The text

On close examination of the Nyangumarta text, it is immediately obvious that the form is very different from that of English. Because of the different structure, it is extremely difficult to translate back into English. This is particularly so for utterances including the morpheme -*naku*, originally glossed

84   Barbara J. Sayers

HORT (hortatory mood)[2] by the Geytenbeeks. Two questions immediately
arise. Firstly, considering the morpheme -naku, is there a more appropriate
gloss that would reflect the cultural situation in which Horace is operating,
and, secondly, how did Horace express in English what he reported he had
said when he recorded his version of the encounter in Nyangumarta? We
will look at these in the order given.

5.1 Gloss of morpheme -naku

The opening quote from Horace shows the degree of frustration and anger that he felt regarding his encounter with the young Social Security man.
Brian and Helen Geytenbeek's translation of -naku HORT as 'should' does
not seem to be a strong enough term considering Horace's state of mind.
The words 'should' and 'ought to' which are the Geytenbeeks' usual translation for this form, convey a weak sense of obligation, allowing some possible alternative response, as in 'I should go, but won't today'. But Horace's
request in line 31 seems to be much stronger than this. It is more like a demand for the Social Service men to do something about the situation. The
Geytenbeeks indicated that this form is a polite imperative which, in certain
social situations, must be used instead of the regular imperative, but pragmatically it carries the form of a strongly worded imperative.

Similarly, with negatives, at least for some speakers, the strongest negative imperative that can be used in Nyangumarta is NEG + HORT. This perceived lack of a stronger imperative leaves the linguist with a wide range of
possible translations back into English—translations which range from weak
to strong. The particular choice for an utterance is best decided in relation to
the context of that utterance and includes the forms such as 'mustn't', 'can't
(have no right to)', and 'won't'—negated indicative forms; and 'oughtn't',
'wouldn't', 'shouldn't (should not have to/have no right to)', and 'couldn't
(not allowed to)'—negated nonindicative forms. Amee Glass (personal
communication) notes similar choices when translating Ngaanyatjara back
into English when context is not known, but states that when the utterance is
in context the choice is usually clear. In other words, the choice of free
translation is dictated by pragmatic issues rather than grammatical ones.

---

[2] Abbreviations: [...] Geytenbeek's original translation, (...) inserted for clarification, ABL.
ablative; ACC. accusative; ALL. allative; CF. contrafactual; CONJ. conjunction, DAT. dative; EMPH.
emphatic, ERG. ergative; FUT. future; GEN. genitive; HORT. hortatory mood; IMFUT. immediate
future; INCHO. inchoative; INST. instrument; INTENS. intensifier; LOC. locative; NEG. negative; NF.
nonfuture; NOM. nominative; NMZR. nominalizer; PL/p, plural; pin, plural inclusive; pex, plural
exclusive; PRES present; REP. repetitive; ROM, marker of rights and obligations; SG/s, singular;
VB. verbalizer; 1 2 3, first, second, and third person.

A Pragmatic Analysis of a Failed Cross-Cultural Communication 85

It is helpful to note that *-naku*, which was glossed by the Geytenbeeks as HORT, is used in this text by Horace as though the encounter involved traditional Aboriginal reciprocal rights and obligations. In traditional encounters the original donor had the right to expect some kind of return for the gift or service such as a reciprocal gift, or cooperation from the recipient. This could give the donor a degree of authority over the recipient since the recipient had a reciprocal obligation to the donor. These various aspects of reciprocity are reflected in the free translation of specific examples.

One of the problems that led Sayers to seek an alternative gloss for *-naku* was the use of HORT in first-person examples, such as those in (1) and (2). While 'let us go' is recognized as a first-person hortatory form, the above use is not usually thought of as hortatory. The Geytenbeeks also report that third-person examples occur. These examples were equally difficult to accept as hortatory since hortatory normally means "...to encourage, exhort, urge a course of action" (*Macquarie Dictionary*, 1982). As a result Sayers suggested that an appropriate technical gloss for this form would be a "marker of rights and obligations" (ROM). By making this change, the morpheme gloss of these lines now relates to the cultural context of the speaker, while the choice of the free English translation indicates the pragmatic perspective of the particular utterance under consideration. It is salutary to note that the use of traditional technical terms for morphemes that only partially overlap in meaning with the traditional usage can mask what is really happening in the language.

(1) *munu kunta   ji-naku*
     NEG   stop   VB-ROM[HORT]
     (We) have no right/authority to [should not have to] stop them.

(2) *jawujul japij   puluku pala ngani-ku-pa   ji-naku*
     Social Service bloke   that what-DAT-CONJ VB-ROM[HORT]
     The Social Service blokes have right/authority to [should] do something about that.

5.2 What did Horace actually say in English?

Geytenbeek confirmed our suspicions that in the context of this text Horace's English could well have contained the form 'gotta' that appears related to our proposed translation 'must' or 'right/authority to'. In making any request in English, Nyangumarta people customarily use the form 'gotta' such as in 'you gotta take me to Port Hedland' when in standard English such a request would be couched in very different terms such as 'I wonder if you

86 Barbara J. Sayers

could take me to Port Hedland?' or 'Please would you take me to Port Hedland?'

It is our experience, and that of a number of colleagues, that 'gotta' is frequently used in requests. There are also many examples in the literature indicating the demanding nature of Aboriginal requests (Elkin 1951:167–72; Gould 1969:189). By glossing the form -*naku* as 'rights/obligations marker', and thus reflecting the cultural values of the speakers, it is easy to see why an Aboriginal speaker, when using English, would use a term that reflected his/her values when interacting with Westerners. Once Horace's perspective on reciprocal rights and obligations is understood, as well as his difficulty with understanding Western bureaucratic practice, it is quite probable that Horace intended what he said to be a demand, that is, a demand that the Social Security man exercise his perceived perogatives. It is less likely that he meant it as an urgent polite request for help which just happened to sound like a demand to the white man. In either case it is easy to understand why the white man could become irritated, if not angry, if he thought an Aboriginal was making unreasonable demands. Furthermore, this analysis gives a reason for the many references to 'the demanding nature of Aboriginal requests' that are found in the literature. Such perceived demands do not indicate impoliteness, but rather, the traditional Aboriginal's perspective on his rights in an established quasi-kin situation, that is, in an interactional encounter.

5.3 The pragmatic role of repetition and the associated absence of conjunctions

The text appears to be quite repetitious. Such repetition is a structural feature of many Aboriginal languages and has been discussed by Sayers (1976), Marsh (1970), and Hudson (1970). What does the repetition mean, that is, what is the pragmatic effect of the structural repetition? The repetition that is used in Australian Aboriginal languages frequently includes cyclic structures (sometimes called sandwich or chiastic structures), and positive-negative and generic-specific paraphrase. Sayers discusses this repetition in detail (1976:11–31, 166–82) in relation to Wik-Mungkan sentences, and the meaning frequently includes emphasis. In some instances it simply provides more information by means of restatement rather than by clause expansion. In cyclic structures it also includes closure of the particular argument. In this text by Jack Horace he uses the same varieties of repetition that Sayers has discussed for Wik-Mungkan, and at this point the functions appear to be the same.

Again, like Wik-Mungkan, Nyangumarta does not include logical conjunctions such as 'because' and 'therefore' in these repetitive amplification

A Pragmatic Analysis of a Failed Cross-Cultural Communication   87

constructions. They are not just absent, there is no place for them since the point is made either by opposing (juxtaposing) a positive and negative repeat of the information or by juxtaposing a generic and specific statement. Overt reasons are rarely given, especially when the reason relates back to assumed shared cultural or social information. Neither are overt results stated, hence the absence of a connective such as 'therefore'. In some discourses, what appears to be the conclusion from a Western perspective actually occurs as the opening statement of the discourse, and may not be overtly referred to again.

As previously discussed, in Nyangumarta as in Wik-Mungkan, repetition is used to emphasize various points and also in chiastic structures to indicate closure of a particular argument. We will exemplify a negative-positive chiastic structure by looking at (3)–(6). It is relevant to note that restatement does not need to be complete. In fact, elliptical structures are common. It is also relevant to note that these lines indicate the build-up of Horace's frustration at not being understood when he feels he has made his point clear. Other examples of repetition are discussed as they occur throughout the text in §5.4.[3]

(3) *munu kunta ji-naku-pa*
NEG stop VB-ROM[HORT]-CONJ
(We) have no right to [should not have to] stop them,

(4) *pala nyuntu-mili*
that 2s-GEN
that's *your* (right/responsibility (job)).

(5) *ngaju-lu nyungu yimpi-rna-rni-ngu muwarr*
I-ERG this explain-NF-1s^ERG-2s^DAT word
I've already explained this word to you.

(6) *munu kunta ji-naku*
NEG stop VB-ROM[HORT]
(We) have no right to [should not have to] stop them.

---

[3] The text contains a more extensive example of chiastic structure in lines 8–19 where 8 links to 18–19; 9–11 link to 15–17; and lines 12–14 are the core of the argument.

88   Barbara J. Sayers

5.4 A pragmatic description of the text

Like Sperber and Wilson (1986:194) "...we will argue that the implicatures of an utterance are recovered by reference to the speaker's manifest expectations about how her [in this case his] utterances should achieve optimal relevance." In this section we assume that both Horace and the Social Security man at least began by aiming to achieve relevance. Identifying the implicatures (referred to as presuppositions in this analysis) behind Horace's utterances, however, we can see why they failed. They were diametrically opposed to the presuppositions of the white man. In this encounter, each man unwittingly left implicit most of the information that was needed to lead to mutual understanding.

In this description, the presuppositions of the white man are not dealt with in detail except to clarify any point that might not be familiar to a non-Australian. However, a detailed analysis of both parties' position is supplied in the charted analysis in §6. Comments on the pragmatic role of structural features are also included in this description.

The text of Jack Horace's description of his encounter with the Social Security man begins by Horace explaining briefly to Geytenbeek in lines (7)–(10) how he went west to Port Hedland to explain 'that word' to the Social Security man.

(7) *ngaju ya-na-rna   marntu-ngu muwarr-karti kara*
     I   go-NF-1s^NOM   cool-LOC   word-ALL   west
     I went this morning to the meeting west.

(8) *wurra-rna-rna-la*
     tell-NF-1s^ERG-3s^DAT
     I spoke to him,

(9) *yimpi-rni-rni-li*
     explain-NF-1s^ERG-3s^DAT
     I explained to him,

(10) *jawujul jikuriti   yimpi-rni-rni-li   pala muwarr*
     Social   Security explain-NF-1s^ERG-3s^DAT that word
     I explained that word to the Social Security (man).

'West' implies the town of Port Hedland and it contrasts with Horace's reference to his own people at Tjalku Wara as 'east dwellers' in (13). It is common for Aborigines to refer to locations by the use of compass points. An understanding of the geography of the area provides the information for

A Pragmatic Analysis of a Failed Cross-Cultural Communication   89

this implication. 'That word' in (10) refers back to what Horace had told Geytenbeek about the meeting with the Social Security man in Port Hedland before Geytenbeek began recording this text. It also points forward to the description in (11) and (12) of the interaction he had just had with the Social Security man.

(11) *nyuntu-mili-rrangu   nyarra-rrangu   marrngu-rrangu*
      2s-GEN-PL   this-PL   men-PL
      These men of yours

(12) *warnku-pa   yi-nganya-yi-janinya*
      money-CONJ   give-PRES-3p^ERG-3p^ACC
      are giving them (the troublesome transients) money,

While the meaning of (11) and (12) looks obvious from the white man's perspective, the anthropological information in the preceding section leads us to identify Horace's presuppositions which are crucial to understanding Horace's position and his associated anger and frustration. These presuppositions (implicatures) are:

a. people who give food, money, etc. set up a quasi-kin relationship with the recipients.

The implication is that the Social Security men are quasi-kin.

b. Reciprocal relationships are on a one-to-one basis, and
c. givers in a kin/quasi-kin relationship have a measure of authority over the recipients.
d. Those not involved in a particular relationship have no authority in it.

The implication from (b), (c), and (d) is that the Tjalku Wara residents have no authority over the drunken transients in relation to the money since they were not involved in the giving and receiving of it. It was the money that led to the transients, drunkenness and their incessant demands on the residents for food and shelter. The residents had tried to use the authority they had as providers of food and shelter but they were unable to deal effectively with the situation. So they, via Horace, went to the source of trouble, the Social Security men who gave the money without requiring anything from the recipients in return.

(13) *kalku-rna-nyi(-janinyi)   kakarra-ra*
      care^for-NF-1pin^ERG(-3p^ACC)   east-dwellers
      (but [while]) we who live out east are looking after (them).

90   Barbara J. Sayers

As in examples (11) and (12), the meaning of (13) looks obvious to the Social Security man. He assumes that after the Social Security benefits are paid to the unemployed, any further responsibility for the recipients of those funds is not his. He understands that Aborigines usually share with each other, so Horace's statement in (13) does not appear to be anything other that what the white man would expect.

The juxtaposed clause in (13) contrasts with what has gone before, and the implied conjunction could better be 'but' which more strongly indicates the contrast. Once the anthropology related to (11) and (12) is understood, it can be seen that Horace's presuppositions are different. His presuppositions are:

e. Kinship involves sharing food, money, etc. without restrictions on quantity—regardless of the reason why the recipients have no food of their own. In this way, the residents are fulfilling their kin obligations to the transients.

f. The residents have no food left for themselves.

The implications are that the residents' food is getting used up while, in contrast, the Social Security man is not fulfilling his rights/responsibility by using his authority as quasi-kin to deal with the transients.

(14)   *kara   wurrp*
       west   IDIOPHONE
       (They are going) west rapidly.

Example (14) is highly elliptical, and it is not clear what the implications were to the white man. He knew that the situation at Tjalku Wara was bad, in fact, that is one reason why he was having this meeting with Horace. He would probably have recognized 'west' as Port Hedland as it is west of Tjalku Wara, but white men are not always aware of compass directions.

Horace's elliptical statement involved a number of presuppositions which are:

g. The transients go west to Port Hedland to collect their unemployment benefits.

h. The transients buy and drink excessive amounts of alcohol and use up all their money.

The implication is that the transients' behavior is bad.

i. The people in the west who give them money have set up a quasi-kin relationship with them.

A Pragmatic Analysis of a Failed Cross-Cultural Communication   91

    j. Quasi-kin have the right and authority to deal with the transient drunks.

The implication is that the Social Security men are responsible for the transients' behavior.

(15)   *warrkamu-ku   wurra-rna-rni-janaku*
        work-DAT   tell-NF-1s^ERG-3p^DAT
        I tell them they should work (lit., about work).

(16)   *munu*
        NEG
        No.

(17)   *munu warrkamu jarri-nya-ka-yi*
        NEG   work   INCHO-NF-PRES^CF-3p^NOM
        They are not working.

(15)–(17) seem to be patently clear to the white man. From his perspective there is only one possible meaning—that Horace wanted the troublesome transients to work for paid employment, but they were not working. However, again he did not understand Horace's presupposition which was:

    k. Work means to have the transients work at Tjalku Wara (validated by example (32)). It is highly probable that Horace had the Community Development and Employment Program (C.D.E.P.; see the end of §2) in mind.

The implication is that they are not working at Tjalku Wara (for C.D.E.P.).

Horace used the exclamation 'no' to contrast what he wanted with what was happening. Horace had the same presuppositions here as he had in (9) and (10).

    l. People who initiate a relationship by giving money have a degree of authority over the recipients.

The implication is that the Social Security men are responsible for the transients not working.

    m. People who do not have any part in a reciprocal relationship between other parties have no authority over the recipients of benefits received (validated by (24) and (31)).

92   Barbara J. Sayers

The implication is that Horace and the residents do not have the necessary
authority to deal with the transients because they had no part in the arrangement between the Social Security men and the transients regarding
the money which led to the drunkenness and the associated problems for
themselves.

(18)   *nyungu ngulyu ngala   wani-nya-yi   nganarna-mili-nga*
       this   same   EMPH   stay-NF-3p^NOM   1pex-GEN-LOC
       This is the way they are staying at our (place).

(19)   *mayi nganarna-mili nga-nanya-yi-Ø*
       food 1pex-GEN   eat-PRES-3p^ERG-3s^ACC
       They are eating our food;

(20)   *wurru-karra   nganarna-mili   ngarta-rna-yi-ɲ*
       belongings-PL 1pex-GEN   break-NF-3p^ERG-3s^ACC
       they are smashing our belongings.

(21)   *pala   warrkamu-ku   wurra-rna-rni-janaku*
       that   work-DAT   tell-NF-1s^ERG-3p^DAT
       I tell them about that work.

(22)   *munu*
       NEG
       No.

(23)   *munu   warrkamu   jarri-nya-ka-y*
       NEG   work   INCHO-NF-PRES^CF-3p^NOM
       They are not working.

(24)   *marntu-ngu   kara-jakurn   turlpa-nya-ya*
       cool-LOC   west-just   appear-NF-3p^NOM
       In the morning they just turn up west (at Port Hedland Social Security
       Office).

(25)   *mima-rna-ya   pala-ku   warnku-ku*
       wait-NF-3p^NOM that-DAT   money-DAT
       They are waiting for that money.

Here Horace makes a generic statement in (18) about what follows in
specific detail in (19) and (20). (These lines were not in the original recording, but were added by Horace when he realized he had omitted this specific

A Pragmatic Analysis of a Failed Cross-Cultural Communication 93

information.) He then goes on in (21)–(25) with a repeat of the information in (14)–(17). There are two features of Aboriginal discourse structure that are exemplified here. The first is the generic-specific (amplification) statements which are common in Aboriginal languages, and the second is the feature of cycling back and closing a point with the same information with which it began. In the center of this repetitive structure are (18) to (20). These lines are pivotal in that they are the things that Horace is seeing as a problem and over which he has no authority. His solution to the problem is to remind the Social Security man of his obligation to do something. The presuppositions and implications in the repeated material are the same as in the original.

(26) *yimpi-rni-rna-la*
explain-NF-1s^ERG-3s^DAT
I explained (that) to him.

(27) *paliny-ju   wurra-rna-ji-ɲ*
3s-ERG   tell-NF-1s^DAT-3s^ERG
He said to me,

(26) and (27) are comments by Horace to Geytenbeek which move the reported dialogue on to the Social Security man's response to Horace.

(28) *wunyjurru-rti   pala   kunta   ji-lama-n-janaka*
which^way-EMPH   that   stop   VB-FUT-2s^ERG-3p^DAT
"How are you going to stop them?"

The Social Security man, since he assumes that the responsibility for dealing with problems at the community belongs to Horace, asks this question which upsets Horace.

(29) *munu kunta   ji-naku-pa*
NEG stop   VB-ROM[HORT]-CONJ
(We) have no right to [should not have to] stop them,

(30) *pala   nyuntu-mili*
that   2s-GEN
that's *your* (right/responsibility (job)).

(31) *ngaju-lu   nyungu yimpi-rna-rni-ngu   muwarr*
I-ERG   this   explain-NF-1s^ERG-2s^DAT word
I've already explained this word to you.

94 Barbara J. Sayers

(32) *munu kunta   ji-na...*
      NEG   stop   VB-ROM[HORT]
      (We) have no right to [should not have to] stop them.

Horace's frustration can be seen in his response to the question. He replies by means of a negative-positive cyclic or chiastic statement. Such statements are frequently used for emphasis and, as in these examples, are often elliptical. In (30) the intonation center is on 'yours'. This line contrasts with (29) and (32) in this negative-positive-negative structure; therefore, from a structural perspective the only subject possible for (29) and (32) is 'we'. In the same way, from a structural perspective, the only possible translation for the ellipses in (30) is the contrast with what was stated in (29) and (32), that is, an appropriate translation would be 'it is your job [responsibility/right] to stop them'.

From a pragmatic perspective the ellipses of both the subject in (29) and (32) and the predicate in (30) need to be explained. The presupposition that someone should stop the men is behind the elision in all these lines. The best account of the ellipses of the subject in (29) and (32) is that it contradicts the Social Security man's presupposition that the residents should stop the men. The intonation center is on 'yours' in (30) and this strengthens the contradiction while still presupposing that someone should stop the men. The presupposition that someone should stop the men makes an appropriate translation of the elided predicate in (30) 'that is your (right/responsibility (job))'. Furthermore, since the intonation center is on 'your' and this is the central statement in this cyclic structure, the focus is clearly on the one who was seen to have the authority. It is interesting to note in this elliptical structure that it is the verb which is elided in (30), while it is 'we' which is elided in (29) and (32). These structural features add to the force of Horace's argument and indicate clearly the person with whom Horace thought the responsibility lay.

The content of (29)–(32) can only lead to difficulty for the white man. The only interpretation he can come up with is that the Tjalku Wara residents are avoiding their responsibility and at the same time asking him to do something for which he has no authority. He can see Horace's frustration when Horace tells him that he had already explained 'that word', but since he doesn't know what 'that word' is he has no way of knowing why Horace is frustrated.

Horace's perspective can be easily understood once the relevant anthropology is considered. The presuppositions here are the same as in (b), (c)/(l), and (d)/(m). For convenience they are listed again:

n. Reciprocal relationships are on a one-to-one basis.

A Pragmatic Analysis of a Failed Cross-Cultural Communication

o. People who give money initiate a relationship and thus have a degree of authority over the recipients.

p. People who do not have any part in a reciprocal relationship between other parties have no authority over the recipients of the benefits received via that relationship.

The implications are as stated by Horace that he and the residents have no authority to deal with the transients but the Social Security man does.

(33) *wunyjurru-rti*   *warrkamu-ja* *pala*
    which^way-EMPH   work-ABL   that

(34)   *yungku-luma-n-janinya*   *warnku-ku*
      give-FUT-2s^ERG-3p^ACC   money-DAT
    How, after (that work), will you pay them?

The white man, having totally missed the point Horace thought he had made so strongly, goes back to the one thing he did grasp, which was Horace's expressed desire for the men to work, so he asks Horace, 'How will you pay them?'. One can only sympathize with Horace on hearing this question. From his frustrated outburst to Geytenbeek at the completion of reporting his account of his interview with the Social Security man, we can understand why he says the white man didn't listen to him in (45)–(56). Horace interpreted 'how will you pay them?' as the white man butting in with 'that word of his'. The amount of repetition in (45)–(56) shows the degree of his frustration.

(35)   *munu*
    NEG
    No.

(36)   *nyungu yimpi-rna-rni-ngu*   *wunyjurru-ku*
      this   explain-NF-1s^ERG-2s^DAT   which^way-DAT
    I've (already) explained to you what ought to be done about this.

(37)   *jawujul japij*   *puluku pala*   *ngani-ku-pa*   *ji-naku*
      Social   Service   bloke   that   what-DAT-CONJ VB-ROM[HORT]
    The Social Service bloke has the right/authority [should] do something about that.

(38)   *pala-nga*   *nganarna-mili-ngi*   *jungka-nga*   *warrkamu*
      that-LOC   1pex-GEN-LOC   ground-LOC   work

ji-naku-pa
VB-ROM[HORT]-CONJ
In that community of ours they are obligated to [should] work.

Horace begins his response to the Social Security man's question with an emphatic 'no' (35) indicating that the question about paying the transients was, at the least, inappropriate. (36)–(38) are an example of generic-specific structure with (36) giving the generic. The Nyangumarta is difficult to back-translate into natural English. Geytenbeek has included the implied 'already' in his English gloss to help handle this. Sayers prefers the back translation 'which way (how) to do it' to the Geytenbeeks' translation 'what ought to be done' as it is closer to the morphology in Nyangumarta and avoids the use of 'ought' for which there is no equivalent in the morphology.

Regardless of the difficulties in back-translating what Horace said, the generic statement in (35) both refers back to what he had previously said in (11)–(12) and (30), and in (15)–(17) and (21)–(23), as well as giving the generic statement for what follows in specific detail in (37) and (38). These are the two crucial points of Horace's argument; namely, that the responsibility for the situation with the transients belongs to the Social Security man, and that the Social Security man should expect the men to work for the money he was already giving them and which created the problem Horace was concerned about. In (38) we have the most overt reference to what Horace was probably thinking, that is, that he expected the men to work in 'that community of ours', probably for C.D.E.P. with which he was familiar from his recent trip to the Northern Territory. The Geytenbeeks assured Sayers that Horace was familiar with C.D.E.P. The literal translation for his reference to Tjalku Wara is 'that ground' which normally covers 'place', 'country', or 'ground'. In more recent days it is also used to cover locations such as modern Aboriginal communities.

Horace's presuppositions with their following implications are the same as in the previous lines with the addition of:

q. The transients are living at Tjalku Wara.
r. People who live in a community should work in it (for C.D.E.P.).

The implication is that the transients should work at Tjalku Wara for C.D.E.P.

A further implication is that the work would benefit the community and that the men would not get drunk and destroy things—at least as easily or as often.

A further implication is that the transients would meet their reciprocal responsibilities, both to the Social Security man by working and to the community by providing useful service in return for the food they had received. (39) moves the reported dialogue on to the Social Security man.

A Pragmatic Analysis of a Failed Cross-Cultural Communication 97

(39) *wurra-rna-ji-ɲ*
       tell-NF-1sˆDAT-3sˆERG
       He said to me,

(40) *wunyjurru-rti   warnku yungku-luma-n-janinya*
       whichˆway-EMPH money   give-FUT-2sˆERG-3pˆACC
       "How are you going to pay them?"

It is now clear to the Social Security man that Horace expects the men to work at Tjalku Wara. His question in (40), which is a repeat of his previous one in (33)–(34), is asked for the same reasons as on the previous occasion. The Social Security man appears to make no link to the C.D.E.P. system which at that time was not operative in the Pilbara region of Western Australia. A further reason could be that Tjalku Wara, with a number of Age and Invalid pensioners as residents and these young men as transients, would not be a suitable community in which the system could operate. As a result the Social Security man saw work, and in particular work at Tjalku Wara, as the community responsibility. Hence, he asked the question again which so upset Horace and led to his outburst about the man to Geytenbeek in (41)–(50).

(40) completes the reported dialogue between Horace and the Social Security man. What follows in (41)–(50) is an expression of Horace's frustration to Geytenbeek. Following this Horace closes the discourse by sharing his plans to have what he had just said put into a letter in English for him to take back to the second day of the meetings with the Social Security man in Port Hedland.

(41) *munu   pinakarri-ɲ-ma-ji-ɲ*
       NEG   listen-NF-CF-1sˆDAT-3sˆERG
       He didn't listen to me.

(42) *purrpi ma-rni-kinyi-nyi-ɲ   ngarrany muwarr-ju pala-lu*
       butt   VB-NF-REP-1sˆACC-3sˆERG INTENS   word-INST that-INST

       paliny-mila-lu
       3s-GEN-INST
       He kept on butting right in on me with that word of his.

(43) *munu pinakarri-ɲ-mi-ji-ɲ   milya-karti-jakurn*
       NEG   listen-NF-CF-1sˆDAT-3sˆERG nose-ALL-allˆtheˆway
       He didn't hear me right through to the end.

(44) *munu   pinakarri-ɲ-mi-ji-ɲ*
      NEG   listen-NF-CF-1sˆDAT-3sˆERG
      He didn't listen to me.

(45) *pala   purrpi   ma-rna-nyi-ɲ*
      that   butt   VB-NF-1sˆACC-3sˆERG
      That (chap) butted in on me.

(46) *pala   yarrpany-ju-rla   purrpi   ma-rna-nyi-ɲ*
      that   youngˆfellow-ERG-EMPH   butt   VB-NF-1sˆACC-3sˆERG
      That young fellow butted in on me.

(47) *munu   pirirri   nyarra   wirtu*
      NEG   man   that   big
      That man is not big (viz, not a high-ranking official),

(48) *pinakarri-nya-pinti*
      listen-NMZR-associatedˆwith
      one trained in listening.

(49) *pirirri-lu   wirtu-lu   pinakarri-nya-ɲ   muwarr-ku*
      man-ERG   big-ERG   listen-NF-3sˆERG   word-DAT
      A big man listens to what a person has to say.

(50) *nyungu yarrpany-ju   purrpi   ma-rna-nyi-ɲ   munumpa-lu*
      this   youngˆfellow-ERG   butt   VB-NF-1sˆDAT-3sˆERG   ignorance-INST
      This young man butted in on me with ignorance.

There are a number of linguistic features and some further cultural issues in this section which help us to understand the degree of Horace's problem. Structurally, the amount of repetition indicates how angry Horace felt. 'Butting in on me with that word of his' was said because Horace saw the white man's responses as totally inappropriate. Furthermore, 'butting in' indicated that the Social Security man was ignorant from the Aboriginal perspective because knowledgeable men would not do such a thing. The contrast between 'ignorant' and 'knowledgeable' men is an important one in traditional Aboriginal society. An ignorant man has not yet been exposed to (initiated into) the appropriate knowledge and, therefore, doesn't know the appropriate behavior. Here the situation is even worse. The Social Security man is displaying his ignorance of one of the most basic concepts of Aboriginal society—that of reciprocal rights and obligations (responsibilities) or, in more abstract terminology, the principle of reciprocity. Any Aboriginal

A Pragmatic Analysis of a Failed Cross-Cultural Communication   99

child would recognize this. Since the Social Security man has displayed ignorance of the most basic acceptable behavior, he has clearly shown that he is not an 'important' (or knowledgeable) man.

The white man had no way of knowing Horace's perspective so could only act in accordance with his own understanding of the situation. In this interaction, each man's argument is congruent with his own world view and its underlying assumptions. Therefore, it is not surprising that there was a breakdown of communication with its associated anger and frustration.

(51) *pala*
       that
       There.

(52) *nyungu wirri-lima-rna-lu   milimili-ngi*
       this   put-FUT-1s^ERG-3s^DAT paper-LOC
       I will put this down in a letter.

(53) *parrja-lku-liny-n   pala-lu   paliny-ju marntu-ngu*
       see-IMFUT-3s-3s^ERG   that-INST   3s-ERG   cool-LOC
       He will see (it) with that (letter) in the morning.

(54) *marntu-ngu kulpu-luma-rna   kin   muwarr-karti pala-karti*
       cool-in   return-FUT-1s^NOM again   word-ALL   that-ALL
       In the morning I will return again to that meeting.

(55) *muwarr pi-lipi-yirni   kin   marntu-ngu*
       talk   VB-FUT-1pex^NOM   again   cool-LOC
       We will talk again in the morning.

(56) *jipi*
       finish
       The end.

The text concludes with Horace explaining to Geytenbeek what should happen next. He had already discussed his problem with Geytenbeek before beginning this recording so Geytenbeek was familiar with what he wanted. Geytenbeek was to translate this text into English for Horace to take back on the second day of the two-day meeting. The next morning the Social Security man would see what he had written down via Geytenbeek and his translation into English. Unfortunately, we have no record of the next day's events.

Appendix 1

Letter of Explanation to the Social Security Man

1 *ngaju ya-na-rna   marntu-ngu muwarr-karti kara*
   I   go-NF-1sˆNOM cool-LOC   word-ALL   west
   I went this morning to the meeting west.

2 *wurra-rna-rna-la*
   tell-NF-1sˆERG-3sˆDAT
   I spoke to him,

3 *yimpi-rni-rni-li*
   explain-NF-1sˆERG-3sˆDAT
   I explained to him,

4 *jawujul jikuriti yimpi-rni-rni-li   pala muwarr*
   Social Security explain-NF-1sˆERG-3sˆDAT that word
   I explained that word to the Social Security (man).

5 *nyuntu-mili-rrangu nyarra-rrangu   marrngu-rrangu*
   2s-GEN-PL   this-PL   men-PL
   These men of yours

6 *warnku-pa   yi-nganya-yi-janinya*
   money-CONJ give-PRES-3pˆERG-3pˆACC
   are giving them [the troublesome transients] money,

7 *kalku-rna-nyi(-janinyi)   kakarra-ra*
   careˆfor-NF-1pinˆERG(-3pˆACC)   east-dwellers
   (but[while]) we who live out east are looking after (them).

8 *kara   wurrp*
   west   IDIOPHONE
   (They are going) west 'rapidly'.

9 *warrkamu-ku wurra-rna-rni-janaku*
   work-DAT   tell-NF-1sˆERG-3pˆDAT
   I tell them they should work (lit., 'about work').

10 *munu*
    No.

A Pragmatic Analysis of a Failed Cross-Cultural Communication 101

11   *munu*   *warrkamu* *jarri-nya-ka-yi*
    NEG   work   INCHO-NF-PRES^CF-3p^NOM
    They are not working.

12   *nyungu ngulyu ngala*   *wani-nya-yi*   *nganarna-mili-nga*
    this   same   EMPH   stay-NF-3p^NOM   1pex-GEN-LOC
    This is the way they are staying at our (place).

13   *mayi* *nganarna-mili*   *nga-nanya-yi-0*
    food   1pex-GEN   eat-PRES-3p^ERG-3s^ACC
    They are eating our food

14   *wurru-karra*   *nganarna-mili*   *ngarta-rna-yi-0*
    belongings-PL 1pex-GEN   break-NF-3p^ERG-3s^ACC
    they are smashing our belongings.

15   *pala* *warrkamu-ku* *wurra-rna-rni-janaku*
    that   work-DAT   tell-NF-1s^ERG-3p^DAT
    I tell them about that work.

16   *munu*
    No.

17   *munu warrkamu* *jarri-nya-ka-yi*
    NEG   work   INCHO-NF-PRES^CF-3p^NOM
    They are not working.

18   *marntu-ngu*   *kara-jakurn* *turlpa-nya-ya*
    cool-LOC   west-just   appear-NF-3p^NOM
    In the morning they just turn up west (at Port Hedland Soc. Sec. Office).

19   *mima-rna-ya*   *pala-ku*   *warnku-ku*
    wait-NF-3p^NOM   that-DAT   money-DAT
    They are waiting for that money.

20   *yimpi-rni-rna-la*
    explain-NF-1s^ERG-3s^DAT
    I explained (that) to him.

21   *paliny-ju*   *wurra-rna-ji-ɲ*
    3s-ERG   tell-NF-1s^DAT-3s^ERG
    He said to me,

22   *wunyjurru-rti*   *pala*   *kunta*   *ji-lama-n-janaka*
       which^way-EMPH   that   stop   VB-FUT-2s^ERG-3p^DAT
       How are you going to stop them?

23   *munu*   *kunta*   *ji-naku-pa*
       NEG   stop   VB-ROM[HORT]-CONJ
       (We) have no right to [should not have to] stop them,

24   *pala*   *nyuntu-mili*
       that   2s-GEN
       that's *yours* (right/responsibility [job]).

25   *ngaju-lu*   *nyungu*   *yimpi-rna-rni-ngu*   *muwarr*
       I-ERG   this   explain-NF-1s^ERG-2s^DAT   word
       I've already explained this word to you.

26   *munu*   *kunta*   *ji-naku*
       NEG   stop   VB-ROM[HORT]
       (We) have no right to [should not have to] stop them.

27   *wunyjurru-rti*   *warrkamu-ja* *pala*
       which^way-EMPH   work-ABL   that

28   *yungku-luma-n-janinya*   *warnku-ku*
       give-FUT-2s^ERG-3p^ACC   money-DAT
       How, after that work, will you pay them?

29   *munu*
       NEG
       No.

30   *nyungu*   *yimpi-rna-rni-ngu*   *wunyjurru-ku*
       this   explain-NF-1s^ERG-2s^DAT   which^way-DAT
       I've (already) explained to you how to do [what ought to be done about] this.

31   *jawujul japij*   *puluku pala* *ngani-ku-pa*   *ji-naku*
       Social Service bloke   that   what-DAT-CONJ   VB-ROM[HORT]
       The Social Service blokes should [is obligated to] do something about that.

A Pragmatic Analysis of a Failed Cross-Cultural Communication 103

32   *pala-nga nganarna-mili-ngi   jungka-nga   warrkamu*
that-LOC 1pex-GEN-LOC   ground-LOC work

       ji-naku-pa
       VB-ROM[HORT]-CONJ
In that country [community] of ours they are obligated to [should] work.

33   *wurra-rna-ji-ɲ*
tell-NF-1sˆDAT-3sˆERG
He said to me,

34   *wunyjurru-rti   warnku   yungku-luma-n-janinya*
whichˆway-EMPH   money   give-FUT-2sˆERG-3pˆACC
"How are you going to pay them?"

35   *munu   pinakarri-ɲ-ma-ji-ɲ*
NEG   listen-NF-CF-1sˆDAT-3sˆERG
He didn't listen to me.

36   *purrpi ma-rni-kinyi-nyi-ɲ   ngarrany   muwarr-ju   pala-lu*
butt   VB-NF-REP-1sˆACC-3sˆERG INTENS   word-INST   that-INST

       paliny-mila-lu
       3s-GEN-INST
He kept on butting right in on me with that word of his.

37   *munu   pinakarri-ɲ-mi-ji-ɲ   milya-karti-jakurn*
NEG   listen-NF-CF-1sˆDAT-3sˆERG   nose-ALL-allˆtheˆway
He didn't hear me right through to the end.

38   *munu   pinakarri-ɲ-mi-ji-ɲ*
NEG   listen-NF-CF-1sˆDAT-3sˆERG
He didn't listen to me.

39   *pala purrpi ma-rna-nyi-ɲ*
that   butt   VB-NF-1sˆACC-3sˆERG
That (chap) butted in on me.

40   *pala yarrpany-ju-rla   purrpi ma-rna-nyi-ɲ*
that   youngˆfellow-ERG-EMPH butt   VB-NF-1sˆACC-3sˆERG
That young fellow butted in on me.

104 Barbara J. Sayers

41 *munu pirirri nyarra wirtu*
NEG man that big
That man is not big, (viz, not a high-ranking official)

42 *pinakarri-nya-pinti*
listen-NMZR-associated^with
one trained in listening.

43 *pirirri-lu wirtu-lu pinakarri-nya-ɲ muwarr-ku*
man-ERG big-ERG listen-NF-3s^ERG word-DAT
A big man listens to what a person has to say.

44 *nyungu yarrpany-ju purrpi ma-rna-nyi-ɲ munumpa-lu*
this young^fellow-ERG butt VB-NF-1s^DAT-3s^ERG ignorance-INST
This young man butted in on me with ignorance.

45 *pala*
that
There.

46 *nyungu wirri-lima-rna-lu milimili-ngi*
this put-FUT-1s^ERG-3s^DAT paper-LOC
I will put this down in a letter.

47 *parrja-lku-liny-ɲ pala-lu paliny-ju marntu-ngu*
see-IMFUT-3s-3s^ERG that-INST 3s-ERG cool-LOC
He will see (it) with that (letter) in the morning.

48 *marntu-ngu kulpu-luma-rna kin muwarr-karti pala-karti*
cool-in return-FUT-1s^NOM again word-ALL that-ALL
In the morning I will return again to that meeting.

49 *muwarr pi-lipi-yirni kin marntu-ngu*
talk VB-FUT-1pex^NOM again cool-LOC
We will talk again in the morning.

50 *jipi*
finish
The end.

A Pragmatic Analysis of a Failed Cross-Cultural Communication 105

Appendix 2
A Pragmatic Analysis of the Letter of Explanation

Literal Translation	Aboriginal Perspective	White Perspective	Aboriginal Message	White Message
5/6 Those people of yours are giving them money	-those people of yours = Social Security Man = SSM -them = transients = T -money = S Security unemployment benefits (dole) = D -people who give money, food, etc., set up a quasi-kin relationship with recipients -reciprocal relationships are on a one-to-one basis -those not involved in a particular relationship have no rights or authority in it -givers in a kin/quasi-kin relationship have a measure of authority over recipients -SSM is a giver to T so has authority over them	-those people of yours = SSM -them = transients = T -Unemployed Ts entitled to money -when entitlement is satisfied there is no further obligation	-SSM are quasi-kin -SSM are in a rights/obligation/ authority relationship to transients	-transients' entitlement has been satisfied
7 (While) we east dwellers are looking after (x)	-we east dwellers = Tjalku Wara -residents = R -x = Transients = T -T are Rs' kin -kinship involves sharing food, money, etc., with kin -food, etc., is shared without restrictions on quantity -R have no food left for themselves	-we = R -x = T -T and R live together -T and R are Aborigines -Aborigines always share and often end up with nothing themselves	-R are fulfilling their obligations to T -Rs' food gets used up -SSM is not fulfilling obligations to Ts	-R are sharing everything they have -R are sharing to their own detriment
8 (They are going) west "rapidly"	-west = Port Hedland -SSM gives money to T -people who give money set up quasi-kin relationship -T buy and drink excessive amounts of alcohol; behavior of T is bad	-people who drink excessive quantities of alcohol deteriorate socially	-the T situation is bad -SSM is responsible	-the T situation is bad

Literal Translation	Aboriginal Perspective	White Perspective	Aboriginal Message	White Message
9 I tell them about work	-SSM as quasi-kin has right and authority to deal with T -I = Horace = H -them = T -work = work for dole scheme = D	-I = H -them = T -work = paid employment -paid employment requires a payer	-H told T that T should work for D -SSM obligated to provide work for D	-H told T that T should get paid employment
10/11 No. They are not working.	-they = T -T do not work for D -people who give money have a degree of authority over recipients -H holds SSM responsible for T not working -H does not give money -H does not have authority to make T work (validated by 24, 31) -H cannot make T work (at Tjalku Wara community—verified by Geytenbeeks' comments regarding Hs expectations)	-they = T -T do not have paid employment	-T do not work for D -SSM responsible (has right/authority) to make T work for D -H not responsible (no right/authority) to make T work for D	-T do not have paid employment
12 They are staying exactly like this at our (place)[generic comment followed by specific points in 13–19]	-they = T -our (place) = Tjalku Wara community = C	-They = T -our (place) = Tjalku Wara community = C	-T are staying at C -T are doing all the things in 13–19	-T are staying at C
13 They are eating our food	-they = T -our = Rs -kin are obligated to share food with other kin	-they = T -our = Rs -Aboriginal people share everything	-R are meeting obligations -R share all food with T	-R are sharing with other Aborigines -R without food

A Pragmatic Analysis of a Failed Cross-Cultural Communication   107

Literal Translation	Aboriginal Perspective	White Perspective	Aboriginal Message	White Message
14 They are smashing our belongings	-food is shared until it is all gone [Aborigines don't keep back "surplus" for their own use at later date] -they = T -T get drunk -drunks are destructive -destruction of property is unacceptable behavior	-them = T -T get drunk -drunks are destructive -destruction of property is unacceptable behavior	-T do not reciprocate -R left with no food -T get drunk -T destroy property -T's behavior unacceptable	-T get drunk -T destroy property -T's behavior is unacceptable
15 I tell them about that work	-I = Horace -them = T -that work = work for dole scheme (Community Development Employment Program) which is operative in some Aboriginal communities and about which Horace is familiar = D -T being paid D already -T not working for D -repetition in 15 = reinforcement of 9	-I = H -them = T -that work = paid employment -paid work requires a payer	-repetition in 15 = reinforcement of 9 -H told T to get SSM to put T on work for D scheme or H told T that SSM should put T on work for D scheme	-H told T that T should get paid employment -H has already told SSM this
16/17 No. They are not working.	-they = T -as 10/11 -reinforces 10/11	-they = T -T do not have paid employment	-neg repetition = reinforcement -16/17 reinforces 15	-H has just told SSM this
18 In the morning they just turn up West.	-they = T -west = Pt. Hedland -Pt.Hedland = Social Security office -morning = time for D benefits to be paid	-they = T -west = Pt. Hedland Social Security office -morning = any morning	-T go to Pt. Hedland to Social Security office	-T go to Pt. Hedland in the morning
19 They are waiting for that money	-they = T -that money = Social Security unemployment benefits (dole) = D -SSM pays D to T without requiring any work -SSM has right/obligation/authority	-they = T -that money = D -SSM pays D to any unemployed people -T are unemployed -SSM pays D to T	-T wait for payment of D -SSM pays D to T -T should work for D -SSM responsible to make T work for D	-T wait for payment of D -T are unemployed -unemployed entitled to D

Literal Translation Aboriginal Perspective	White Perspective	Aboriginal Message	White Message
to require work from T -T are waiting for D to buy alcohol -T get drunk -T eat Rs' food -T destroy Rs' property	-SSM has no further responsibility to T	NA	NA
20 I explained (that) to him -I = II -that = contents of 15-19 -him = SSM	-I = II -that = contents of 15-19	NA	NA
21 He said to me -he = SSM -ne = II	-he = SSM -ne = II	NA	NA
22 How are you going to stop them -you = II -them = T -II not involved in giving D to T -H has no right/authority to stop T -SSM has given D to T -SSM has established quasi-kin relationship -SSM has obligation and right/authority to deal with the problem	-you = II -them = T -H and Rs responsible for Aborigines living at C -SSMs role is to encourage people to find solution to their own problems	-SSM is asking II to do something that is SSMs responsibility -SSM is explicitly avoiding his responsibility	-SSM encourages II to look for solutions to problem with T
23 (We) have no right/authority to stop [should not stop] (them) -we = R -them = T -R not involved in giving D to T -R have no right/authority to deal with T	-we = C -them = T -R have the possibility for solving their own problems -T causing destruction of Rs' possessions -Rs have possibility to solve Rs problems with T	-H reinforces Rs inability to deal with T -T causing food to be used up	-R are avoiding responsibility for solving their own problems
24 That's your right/responsibility (job) -that = stopping T -yours (sg) = SSMs -SSM give D to T -SSM therefore in quasi-kin relationship -SSM therefore has responsibility and right/authority to deal with T		-reinforcing SSMs obligation to deal with: -T causing food usage -T causing destruction of property -T waiting for money for alcohol	-H is asking SSM to do something that is IIs responsibility

Literal Translation	Aboriginal Perspective	White Perspective	Aboriginal Message	White Message
[25] I've (already) explained this word to you	-I = II -you = SSM -this word = content of 5–19, 23, 24	-I = II -you = SSM -this word = content of 5–19, 23, 24	-T not working for money from D -SSM is not understanding Hs -SSM should understand the message above -H is frustrated	-H is frustrated -SSM doesn't know why
[26] (We) have no right [should not] stop (them)	-we = R including H -them = T -identical beginning and ending of stretch of speech (23 and 26) = reinforcement of whole speech from 23–26	-repetition is redundant	-reinforcing 23–26	-H is saying the same thing again
[27/28] How will you pay them after that work	-you = II -them = T -SSM is already paying D to T -SSM should make them work for D at C (validated by Geytenbeek's comments about Hs expectations regarding C.D.E.P. scheme and Hs further response in 32)	-you = II -them = T -that work = paid employment -H should think through how he will pay T if they work	-SSM is asking H about doing what SSM is already doing himself -SSM is young, rude, ignorant (validated by 35–44)	-H wants T to work -H has to find a way to pay T
[29/30] No! I've (already) explained to you how to do [what ought to be done about] this	-I = H -you = SSM -how = require work in return for D -SSM is not understanding Hs message -SSM has to make T work for the money SSM is paying them	-I = H -you = SSM -how = ? i.e., SSM does not know what H is referring to	-SSM is wrong in all the implications arising from the question in 27/28	-H is frustrated -SSM doesn't know what it is H has explained
[31] Social Service bloke is obligated to [should] dosomething about that	-Social Service bloke = SSM -that = require work in return for D	-Social Service bloke = SSM -that = ? i.e., SSM doesn't know what "that" refers to	-SSM is obligated to make Ts work for D	-H is frustrated -SSM doesn't know what "that" refers to

110 — Barbara J. Sayers

Literal Translation	Aboriginal Perspective	White Perspective	Aboriginal Message	White Message
[32] On that land of ours (Tjalku Wara) they should [are obligated to] work	-land = Tjalku Wara = C -ours = Rs -they = T -work = work for D = working in Aborigines' own community on C.D.E.P. scheme -R worked to develop C -T should work for D -if T worked for D, T would work at C -T's work would benefit R -T would meet reciprocal responsibilities	-land = Tjalku Wara = C -ours = Rs -they = T -if T work at C, somebody has to pay them	-if T live at C, T obligated to work to help maintain and develop C	-II tells SSM that T should work for paid employment at C
[33] He said to me	-he = SSM -me = II	-he = SSM -me = II	NA	NA
[34] How are you going to pay then?	-you = II -them = T -SSM is butting in with his own word -SSM is ignorant, rude, and not important because -SSM has not listened to IIs explanation (validated by IIs repetitive accusations about the SSM to Geytenbeek, 35–44)	-you = II -them = T -pay = wages for paid employment -when a man wants someone to work it is legitimate to expect to have to pay them	-SSM is asking II about doing what SSM is already doing himself -SSM is young, rude, ignorant (validated by 35–44)	-II wants T to work -II has to find way to pay T

End of reported dialogue

Comments by H about SSM to Geytenbeek

Literal Translation	Aboriginal Perspective	Summary of Aboriginal and White Perspectives
[35] He didn't listen to me	-he = SSM -me = H	-SSMs responses were not appropriate to message Horace wanted to convey. -H was very angry as shown by the amount of repetition when reporting about the SSM to Geytenbeek. -"Butting in with his own word" was said because SSMs response was not appropriate from Hs perspective. -Contrast between important men and ignorant men is an important distinction in Aboriginal thinking: an ignorant man hasn't been exposed to (initiated into) the appropriate knowledge. -Knowledge makes a man knowledgeable and thus important. -The knowledge not known here was in relationship to reciprocal responsibilities and the authority of kin and quasi-kin. -The quasi-kin relationship set up by the giving of the D to T required the SSM to exert his authority and make the T work for the money. -The SSM had no way of knowing the preceding two points. He spoke in accordance with his own understanding of the situation. -H had no way of understanding the SSMs perspective. H interpreted the SSMs response in terms of Hs own understanding.
[36] He kept on butting in on me with that word of his	-he = SSM -me = H -that word of his = content of 32, 27, 34	
[37] He didn't listen to me through to the end	-he = SSM -me = H	
[38] He didn't listen to me	-he = SSM -me = H	
[39] That (man) butted in on me	-that = SSM -me = H	
[41] He is not an important man	-he = SSM	
[42] one trained in listening		
[43] (An) important man listens to the message (a person's talk)	-important man = one who listens to a message	
[44] This young man butted in on me with (his) ignorance	-this young man = SSM -me = H	

The argument of both H and SSM throughout the reported dialogue was congruent with each man's world view and its underlying assumptions. Therefore, there was a breakdown of communication since each man thought the other had the authority and responsibility to do something. Anger and frustration was all that could follow.

References

Albrecht, P. G. E. 1974. The social and psychological reasons for the alcohol problem among Aborigines. In Basil S. Hetzel, Malcolm Dobbins, Lorna Lippman, and Elizabeth Eggleston (eds.), Better health for Aborigines, 283. Brisbane: University of Queensland Press.

————. n.d. Aboriginal Australians. Adelaide: Lutheran Publishing House. (edited version of a paper presented to the Lutheran Youth Assembly, Canberra, January 1988.)

Bain, Margaret S. 1992. The Aboriginal-white encounter: Towards better communication. SIL-AAIB Occasional Papers 2. Darwin: Summer Institute of Linguistics.

Berndt, Ronald M. and Catherine H. Berndt. 1964. The world of the first Australians: An introduction to the traditional life of the Australian Aborigines. Sydney: Ure Smith.

Budget Macquarie Dictionary. 1982. Macquarie Library: McMahon's Point, N. S. W., Australia.

Elkin, Adolphus P. 1951. Reaction and interaction: A food gathering people and European settlement in Australia. American Anthropologist 53:164–86.

————. 1974. The Australian Aborigines, 5th ed. Sydney: Angus and Robertson.

Gould, Richard A. 1969. Yiwara: Foragers of the Australian desert. London, Sydney: Collins.

Hasan, Ruqaiya. 1985. Meaning, context and text: Fifty years after Malinowski. In James D. Benson and William S. Greaves (eds.), Systemic perspectives on discourse, 1:16–49. Selected Applied Papers from the 9th International Systemic Workshop. Norwood, New Jersey: Ablex.

Hudson, Joyce. 1970. Walmatjari paragraph types. Unpublished ms.

Levinson, Stephen C. 1983. Pragmatics. Cambridge: Cambridge University Press.

Marsh, James. 1970. Paragraph structure in Mantjiltjara. Unpublished ms.

Malinowski, Bronislaw. 1935. Coral gardens and their magic, 2. London: George Allen and Unwin.

Meggitt, Mervyn J. 1965. Desert people: A study of the Warlpiri Aborigines of Central Australia. Chicago: The University of Chicago Press.

Sayers, Barbara J. 1976. The sentence in Wik-Mungkan: A description of propositional relationships. Pacific Linguistics, Series B 44:183–85. Canberra: The Australian National University.

———— and Margaret S. Bain. 1990. A communication dilemma: Contrasting degrees of abstraction and the associated logic. Unpublished paper presented at a Summer Institute of Linguistics Consultants Seminar, Dallas, 1989.

Sperber, Dan and Deirdre Wilson. 1986. Relevance: Communication and cognition. Oxford: Blackwell.

A Beginning Look at
Brahui Connectives

David A. Ross

1. Introduction

1.1 Motivation

This article arises out of a concern to apply some methodical approach to the discovery of the uses of the various connectives in the Brahui language. As such, it is part of a larger effort being undertaken to gain a greater understanding of the way connectives function in the languages of the world.

This article does not attempt to provide an exhaustive analysis of the way connectives function in the Brahui language. Rather, the methodology is applied to a limited subset of connectives, with a view to distinguishing their uses. The technique adopted is to consider all examples of a particular connective found in a limited corpus of texts, in an attempt to define the range of uses of that particular connective. When this process has been repeated for several related connectives, then an attempt to define "regions of mutually-exclusive influence" for each connective can begin.

The interest in diachronic change in the use of connectives in Brahui has arisen from a previous investigation into the discourse features of Brahui narratives (Ross 1987). Using narratives collected approximately a century apart, it was shown that there was surprisingly little change in the narrative discourse features of the language in that period. The corpus used for that investigation has been expanded somewhat in the present investigation, and it will be shown that there have been significant changes in the uses of connectives in Brahui in that time period.

113

114 David A. Ross

1.2 Language situation

Brahui is a language spoken by up to 2 million people, living largely in North-central Baluchistan, Pakistan. The Brahui people are traditionally nomadic herdsmen, although a growing proportion now lead a more settled existence as farm workers or city dwellers.

The Brahui language is usually thought to be Dravidian in origin, although it has been separated geographically from other Dravidian languages for at least three millennia (Andronov (1980:18) estimates five millennia). Its links with other Dravidian languages are, thus, tenuous at best. It is largely through historical linguistics, coupled with a knowledge of kinds of morphemes which are resistant to change, that the Dravidian linkage has been established. For the past century, however, the subject of the classification of Brahui by language family has provoked considerable discussion, e.g., Bray 1907, 1934, Elfenbein 1983a, 1983b, McAlpin 1981.

During the past fifty years or so Brahui has had increasing contact with the national language of Pakistan, Urdu. Since the formation of Pakistan in 1947 the language of instruction in government schools in Baluchistan has been Urdu. Thus, the small percentage of literate Brahui people are nearly all literate in Urdu. This investigation places considerable emphasis on connectors that appear to have been borrowed from Urdu during the last century.

1.3 Text corpus and phonetic conventions

The investigation reported here is based on analysis of eight Brahui texts. Three of these are narratives collected and written down approximately a century ago. In listing these, the title of the text is given first, followed (in parentheses) by the letter abbreviation by which it will be referred to in this investigation. For the purposes of comparison, the approximate number of words of the English gloss of the text are given as well as the source of the text.

A miser and a cheat (MC)   400 words   Jamait and Diwan (1907)
The war between the Mengals and the Bizanjaus (WMB)
                            600 words   Jamait and Diwan (1907)
The war between the Mengals and the Lasis (WML)
                            600 words   Jamait and Diwan (1907)

A Beginning Look at Brahui Connectives 115

In addition to this, there are five contemporary texts. These are all translated from published material. The first two of these are narratives.

Teardrop (T)	700 words	Hussein (1985)
Kick (K)	1800 words	Godi (1985)

Two other descriptive texts are also analyzed as well as an expository text (as defined by Larson (1984:366)).

Descriptive:

Marriage (N)	900 words	Arif (1984)
God's Wish (XND)	1200 words	Arif (1984)

Expository:

By the status of the Holy Prophet (XB)

	1800 words	Ghulam (1981)

It is impossible to give all of these texts in this work. Thus, a representative sample of texts is included as appendices to this article. Specifically, the texts MC and N are given, in both free translation and morpheme-by-morpheme gloss in appendices A and B. When referring to other texts, I will give an extract from the text to illustrate, but space does not permit inclusion of extensive contexts.

In giving examples from the texts, I shall use a reduced nomenclature which is still readily recoverable. The texts are divided into sentences with the clauses being separated by the free glosses (on a clause-by-clause basis). Thus, for example, the designation MC20.2 refers to the second clause in sentence 20 of the the text *A miser and a cheat*.

The other major issue to be faced in the sharing of text data is that of the phonetic convention to be used. The convention used here will largely be that in common usage in South Asia linguistics. The basic approach has been to modify the IPA phonetic system in such a way that sounds can be represented on a typewriter without special symbols. However, the convention has been modified somewhat to allow representation of peculiarities of the Brahui phonetic system in an efficient manner. The basic conventions to be adopted in this article (from Ross 1989) are shown in (1) and (2), for consonants and vowels, respectively.

116   David A. Ross

(1)   Phonetic consonant chart

		Bi-labial	Labio-dental	Alveo-lar	Retro-flex	Palatal	Velar	Laryn-geal
Stop	vl	p		t	T		k	
	vd	b		d	D		g	
Fricative	vl		f	s		S	x	h
	vd			z		Z	G	
Affricate	vl					c		
	vd					j		
Lateral	vl			L				
	vd			l				
Flap				r	R			
Nasal		m		n			N	
Semivowel		v			y			

   In the phonetic consonant chart capital letters are used for retroflexed sounds, as well as for sounds which require some care. Of some interest is the lateral fricative /L/ which does not occur in neighboring languages. The velar nasal /N/ is not phonemic. The symbols /S/ and /Z/ have been adopted to avoid the necessity of wedges over symbols, and the /G/ avoids the necessity of a barred g.
   Some mention must also be made about the absence of a glottal stop in the phonetic consonant chart. There are a number of Arabic borrowed words in Brahui, some cf which are spelled with the "ein" which is sometimes interpreted as a glottal stop. Despite this, it seems to me that, when an "ein" occurs word medially (the easiest place to spot a glottal stop), the word is invariably sounded with a vowel (usually a short vowel) substituted.

(2)   Phonetic vowel chart

		Front	Central	Back
High	open	ii		uu
	close	i		u
Mid	open	ee		oo
	close	e		o
Low	open	ae	a aa	
		ai		au

   The phonetic vowel chart includes some unusual representations, which need some explanation. As is common in regional linguistics, long vowels are indicated by duplicated vowels (/ii/, /uu/, /ee/, /oo/, and /aa/). The sound marked /ae/ occurs in the English 'cat' /kaet/ and in the Brahui /baevas/ 'upset'.

A Beginning Look at Brahui Connectives 117

The two other sounds, represented as /ai/ and /au/, are usually thought of as dipthongs. The /ai/ occurs in the English (and Brahui) 'bicycle' /baisakil/, while the /au/ occurs in the English 'out' /aut/ and the Brahui /katau/ '(he) did not do'.

1.4 Theoretical background

Another major issue to be faced in an investigation of this sort is the theoretical background to be adopted. In particular, since interclausal relations are involved, how are clauses determined?

As far as possible, this investigation attempts to be independent of any theoretical framework, since it is thought of as a piece of basic research which will, hopefully, contribute to the development of a better theory of connectives. There is, however, a basic dependence on analysis of interclausal relationships, and thus a basic terminology needs to be adopted. The author has a high regard for both SEMANTIC STRUCTURE ANALYSIS, e.g., Beekman et al. (1981), and RHETORICAL STRUCTURE THEORY, e.g., Mann and Thompson (1987), as means of specifying the basic types of interclausal relationships.

Nonetheless, I also believe that both of these analytical approaches have significant liabilities. On the one hand, semantic structure analysis has no clear definitions of the various interclausal definitions proposed. The analyst is thus reduced to comparing his clause relationships to those of examples given in the literature, e.g., Larson (1984). On the other hand, rhetorical structure theory, which has made a significant advance in the direction of tightly specifying the type(s) of relations to be included in a particular category, has tended to define the categories in terms of surface structure rather than function.

Furthermore, neither analytical approach would claim that there is one unique analysis of a particular interclausal relationship. This leaves the analyst in a difficulty—if there is no unique analysis, how can he know whether he has analyzed the connective correctly?

Passing reference should also be made to the categories proposed by Longacre (1983). No serious attempt is made to apply this approach, largely because it seems just as hard as the other two approaches to apply.

For all of these reasons I have chosen to conduct this investigation without rigid attachment to a particular theoretical approach. The terminology used is largely that of semantic structure analysis. It would be untrue, however, to suggest that the categories proposed by semantic structure analysis have been assumed to be valid for this investigation. Rather, when analyzing a particular connective, I permit its uses to cover uses expected by (perhaps) several categories, but nonetheless having the "flavors" expected by those categories. Then, when all examples have been considered, I attempt to

118 David A. Ross

define a "megacategory" valid for that particular connective, and mutually exclusive of the categories of all other Brahui connectives.

1.5 Organization of the article

We have previously noted that we would not be able to cover all aspects of the use of connectives in Brahui. We will concentrate our investigations under three main topics—the coordinating connectives, e.g., *and*, the adversative connectives, e.g., *but*, and the logical connectives such as reason/result-type. Any such categorizing has a major problem associated with it, namely, that there is no formal way of identifying implied connectives. Recognizing this, we will attempt to note clear occurrences of implied interclausal relationships under each of these categories where possible.

2. Coordinating connectives

In this section we specifically analyze three Brahui morphemes: /too/, usually glossed as 'then', /oo/ 'and', and /ham/ 'also'. Interest in these connectives was first piqued by the observation that /too/ only occurs in the newer texts, i.e., it is not found at all as a connector in the older texts. The use of /too/ as a connector is quite common in contemporary literature (and in speech). It seems that the use of /too/ has been recently borrowed from Urdu. Several questions immediately arise concerning the use of /too/. How does it function in the newer texts? How were these functions denoted in older texts? What is the current relationship between /too/ and /oo/? This section is an attempt to answer questions of this sort.

2.1 The morpheme /too/

2.1.1 Homophonous morphemes. It is not quite correct to state that the morpheme /too/ is not present in older texts. There is a morpheme /too/, used as a postposition meaning 'with' (accompaniment), which has been, and still is, in common use. Because it is not a connective but a postposition, I consider it to be a homophonous morpheme, and thus exclude it from the present analysis. Examples of /too/ as a postposition are given in (3).

(3) /baava too/   with father
     /kan too/   with me
     /Saam too/   at evening
     /soob too/   in the morning   e.g., WML22

A Beginning Look at Brahui Connectives

The second two examples above are part of an adverbial phrase and, thus, constitute a problem in that adverbials (particularly of time) frequently form discourse-level connectives. The use of /too/ in this context is idiomatic, however, reflecting the Brahui preference for single-clause sentences. Thus, /Saam too/ might be 'with the coming of evening' or be contraction of 'when evening had come'.

The morpheme /too/ is also used as a connector, recently replacing another morpheme in constructions of the type 'if ... then ...'. Specifically, older texts used constructions in (4).

(4) /agar ... guRaa .../ e.g., WML9
     /agar ... 0 .../   e.g., MC1.3–5

In contrast to this there is a common construction in newer texts where the morpheme /too/ introduces the second half of the conditional expression as in (5).

(5) /agar ... too .../   e.g., MC137

Since this type of construction is really a conditional construction we will not make further reference to it in this discussion of coordinating connectives. It is interesting to note, however, that this use of /too/ also appears to have undergone diachronic change parallel with the coordinating functions.

2.1.2 /too/ as a facet introducer. The term FACET INTRODUCER will be used extensively throughout this article. It is defined as a connective which links constructions in which two different aspects of the same event or state are being compared or contrasted. We may need to modify this definition slightly as we go along, but this will serve as an adequate starting definition. When we consider how this is applied to use of the morpheme /too/, we note also that the two constructions being linked typically make considerable use of parallel constructions, with much use of lexical or syntactic overlap.

Let us illustrate this construction with some examples.[1]

(6) N4
     A   1   2   B   3   4
     asa paar-Gaa masink diira aa maS-ook xal-iN Tii as-ura

---

[1] In the examples which come from the texts N or MC morpheme-by-morpheme glosses will not be given, since these can be readily recovered from the texts in the appendices.

120   David A. Ross

A   1   2
too eloo paar-Gaa uraa naa piir-angaa nariina

B   3   4
zaaifa-Gak nikaah naa tiiaar-ii Tii lag-ook as-ura
On one side the girls were starting up to the drum, *and* elsewhere, the old people of the house, men and their wives were making ready for the engagement.

We note many similarities between the clauses linked by /too/. First of all, we note that semantically they both refer to aspects of preparation for the wedding. Different groups of people (the young girls and the old people) are performing different activities in different locations (probably all within the same house compound), but they are both related to preparations for the engagement.

We note next a high degree of lexical overlap and parallelism. In the example, lexical items which are repeated in the second clause are given a number (1, 2, 3...), while those lexical items which have a parallel but different word in the second clause are given a letter (A, B, C...) in order to highlight this overlap and parallelism.

Finally, we note that both clauses are stative in nature, both featuring a construction using the present participle (the word ending with /-ook/) and the imperfect of the verb to be, /as-ura/. The verb constructions are different in that only the first clause uses the past continuous tense, but they both suggest continuing activities in the past. (7) illustrates the same phenomena.

(7)   MC9
A   B 1   2   C   3 D   4 5   6
uraa Tii uraa naa goodii-k mehmaan-taa xidmat-ee kan-iN   aT

E   A   B 1   2   C   3
damdar-iN-tav-asa too vataax aT uraa naa xuuaaja-ak

D   4   5   6 E
nariina-taa xidmat   aT axtajaan as-ura
In the house the ladies of the house were not becoming tired as they served the guests, *and* in the guest room the men of the house were busy serving the men guests.

In this example again, we note a high degree of lexical overlap and parallelism, as well as syntactic parallelism. Again, the events being described are merely different aspects of the same event, namely, the serving of the guests

A Beginning Look at Brahui Connectives

at the wedding feast. There is, in both clauses, a continuing connotation of contented business.

Now let us take this one step further, and note that sometimes the interdependence of the two clauses linked by /too/ is such that portions of one of the clauses is ellipsed, and is meant to be inferred by the other half of the construction as in (8).

(8) N11

1   A   2   1   B   2
kas-as brinj naa rakaabii-tee arf-eenee, **too** *kas zaRdah naa ∅*
Someone (guest) asked for plates of rice, *and* another (asked for plates of) sweet rice.

In (8), the two clauses are so closely linked that it is possible to infer a large portion of the content of the second clause from the first clause. Not only is the verb completely ellipsed, but also a large portion of the syntactic object. Once again, however, the /too/ is serving as a facet introducer, making it clear that two clauses are linked strongly together. Moreover, there is almost complete syntactic overlap and/or parallelism. Both clauses are elaborating on the food requirements of the guests.

2.1.3 /too/ as it relates to time. Since we glossed the morpheme /too/ as 'then', we might expect that the usual use of this morpheme would be as an indicator of time. Further, we might expect that it would indicate concurrent or subsequent time. It seems that /too/ may be used in both of these situations. Rather than extensively discussing these uses, let us merely note uses of /too/ in both these contexts.

(9) N62: Identical time
riihaana   naa noo-miikoo saal raseeNg-aa **too** *oo-naaluma am daa duniiaa-eefaanii aa al-aa*

When Rihaana was nine years old, her mother also died (lit., R's ninth year arrived, *then* her mother also brought this world to mortality).

(10) XB127: Immediately subsequent time
nabii   kariim   saii allah aliia oo aala oo salaam vaxt-as
prophet Kariim [Arabic   ] time-INDEF[2]

---

[2] Abbreviations: ADV, adverb; CAUS, causative; COND, conditional; CONT, continuous; DEF, definite; DEM, demonstrative; dist, distant; EMPH, emphatic; IMPER, imperative; IMPF, imperfect; IMPL, implied; INCOMPL, incompletive; INDEF, indefinite; INF, infinitive; med, medial; NEG,

kih	*musaafir-ii*	*aan*	*bas-akaa*	***too***	*kul*	*aan*	*must*
that	traveler-NN	from	come-IMPF^3s	then	all	from	before

hazrat	*faatima-ee*	*in-aa*
Hazrat	Faatima-OBL	go-PAST^3s

The Holy Prophet [Peace Be Upon Him] when he came (home) from travelling *then* went first (to see) Hazrat Faatima.

In (9), the first clause establishes the time at which the second clause takes place; the /too/ serves to indicate this relationship. In (10), the Holy Prophet must return home before going to see his daughter (Hazrat Faatima); the /too/ indicates an immediately subsequent event.

We should also note, in passing, that the morpheme /too/ is not the only time word in Brahui. Both older and newer texts use /guRaa/ 'then', e.g., XB86, WML9, and /davaara/ 'then', e.g., XB110. It is not relevant to this discussion to delve into the nuances of these connectives.

2.1.4 /too/ with a result orientation. The situation now begins to get a bit complicated by other somewhat unexpected uses of /too/. In particular, let us mention first an example which seems to emphasize a result-type relationship between the two clauses in (11).

(11) XB120

oo-naa	*vafaat*	*aan*	*pad*	*xuuaaja-ee*	*yaat*	*bas-akaa*
she-of	death	from	later	Sir-OBL	memory	come-IMPF^3s

too	*xan-k*	*xaRiink*	*aan*	*pur*	*mas-uura*
then	eye-PL	teardrop	from	full	become-IMPF^3p

...after her death (whenever) the Prophet remembered *then* tears filled his eyes.

There seems little doubt here that the tears were a result of the Prophet remembering his daughter, for whom he was still grieving.

This does not seem to be a very common use of the /too/ morpheme, so one more example will suffice.

---

negative; NN, noun; NOM, nominative; OBLIG, obligative; OBL, oblique PART, participle; PASS, passive; PAST, past; PERF, perfect; PLE, participle; PL/p, plural; PLUP, pluperfect; PRES/FUT, present/future; PRO, pronoun; PROB^FUT, probable future; RESPRO, resumptive pronoun, SG/s, singular; 1 2 3, first, second, and third person.

A Beginning Look at Brahui Connectives

(12) K18

uraa	naa	talaaSii	dee	niiaama	aa	man-iN	Ø	too
house of		search	day	middle	to	become-INF	IMPL	then

hic-oo	iit-as	al-au
something-INDEF	thing-INDEF	be-NEG^PAST^3s

A house search was mounted until midday *but* nothing was found.

It would be convenient to say that this was an example of contraexpectation. The context really gives no clue, however, that anything was ever expected to be found in the house search, and so I have preferred to consider it as a result-oriented example. This example leads nicely into our next use of the morpheme /too/.

2.1.5 /too/ as indicating contraexpectation. It is perhaps with some surprise that we find that the morpheme /too/ is quite often used to indicate a contraexpectational relationship between the two clauses being linked as in (13).

(13) T48

naasar	iskuul	aan	uraa-Gaa	bas	too
Nasser	school	from	house-to	come^PAST^3s	then

maatuna-ta	kalk-ta
stepmother-RESPRO	seize^PAST^3s-RESPRO

Nasser came home from school *then* his stepmother hit him

In this instance the context indicates that, not only an inappropriate activity for the stepmother, but also that no one expected her to strike her stepson (least of all Nasser himself).

(14) XND104

dam-as	aaraam	kan	kaT	aa	leeT-aa	too
breath-INDEF	rest	for	cot	to	lie^down-PAST^3s	then

samaah	tam-tau-ta	kih	hamar	taNg	aan
information	fall-NEG^PAST^3s-RESPRO	that	how	upset	from

in-aa
go-PAST^3s

she lay down for a while to rest on a bed *then* she was not aware how her upsetness went...

124 David A. Ross

In (14), a young lady is under severe criticism for being barren. Unknown to her, her husband is infertile. She visits a faith-healer who prescribes a mixture of medicine, spells, and rest. At the third visit, described here, she undergoes a transformation and conceives in an unexpected (and supposedly miraculous) manner.

2.1.6 Summary of /too/. We have considered above the various uses of /too/ readily discoverable in our text corpus. We have found examples of this morpheme, functioning as a nonconditional connective, in the following contexts: as a facet introducer, as a time indicator (either concurrent or immediately subsequent), with result orientation, and to indicate contraexpectation. The range of functions for /too/ is difficult to define, especially when we have uses as different as result and contraexpectation.

One way out of this dilemma is to propose that /too/ functions as a general connector in contemporary Brahui texts and, thus, encompasses a wide variety of uses. If we are to adopt this solution, however, we will need to demonstrate that all other connectives have a severely restricted, or welldefined, set of functions. As we move to a discussion of /oo/ and /ham/ we will need to keep this in mind.

2.2 The morpheme /oo/

2.2.1 Homophonous morphemes. There are several morphemes with the Brahui form of /oo/, and it is not always easy to sort them out. The homophonous morphemes will be listed with an example each.

(15) Indefinite affix for adjectives
    bal-oo   bandaG-as
    big-INDEF man-INDEF
    a big man

(16) Third-person plural of 'to be' in present/future tense
    daak   oo
    3p   beˆPRES/FUTˆ3p
    they are

(17) Third-person singular medial pronoun
    oo   k-eek
    PROˆ3s(med) doˆPRES/FUTˆ3s
    he, she, it does

A Beginning Look at Brahui Connectives 125

Unfortunately the last of these morphemes occurs frequently at the beginning of clauses, so extra care needs to be taken not to confuse it with the use of /oo/ as a connector. Situations in which there can be no confusion include situations where there is another explicit subject, and where the verb has a plural person ending, since a plural verb does not usually agree with a singular subject.

2.2.2 Other uses of the connective /oo/. In this investigation we are particularly concerned with the use of /oo/ as a logical connector between clauses. Despite being the most common form in which propositions are expressed, we should also note that /oo/ may connect elements of constructions other than clauses. (18) and (19) will suffice to illustrate this.

(18) Joining two nouns [N53, 39]
gul biibii oo riihaana
Gul Bibi and Rihana

raN oo xuuSboo
color and scent

(19) Joining two adjectives [N31, 71]
ooliikoo oo aaxir-ii uhabat
first and last love

paak oo saaf
holy and clean

2.2.3 /oo/ in chronological sequences. As might be expected for a morpheme glossed as 'and', /oo/ is very frequently used as an indicator of chronological sequencing. This may be indicated either by juxtaposing the initial clauses and inserting /oo/ before the last clause, or by inserting /oo/ between all the clauses in the sequence.

(20) WMB18
teenaa silaa-tee biT oo ba-ee baa Tii
self of weapon-OBL^PL throw^IMPER^SG and grass-OBL mouth in

kar oo xaraas aan baar caar-pada
do^IMPER^SG and bull from like four-footed

126   David A. Ross

> *bax-isa*   *bar*
> bellow-PRES^ADV^PART   come^MPER^SG
>
> throw your weapons away, *(and)* put grass in your mouth, *(and)*, like
> a bull, four-footed and bellowing, come (down)...

(21) MC4
> *iilum kan-aa uraa Tii aenoo mehmaan-as bas-uunee, teenaa bala*
> *xoo-ee kan-ee eetee... oo pagar soob too padai hatar-eeva-ta*
>
> "Brother, today a guest has come to my house, give me your big
> cooking pot... *and* I will bring it back again tomorrow morning."

(22) WMB16
> *guRaa   laSkar-ee muc   kar-ee   bas   awaaliikoo*
> then   army-OBL assemble do-PAST^3p come^PAST^3s first
>
> *jaN-ee   mengal too   drakalav Tii   tis   oo*
> fight-OBL Mengal with Drakalav in   give^PAST^3s and
>
> *Saa=zda Saahizai   han   daa jaN   Tii   kas-f-ee*
> sixteen   Shahizai just this fight in   die-CAUS-PAST^3s
>
> Then he assembled an army, came, first fought the Mengals in
> Drakalav, *and* killed sixteen Shahizai in just this one fight.

2.2.4 /oo/ as a facet introducer. There are other uses of the morpheme
/oo/ in which temporal sequencing is not in focus. In particular, there is a
use of the morpheme in a similar manner to the use of /too/ as a facet introducer described in §2.1.2. For this use, there is a continuity of topic, but
some other aspect is being considered. Consider (23) describing wedding
customs pertaining in Arabia at the time of the Prophet.

(23) XB54, 55
> *uraa-k   soodaa mas-uur   jaaiidar aan   garooii*
> house-PL   sell   become-PAST^3p property from collateral
>
> *mas-uur   oo   waam   naa boojh   moox-ee*
> become-PAST^3p and debt   of load   waist-OBL
>
> *pirG-aa*
> broken-PAST^3s
>
> Houses were sold. Property was taken/given as collateral, *and* the
> load of debt was ruinous.

A Beginning Look at Brahui Connectives

The whole idea in this example is that these methods of raising a huge marriage dowry were occurring simultaneously. In particular, the selling of houses, the giving of collateral, and the assumption of large debts was all part of collecting the cash payment required for the dowry. We can, therefore, no longer claim that the /oo/ indicates temporal sequencing.

In this example there would be some justification for saying that the /oo/ points to the result of the practice. We will return to this use of the morpheme /oo/. I believe that the resultative aspect is not in focus here; however, let us consider that the /oo/ is acting here as a facet introducer. If there is a need to be more specific, we could say that the events described and connected by the /oo/ being used in this function are usually concurrent.

It seems that the use of /oo/ as an indicator of chronological sequencing or as a facet introducer cover about seventy-five percent of the occurrences of the morpheme as a connector in the text corpus considered. Furthermore, in these uses there does not seem to be serious interference with the uses of the morpheme /too/ described above. (We should remember that when /too/ was used as a facet introducer it was characterized by extensive lexical and syntactic overlap. This is not the case when the morpheme /oo/ is used.) When we start to consider the residue, the situation becomes more complicated.

2.2.5 /oo/ as a concessive marker. In its use as a concessive marker the morpheme /oo/ could be glossed approximately as 'furthermore'.

(24) XB51

walaad	*naa*	*taliimnaghadaaSt*	*oo*	*baraam*	*kul*	*kaariim-tee*
child^of	study	care	and	wedding	all	work-OBL^PL

daa	*xoobii*	*aT*	*k-eek*	*kih*	*na*	*daa*	*Tii*
this	well^done	by	do-PRES/FUT^3s	that	no	this	in

kas-ee	*Sakaaeest*	*naa*	*mooka*	*duu*
someone-OBL	complaint	of	opportunity	hand

bar-eek	*oo*	*na*	*xuuaaja*	*daa-dee*	*teen*	*kan*
come-PRES/FUT^3s	and	no	Sir	PRO^3s(near)-OBL	self	for

baareem-as	*xiiaal*	*kar-ee*
responsibility-INDEF	care	do-PAST^3s

He took great care with his children's education and all the works associated with weddings, so that in this no one would have any opportunity for complaint and *(furthermore)* the Prophet did not care for himself in this (matter).

128   David A. Ross

(25)   WMB6
    daasa   nan   ee   oo   drakalav muur ee
    now   night beˆPRES/FUTˆ3s   and Drakalav far   beˆPRES/FUTˆ3s
    Now it is dark, and *(furthermore)* Drakalav is (still) far away.

This use of /oo/ may have been somewhat unexpected, but might be
considered as an extension of the facet introducer concept. As such it can be
accommodated within our analysis satisfactorily.

2.2.6 /oo/ with result orientation. As we discovered before, there is
some reason to suspect that /oo/ can indicate a resultative relationship
between two prepositions. Let us see now if we can illustrate this more
conclusively.

(26)   WML16
    jaam naa asi mee-as   as   kih kukuR aan
    Jam   of   one maleˆslave-INDEF beˆPASTˆ3s that cock   from

    baar   baaN   tis-aka   oo handaaR   kee
    like   crow(ing) give-IMPFˆ3s and thisˆsame for

    ood-ee   kukuR paar-eera
    PROˆ3s(med)-OBL cock   say-IMPFˆ3p
    The Jam had a male slave who used to crow like a cock and for this
    (reason) they call him "cock."

For the moment we will not worry about the distinction between reason-
orientation and result-orientation, i.e., did they call him "cock" because he
crowed like one, or did he crow like a cock and as a result they called him
"cock?" What is significant is that the clauses linked by /oo/ are definitely
related by a cause-result-reason-type relationship.

While there are possible examples of /oo/ in this usage in newer texts,
the clearer examples are in the older texts. It, therefore, seems feasible that
the morpheme /too/ has usurped this function from /oo/ in more modern
texts, thus restricting /oo/, so that it is no longer a general connective. We
should note, however, that there are several other connectives which special-
ize in indicating the result-reason-cause-type relations. These include /aaxir/
'finally', e.g., MC13, /andaa hatar aan/ 'therefore', e.g., XB10, XB36,
XB67, /cunaanca/ 'so', e.g., XB70, and /daasa/ 'now', e.g., K36, XB9, N72.

2.2.7 /oo/: the remainder. To demonstrate that there does not yet seem
to be satisfactory closure to this analysis, I return to the idea of /oo/

A Beginning Look at Brahui Connectives

functioning as a facet introducer. In the above analysis I tried to distinguish /too/ and /oo/ being used in this capacity by saying that when /too/ was used there was significant syntactic and lexical overlap and parallelism, whereas this was not a feature when /oo/ was used. Unfortunately, while generally true, this is not always the case. Thus, two examples will be given where /oo/ is used as a facet introducer, and yet there is also significant overlap and parallelism. One example is from an older text, and the other from a contemporary text.

(27) WMB27

A	B	C		1	2
menga l	*aan*	*musiT*	*biist*	*bandaG*	*kas-f-iN-asas*
Mengal	from	three	twenty	man	die-CAUS-PASS-PLUP^3s

A	B					C		
oo	*jadgal*	*naa*	*asiT sad*		*oo*	*sii*	*oo*	*see*
and	Jadgal	of	one hundred		and	thirty	and	three

1	2
bandaG	*kas-f-iN-asas*
man	die-CAUS-PASS-PLUP^3s

Sixty Mengals were killed, *and* one hundred thirty-three Jadgals.

In (27) it is interesting to note that a special construction, 3 x 20, has been used in the first clause to state the number sixty, while there is a perfectly good single word which could have been used instead. One explanation for this would be that the speaker was deliberately trying to increase the syntactic similarity between the two clauses being linked by /oo/.

(28) XB99

A	1	2	3	B	C	D	A	1
xuuaaja	*naa*	*muhabat*	*naa*	*isluub*	*jitaa*	*as*	*oo*	*nanaa*
Sir	of	love	of	method	different	be^PAST^3s	and	our

2	3	B	C	D
muhabat	*naa*	*muyaa*	*past*	*ee*
love	of	standard	lower	be^PRES/FUT^3s

The Prophet's method of loving was different *and* our standard of loving is lower.

130 David A. Ross

2.3 The morpheme /ham/

The morpheme /ham/ (sometimes realized as /am/) was included in this analysis partly because of its ubiquitous appearance, and partly because of its usual gloss of 'also'. It was noted that this morpheme, unlike most connectors, never occurs clause initially. This is not an insurmountable hindrance, however, since adverbials are very commonly used as clause connectors in Brahui. They are usually the second element in the clause; /ham/ also occurs in this position.

After examining the occurrences of /ham/ I came to the conclusion that /ham/ does not usually function as a logical connector. The most common use of /ham/ is as an emphasis marker, or topic highlighter, placing emphasis on the closest preceding noun, noun complex, adverbial, adjective, or postpositional phrase within the same clause. It cannot, however, place emphasis on a resumptive pronoun or on a postposition.

The examples in (29)–(32) are given to illustrate the general principles, rather than to exhaustively illustrate all of the common uses of /ham/. The lines from the /ham/ lead to the item being emphasized.

(29)   WML14
    jaam   bal-oo   laSkar-as   harf-eenee   oo   ira
    Jam   big-INDEF army-INDEF raise-PERFˆ3s and two

    *toop   **ham**   harf-eenee jaam alii **ham** tud*
    cannon also   raise-PERFˆ3s Jam   Ali   also inˆcompany

    ee
    beˆPRES/FUTˆ3s
The Jam has raised a large army... and he *also* has obtained two cannon. Jam Ali is *also* with him.

In (29), the two uses of /ham/ are to emphasize a noun and to emphasize a noun complex (NP). In general, the item being emphasized immediately precedes the /ham/. Consider, however, the different order in (30).

(30)   MC20.2

    *mark kee-ta   **ham** xafa ma-f-a*
    death for-RESPRO also sorry become-NEG-IMPERˆSG
    Don't be upset about its death *either*.

A Beginning Look at Brahui Connectives

131

This example is significant because the /ham/ applies not to the immediately preceding element, but to a noun two elements removed; the application of the /ham/ had to jump over the resumptive pronoun (/-ta/) and the postposition (/kee/) before reaching its head.

For completeness we also note (31) where the /ham/ applies to an adverbial.

(31) MC5

ii   nee   peenduuaar   **ham** xuuaaS k-eeva
1s   2s^OBL another^time also happy   do-PRES/FUT^1s
I will make you happy another time *also*.

With this use of /ham/ established, we can briefly discuss the rare function of /ham/ as a logical connector. In some instances /ham/ qualifies as an element being used an anaphoric reference, e.g., T44, where it qualifies 'in that manner', an anaphoric reference to the preceding clause.

Of more interest, however, is the use of /ham/ to qualify an ellipsed unit, effectively collapsing two propositions into one in (32).

(32) K2

gul xaan iskuul   naa baaz mana Tii **ham** duzii loofaarii
Gul Khan school   of   very few   in   also   theft likewise

kar-eeka
do-IMPF^3s
Just like a few others in school, Gul Khan *also* stole.

The only way this can make sense in English is to use two clauses. Further, there is nothing explicit for the /ham/ to relate to unless we go all the way back to the 'Gul Khan'. The best explanation is that several words have been ellipsed. Rather than try to reconstruct the Brahui, let us attempt to reconstruct the English gloss: 'school of very few in theft DID, Gul Khan also likewise did'. The inserted verb 'did' has been capitalized to indicate ellipsis. Furthermore, the word order has had to be altered from that given. By doing this we see clearly that the /ham/ applies to Gul Khan. Thus, in a sense /ham/ serves as a connector, binding the second half of the construction as given to the first half, where there is explicit mention of Gul Khan.

2.4 Summary of coordinating connectives

Having examined /too/, /oo/, and /ham/ as coordinating connectives in Brahui texts, what can we say about them? First of all, we note that /too/ is a

132   David A. Ross

relatively recent borrowing, probably from Urdu, and that it appears to function as a general connective. We note also that, the much older connective /oo/ is still often used in Brahui texts, although there is some evidence that its use is becoming more restricted. We can also say that /ham/ is not really a connector at all, but rather an emphasis marker, or topic highlighter.

3. Adversative connectives

There are two morphemes often glossed as 'but' in Brahui, /magar/ and /vala/ (the latter sometimes appearing as /valee/). The first interest is to try to distinguish between the uses of these morphemes. We can make the initial observation that /vala/ does not appear in older texts: that it only appears in some newer texts. This immediately widens the scope of our investigation somewhat, with the potential of some diachronic phenomenon also applicable.

While we are initiating this investigation, the infrequent connective /balka/ 'rather' also has a feel which might be adversative. Some remarks about this connective will be made, although it will be more peripheral than central to this section.

One further complication will bear some investigation. In the newer text K, /vala/ does not occur at all, but there is significant use of another connective /valdaa/, usually glossed as 'again'. We will need to ask ourselves whether /valdaa/ has taken over the functions of /vala/ in this text (since there is obvious phonetic similarity), or whether there is something else at work here.

3.1 The morpheme /vala/

Since /vala/ has a more restricted occurrence than /magar/, at least on the surface, occurring exclusively in newer texts, we will attempt to discover its functions before considering those of /magar/.

3.1.1 /vala/ as contraexpectation. It seems that the major use of /vala/ is to indicate contraexpectation. Rather than try to justify this using any quantitative analysis, let us illustrate this use with several examples:

(33)   N51–52
oo-naa baava asa nan jald jik oo jooR mulk-taa diir too naN kan
in-aa **vala** *soob too oofk oo-naa laaSa-ee uraa-Gaa al-eer*

One night her father, in good health, went hurriedly to the watering place (to get water) for (his) wife. *But* in the morning they brought his body to the house.

A Beginning Look at Brahui Connectives

133

In (33), there is clearly a contraexpectational relationship between the clauses. It is, in fact, heightened by the extra adverb /jik oo jooR/ 'in good health' in the first clause. With this the reader is left in no doubt that there was no reason to expect the death of the father at that time.

With this example we can also begin to notice another feature of the use of use of /vala/ in a contraexpectational manner: it is usual for the two propositions being linked to have different grammatical subjects. This may or may not have significance later on.

(34)   N15–17

dun-angaa xuuS-ii naa vaxt aa har asiT zeebaa-oo pusku-oo puuS-aak
*baen-ook daaN eeN carx k-eek **vala** daa kul naa niiaam aT*
riihaana naa ust muunjaa ee

At this happy time everyone is wearing beautiful new clothes (and) is walking hither and thither. *But* in the middle of all this Rihana's heart is sad.

The example begins with an expression which only weakly translates as 'At this happy time...'. The use of /vala/ in this context is clearly contraexpectational. In addition, however, the whole text begins to take on a new connotation at this point. Up until this time the description has been about preparations for the wedding, and the joyfulness of the events is often emphasized. We find expressions of the type in N9 'On such a day of happiness everyone, young and old, was happy', and in N13 'Everywhere wonderful happiness was evident'. It comes as a surprise, therefore, when we are abruptly informed in N17 that Rihana is sad. I conclude that the /vala/ is acting as a contraexpectation indicator. Note again that the grammatical subject has changed after the /vala/.

Another example is given from a different text, discussing the reaction of the Prophet to the death of his son, Abraham.

(35)   XB105–106

xan-tee	*Tii*	*xaRiink-aak*	*oo*		*ust*	*Tii*	*Gam-k*
eye-OBL^PL	in	tear-PL	be^PRES/FUT^3p		heart	in	sorrow-PL

ar-eer		*valee*	*dun-oo*	*iit-as*		*baa*	*aan*
be^PRES^DEF-3p		but	thus-INDEF	concern-INDEF		mouth	from

kaSee-p-eena		*oo*		*kih*	*rab-ee*	*pasand*
pull^out-NEG-PRES/FUT^1p		PRO^3s(med)		that	God-OBL	liking

134   David A. Ross

af
be^NEG^PRES/FUT^3s

There were tears in his eyes, there was (certainly) sorrow in (his) heart *but* we do not find him saying anything because God would not have liked it.

Here the contraexpectation arises from the fact that a natural reaction to grief is to give some verbal expression of it (whether in discussion or wailing), and yet the Prophet (PBUH) rigidly avoids this. One might be tempted to say that this was not contraexpectation if the culture expected this reaction. There are two indications, however, that contraexpectation is indeed implied here. The first is that the author felt it necessary to state the reason for this restraint of reaction, namely, that it does not make God happy. The very fact that the reason was stated indicates that this was not the expected response. Furthermore, contemporary culture does exhibit the noise of grief at the death of a loved one, and thus, the reader would find this an unexpected reaction.

We also note the rather unusual construction necessary to change the grammatical subject following the /vala/. After /vala/, the first-person plural of the verb is used, whereas previously it was the third-person plural. Before /vala/, the subjects are 'tears' and 'sorrows', whereas afterwards the subject is (an indeterminate) 'we'.

3.1.2 /vala/ as contrast. Another important use of /vala/ is to indicate contrast between two propositions. This is typically accompanied by extensive use of syntactic parallelism and lexical overlap. In this connection we recall the use of /too/ as a facet introducer. In that investigation we noted a similar use of overlap and parallelism.

Before continuing this discussion, let us consider some examples of the phenomenon. The same conventions will be used to indicate overlap and parallelism as were used in the discussion of /too/.

(36) N75
      A   1   2   3   B   4   C
      zaahir aT   asa   eloo-Raan mur   man-iN   naa kooSiS Ø

             A   1   2   3   B   4   C
          vala   baatan aT   asa eloo naa diid naa talabgaar Ø
      Outwardly they tried to remain far from each other, *but* in their hearts they sought out meetings of loved ones.

Immediately prior to this, the author has been at pains to point out the mutual affection between the boy and girl is culturally unusual. Thus, one

A Beginning Look at Brahui Connectives

could not really say that this was contraexpectation, in that the activities and attitudes expressed may well have been expected. There is a definite contrast, however, between what was expected of them (namely, that they should keep apart after their engagement) and what they desired to do (namely, meet often).

(37) N83, 84

      1   2   3   A
asa *giRaa-as* *bandaG-ee* *duu* *ba-f-∅*

      4   B   C
     too *oo* *sabar* *k-eek*

          1   3   A
vala *duu naa giRaa kih* *duu aan peeS* *tam-aa*

      4 2   B   C
     too bandaG-ee baaz *armaan bar-eek*
(If) something is not available to a man
then he accepts it.
But when it became (no longer) available
then a great desire comes to a man.

Once again there appear to be two contrasting aspects of behavior or attitude presented here. The letters and numbers included in (37) give some indication of the high degree of lexical overlap and syntactic parallelism.

It is perhaps worth noting that there is no consistency in the matter of grammatical subjects in the two examples. In (36) the same subject is implied in both clauses. In (37), however, where there are two relevant clauses preceding the /vala/ and two afterwards, the same subject is used when one preceding clause is compared with its following correspondent, but a different grammatical subject is used when the other preceding clause is compared to its following correspondent.

Since we want to avoid any suspicion that this phenomenon might only be applicable in one text, an example from another text is given in (38).

(38) XND17, 18

    A   1   2
    oo   *xisun zeeb*   *naa asa mukamal-oo*
    PRO^3s(med) red beautiful of one complete-INDEF

136   David A. Ross

	B	A		
Saahukaar-as	*as-aka* ***vala***	*niiaaRii*	*naa*	*zaat*
merchant^banker-INDEF	be-IMPF^3s but	woman	of	tribe

			1	2	B
bee	*walaad*	*aan*	*naa*	*mukamal*	*ee*
without	child	from	not	complete	be^PRES/FUT^3s

She was the beautiful, golden (daughter) of a prosperous merchant banker, *but* a woman without a child is not complete.

This example is not contraexpectation in that it is possible for a woman to be both beautiful and barren. However, it is definitely a contrast on which the story is based. Without going into details, both of the propositions have somewhat unusual grammatical constructions which tends to emphasize the overlap and parallelism present.

While we are dealing with the topic of contrast it is instructive to note that a contrastive relationship may be implied without any overt connective.

(39)   K79, 80

rahzan-tee	*aan*	*ira*	*jaaga*	*aa*	*raahii*
highway^robber-OBL^PL	from	two	place	towards	start^on^journey

mas	*eeloo-k*	*teenaa*	*giRaa-tee*	*aDa-ee*
become^PAST^3s	other-PL	self^of	thing-OBŁ^PL	shelter-OBL

hal-aar	*nar-aar*
take-PAST^3p	flee-PAST^3p

(One of the men) started on a journey from the robbers to another place. The others (highway robbers) took their things to the shelter, (and) fled.

3.1.3 /vala/ as amplification/restatement. Occasionally /vala/ is used to indicate an amplification or restatement relationship between two propositions. In (40), we note extensive use of lexical overlap and syntactic parallelism, although I hesitate to say at this point that this is always a characteristic of this use of /vala/.

(40)   XND65

1	2	3	4	A		
oo-Raa		*haqiiqat*	*paaS*	*mas*	***vala***	
PRO^3s(med)-to		fact	evident	become^PAST^3s	but	DEMO^3s(near)

A Beginning Look at Brahui Connectives

    3   1 2   4   A

haqiiqat biira oo-Raa paaS as-aka
fact   simply   PRO^3s(med)-to   evident   be-IMPF^3s

The fact became evident to him, *but* this fact was simply clear to him.

This quote occurs in the midst of a man's meditation on the fact of his own infertility, and how he should inform his wife of this. He is thinking about how the facts are undeniable that he is infertile and that he must inform his wife; yet at the same time he is resisting telling his wife. The two propositions are essentially identical (one could argue that the second proposition was an amplification), and so the real question is why the author chose to link them with /vala/. I tentatively conclude that this is one of the potential functions of the morpheme /vala/, at least in newer texts.

3.1.4 The morpheme /valdaa/. Before leaving our discussion of the morpheme /vala/, we should briefly mention the morpheme /valdaa/, usually glossed as 'again', but which has possibly been used in place of /vala/ in one newer text. The usual use of /valdaa/, shown in (41), is to note repeated activity, although this is not the only way of doing this (see Bray 1934:305).

(41)   *xadoo   naa   Tag-ak   **valdaa**   bas-uunoo*
        last^year   of   cheat-PL   again   come-PERF^3p

        (Those) cheats of last year have come back *again.*

If we refer to examples in the text corpus, although such examples outside the K text are rare, we conclude that the /valdaa/ is used for anaphoric reference to a state or event. Sometimes this event or state might have occurred or been mentioned a long way back in the text, e.g., the /valdaa/ in N77.1 refers to N66, 67. Consider an example in (42).

(42)   T15–17

luma   aan   guD   naasar   naa   xiiaal-daarii   ham   abdal   naa
mother   from   later   Nasser   of   thought-NN   also   Abdul   of

*kaaTum aa   bas   **valdaa**   naasar   naa   xiiaal-daarii*
head   to   come^PAST^3s   again   Nasser   of   thought-NN

naa   xaatar   aan   ham   goodii   see   naa
of   reason   from   also   housewife   concerning   of

138   David A. Ross

    zaruur   *aT*   *as*
    certainly by^means^of   be^PAST^3s
After his wife's death Abdul also thought about Nasser.... *Again*, out
of concern for Nasser also, it was necessary to have a housewife.

In (42) the lexical repetition helps to specify which preceding clause is
referred to by the /valdaa/. This, then is the usual use of /valdaa/.

Now, let us consider for a moment the K text, in which there is no example
of /vala/ being used, but in which /valdaa/ appears to be used as a connective.

Example (43) shows /valdaa/ being used in a contraexpectation relationship. In the story, the police are searching Amir Jan's house. At first Amir
Jan sits with his friends in the mosque, but, at the time of the extract, he
returns home, presumably expecting to get some news.

(43)   K15
      masiit   *aan*   *siidaa*   *uraa-Gaa*   *bas-aka*   **valdaa**
      mosque   from   straight   house-to   come-IMPF^3s again

      hic   *peeSaan*   *ma-t-aka*
      something outside   become-NEG-IMPF^3s
He was coming straight from the mosque to (his) house *but* nothing
was happening outside.

Example (44) appears to show /valdaa/ in a contrastive relationship, but
it is necessary to enlarge the quote somewhat to show the accompanying
lexical overlap.

(44)   K28–30
    28   *hamee*   *jaaga*   *aa*   *reseeNg-aa*
         that^same   place   to   arrive-PAST^3s
         He arrived at that place...

    29.2 *xaf-tee*   *asa niiaaRii* *asiT* *naa* *tavaar* *tam-aa*
        ear-OBL^PL one woman one   of   shout   fall-PAST^3s
        he heard the shout of a woman

    29.3 1   2   3
        moon   *aa*   *mas*
        face   to   become^PAST^3s
        she came forward...

A Beginning Look at Brahui Connectives

30.1 *gul xaan asa zid-as xaf toor-ee*
Gul Khan one temper-INDEF ear hold-PAST^3s
Gul Khan held his ears in a rage...

30.3   1   2   3
       valdaa *moon aa mas*
       again face to become^PAST^3s
       but then came forward

In one sense, one could say that this was contraexpectation, in that Gul Khan's action in coming forward (and subsequently supporting the lady's cause) was unexpected. I think an equally good case can be made for a contrastive relationship, where the contrast is between Gul Khan's activities and those of his (fellow) highway robbers, none of whom treats the lady with any deference.

3.2 The morpheme /magar/

The morpheme /magar/ 'but' appears in both older and newer texts, and is much more common in contemporary speech than is /vala/. Since we have concentrated our investigation of /vala/ on newer texts, we will start by considering the use(s) of /magar/ also in newer texts. Of some interest here is the attempt to see whether it is possible to define applications of /magar/ which are mutually exclusive from those of /vala/. We will, of course, also need to consider the older texts and their use of /magar/, which may help our understanding of the diachronic change (if any) in the use of /magar/.

/magar/ does not occur in all newer texts, but, when it does occur, its use is almost exclusively that of a contrastive relationship. In these uses the emphasis appears to be on balancing the reader's opinion with the addition of more data. Typically, the second proposition, preceded by the /magar/, presents a different, off-setting aspect of the problem presented in the first clause. Grammatically, the contrastive function is sometimes accompanied by syntactic parallelism, although this is not essential, and the two clauses usually have different grammatical subjects. Consider (45)–(47).

(45) N47, 48
  too teen-aa iilum abdul kareem-ee am salah tis kih oo am gul biibii oo riihaana-ee arf-ee Shar aa bar-ee

140   David A. Ross

vala abdul kareem xalk naa saada-oo bandaG-as as-aka

Then he also advised his brother that he should also bring Gul Bibi and Rihana (and) come to the city. *But* Abdul Kariim was a simple village man

(46) XB101

xuuaaja-ee	*beeSak*	*walaad*	*naa*	*muhabat*	*as*	*magar*
Sir-ee	doubtless	child	of	love	be^PAST^3s	but

xudaa	*naa*	*muhabat*	*daa*	*Raan*	*ziiaat*	*as*
God	of	love	this	from	great	be^PAST^3s

Doubtless the Prophet loved his children *but* his love for God was greater than this.

(47) XB37, 38

daa	*too*	*xuuaaja*	*naa*	*sublii*	*walaad-ak*	*as-uura*	*magar*
this	with	Sir	of	real	child-PL	be^PAST-3p	but

daaf-tee	*aan*	*baidas*	*xuuaaja*	*naa*	*giRaa-s*	*rabeeba*
DEM(near)^3p-OBL	from	more	Sir	of	thing-INDEF	step

walaad	*ham*	*as*
son	also	be^PAST^3s

These were the Prophet's real children. *But*, more than these, the Prophet also had a stepson.

The real question that this raises is whether this contrastive use of /magar/ overlaps with the contrastive use of /vala/ in newer texts. We first note that the contrastive use of /magar/ is the only significant use noted (within the limits of the text corpus), whereas the contrastive use of /vala/ is statistically a secondary use. We also note that, whereas syntactic parallelism was a notable feature when /vala/ was used as a contrastive connective, it is not so obvious or pervasive when /magar/ is used in this role.

Having said all that, however, there still seems to be an overlap in the use of the two connectives, which it is at present impossible to resolve.

3.3 Contraexpectation in older texts

We have just concluded that /vala/, but not /magar/, may indicate contraexpectation in newer texts. Since /vala/ does not occur in older texts, it is appropriate to ask how contraexpectation is indicated in older texts.

A Beginning Look at Brahui Connectives

141

Probably the most obvious answer is that /magar/ filled this function in older texts, leading to the conclusion that there has been a diachronic change in the use of this connector. While this is not the complete answer, there is evidence of this, as the following examples show.

(48) MC10
kul xoo-k haazir oo, dar-ak-ta
magar *oof-taa cuca-aa-ta sambaal-ee k-ees, kih piD pur oo*

All the pots are here, take them, *but* take care of the small ones, (because) they are pregnant

Not only is the assertion of pregnancy for cooking pots unexpected coming from the speaker (a miser), but it is part of a continuing verbal repartee which gets its humor from its very unexpected nature.

(49) WMB11

mehmaan	*naa*	*rasm*	*handaa*	*ee*		*kih*	*bandaG*
guest	of	custom	just^this	be^PRES/FUT^3s		that	man

ood-ee		*iraG*	*eetee*		**magar**	*kan-ee*
PRO^3s(med)-OBL		bread	give^IMPER^SG		but	PRO^1s-OBL

Saka	*bar-ek*		*oo*	*kan-aa*		*maar-ee*
suspicion	come-PRES/FUT^3s		PRO^3s(med)	PRO^1s^OBL-of		son-OBL

kas-fee-nee
die-CAUS-PERF^3s

(Our) custom (for treating) guests (hospitably) is this, that a man must feed him... *but* I suspect that he has killed my son.

This is classified as contraexpectation because of the unexpectedness of the event that a guest in a house would be suspected of murdering a member of the host's family. However, there would be some justification in saying that this was a contrastive use of the connective, in that two mutually exclusive cultural obligations are being recognized by the host (the speaker): that of being hospitable to a guest and that of avenging a wrong done to the family.

One of the reasons for hesitancy on whether /magar/ indicates contraexpectation in older texts is that it is clearly not the only way contraexpectation is indicated in older texts. Furthermore, there are not many occurrences of /magar/ on which to base the analysis, and, in some of the instances, such as

142   David A. Ross

(49), there is some question as to whether /magar/ is being used to indicate contrast or contraexpectation.

With this in mind, let us widen the discussion a little and look at the various ways contraexpectation is indicated in older texts (in addition to the use of /magar/). There is no other explicit marker of contraexpectation, but one is left with the impression that complex syntactic constructions often accompany contraexpectation. Two of these are illustrated in (50).

(50) MC13.5–15
       luc-ee tavaar kar-ee paar-e, kan-aa xoo-tee hat

       14 *luc paar-ee, oo xuuaaja, ii naa moon Tii Sarmindaa uT, kih
            naa xoo-k kask-uunoo*

       15 *baxiil paar-ee, antae masxara k-eesa? xoo ham gahas
            kask-uunee*

       (The miser) shouted to the cheat, (and) said, "Bring (back) my cooking pots."
       The cheat said, "Oh, Lord, I am ashamed before you, (but) your cooking pots died."
       The miser said, "Why do you jest? (No) cooking pot has died."

The first contraexpectational relation is in the last clause of MC14, where the cheat tells the miser that his pots have died. This is contraexpectational on two counts. First, it is not expected as response to the command to return the pots (MC13.7). Further, it is not expected as a reason why the cheat claims to be ashamed (MC14.2). The interesting fact, however, is that there is no overt marker of contraexpectation, other than the fact that the relative clause construction (/kih/...) is used. This in itself is significant because of a Brahui preference not to use this type of construction if at all possible (see Bray 1907 or Ross 1988).

The other contraexpectational relation is between clauses MC15.2 and MC15.3. (There is lexical overlap also to suggest anaphoric reference to MC14.3.) We note that use has been made of the rhetorical question construction in MC15.5, which is an extremely rare construction. There is, in fact, some reason to believe that its use is reserved for purposes such as this, but this is outside the scope of our discussion here. For the present time let us merely make note that this is another indication of the fact that contraexpectation may be indicated by use of a complex grammatical construction, without any overt connective morpheme.

A Beginning Look at Brahui Connectives

143

Let us conclude this discussion with another example of the phenomenon. There is a connective morpheme which one would not automatically associate with contraexpectation.

(51) MC20
    nii baxiil xoo naa cuca kee xuuaaS mas-us, **daasa** *mark kee-ta ham*
    xafa ma-f-a, Sukr kaS-a

You, miser, were happy when the pot had children; *now* don't be sorry about its death either, (instead) give thanks.

In this example the contraexpectation hinges on the /daasa/ 'now' connective. This morpheme is usually a time adverbial, but in (51) the emphasis is clearly not on time.

3.4 Other adversative connectives

No attempt will be made to make an exhaustive analysis of all adversative connectives in Brahui. Since examples are sparse for other adversative connectives, they will only be mentioned here, with an example. It is not expected that any of these morphemes will affect the analysis thus far.

(52) XB95, 96: /bahar/ 'however'

baaz-aNgaa	*muuarix-ak*	*ira*	*baaz-oo*	*band*	*xiisun*	*naa*
much-DEF	historian-PL	two	much-INDEF	bangle	gold	of

	am	*nooSta*	*kar-eenoo*	**bahar**	*haal*	*daa*	*maxqar*	*oo*
	also	written	do-PERF^3p	however	health	of	limited	and

	saamaan	*as*	*oo*	*kih*	*Daaj*	*tin-iNg-aa*
	baggage	be^PAST^3s	PRO^3s(med)	that	dowry	give-PASS-PAST^3s

Many historians have also written about two large gold bangles. *However,* the gifts were limited which were given as dowry.

(53) WML7: /neeT/ 'finally'

mana	*saal*	*teen^pa^teen*	*mengal*	*oo*	*cuTav*	*maal*
few	year	among^themselves	Mengal	and	Chutta	livestock

	xal-isa	*oo*	*bandaG*	*kas-f-isa*	*hin-aar*
	strike-ADV^PART	and	man	die-CAUS-ADV^PART	go-PAST^3p

144 David A. Ross

neeT *beelav naa jaam jadgal naa mux-ee taf-ee*
finally Bela of Jam Jadgal of cause-OBL bind-PAST^3s
For a few years the Mengal and the Chuttas stole one another's
livestock and killed (opposing) men; *finally*, the Jam of Bela adopted
the Jadgal's cause.

(54) XND98, 99: /aaxir/ 'finally'
fariida daaruu-tee kun-iN aan guD dam-as kaT aa
Farida medicine-OBL^PL eat-INF from later rest-INDEF cot to

leet-aa aaxir paxiir musa vaar hafta Tii
lie^down-PAST^3s finally faith^healer three time week in

asa dee dam daaruu kan ban-iN naa paan-iN too
one day spell medicine for come-INF of say-INF with

raxsat kar-ee-ta
permission do-PAST^3s-RESPRO
After drinking the medicines, Farida lay down on the cot for a rest.
Finally, the faith healer asked permission for her to come (to him)
three times in a week, each time for medicine and a spell.

In each of the last two examples the connective glossed as 'finally' cannot mean that the action is being terminated, since in each case the quote is
far from the end of the text. Furthermore, in each case the connective is introducing a new twist into the text, serving as a sort of occasioning incident
for what is immediately following. Rather than trying to classify these new
connectives we merely observe that they tend to fill roles which other connectives discussed above may also fill.

3.5 The morpheme /balka/

At the beginning of this section we noted one other morpheme, which we
thought might come under the general heading of adversative connectives—
the morpheme /balka/. This is not a common connective, but it appears to
function primarily to introduce a negated antonym construction. Before discussing the limitations on this, consider the prototypical examples:

(55) N34, 35
vala riihaana daa muhabat naa haneen oo giceen aa phul-ee tiiaar
*tiiaar Saax aa kaSka-tav-eesus. **balka** oo daa phul-ee teenaa duu*

A Beginning Look at Brahui Connectives

aT xar-f-eesus

But this flower of love was not fully ready when Rihana had picked it. *Rather* she had caused the flower to grow by herself.

(56) N72
daa jazbah, kih ood-ee hic-oo pin-as tin-iN ma-tav-aka balka beerav mahsoos kan-iNg-aka

this emotion, for which it was not possible for her to give a name, *rather* it was only felt...

In the usual case of /balka/ as a connector indicating negated antonym, the first proposition is expressed in the negative, and the connective precedes the second proposition.

This does not, however, seem to fit the use of /balka/ in (57).

(57) XB58, 59

juuaan-angaa	*iit*	*daa-dee*	*Ø*	*kih*	*baraam-ak*	
good-DEF	thing	PRO^3s(near)-OBL	IMPL	that	wedding-PL	

mas-uur,	*davit*	*(valiima)-ak*	*mas-uur*		/
become-PAST^3p	invitation	(to^marriage)-PL	become-PAST^3p		

mehr	*muqarar*	*mas*	*balka*	*daa*	*am*
love	allowance	become^PAST^3s	rather	DEM(near)^SG	also

mas	*siiaal-ak*	*am*	*bas-uur*
become^PAST^3s	family-PL	also	come-PAST^3p

It is a (very) good thing that weddings happened, wedding invitations were distributed, a love allowance was settled (on the bride), *rather* this also happened, families also came.

Not only is there no negative expression included, but there are no obvious referents which could be classed as negated antonyms. The discussion concerns wedding customs, and in particular is trying to contrast good customs with bad (usually expensive) customs. It seems that the author is attributing to the Prophet (PBUH) a desire that there be no expensive entertaining of guests at a wedding. In this sense the connective /balka/ could be operating in either a contrastive or a contraexpectational mode.

Before leaving this discussion we should also note that it is not essential to use /balka/ to introduce a negated antonym construction. In fact, it is quite

146 David A. Ross

common for there to be no overt connector used when clauses are linked in this relationship as shown in (58).

(58) K62

cir-ta-tee   *Tii*   *leeT-at-aka*   *daaN eeN*
lapse^of^time-RESPRO-OBL^PL   in   lie^down-NEG-IMPF^3s   hither thither

hur-aka
look-IMPF^3s

For a while he was not lying down (to rest) *(but rather)* was looking about...

4. Reason-result-purpose connectives

As we begin our consideration of the broad range of connectives which may be considered as reason-result-purpose connectives, it is appropriate to note that we have already seen the morpheme /too/ functioning with a result-orientation, e.g., N109, 110. Furthermore, we must once again be aware that it is possible to imply one of these relationships, without any overt connective being given.

Notwithstanding these considerations, it makes a fruitful study to examine those connectives which do seem to be used in this context, with a view once again to distinguishing their uses. By far the most common connective with this use is /kih/ and its derivatives, e.g., /antae kih/, and so this will be examined first in the analysis below. Other connectives to be examined include /handaa xaatar aan/ 'therefore' and /dun/ (or its derivatives) 'thus'.

4.1 The morpheme /kih/

In mentioning the morpheme /kih/ above I carefully avoided giving it a gloss, because it has many uses in Brahui. For convenience I have usually glossed it as 'that', but this is not a good indication of its functions.

First of all, since there are no other relative pronouns in Brahui, /kih/ has adopted this means of introducing relative clauses. (In general, Brahui does not like to use subordinate clauses of this type, preferring to use concatenated simple sentences.) These tend to be used in introductions, or at other points in a text where the tension is relatively low. There are two examples of /kih/ in the first sentence of (59).

(59) MC1

maaSed naa Saar Tii asiT baxiil-as as

A Beginning Look at Brahui Connectives

> *kih teenaa umr Tii paxiir-as-eeasa baaxoo-as iraG naa ti-taw-asas oo*
> *agar peen kas-as-ee xan-aka*
> *kih giRa-as kas-as tis-aka baaz xafa mas-aka*

In the city of Mashed was a miser *who* had never given a morsel of bread to a poor man and if he saw anyone else *who* was giving anything (then he) became very angry.

This example highlights several aspects of the use of /kih/ to introduce relative clauses. First, we note that the relative pronoun does not necessarily come immediately adjacent to its head noun, but may rather introduce a following clause. Further, we note that the relative clause qualifies the grammatical subject of the preceding clause in its first use, but qualifies the grammatical object of the preceding clause in the second.

Another use of /kih/ is in the formulae for quotation (see Ross 1987: 274ff.). It is usual to link it to a speech verb, for example the verb 'to say'.

(60) daa   paar-ee   **kih**
      PRO^3s(near) say-PAST^3s   that
      He said...

Particularly in places of high tension in the texts, however, the speech verb tends to get dropped completely, and the morpheme /kih/ alone becomes the indicator of direct speech.

(61) MC17
      aaxir jaN kar-eer hin-aar haakim naa paaraaG-aa
      kih nan-aa Saraa-ee kar-ak

Finally, they fought, (then) went to the judge (*asking*), "Decide between us by Muslim law."

In the last clause of (61), we know that there is direct speech, because the verb appears in the imperative. Yet the /kih/ provides the only evidence of direct speech.

We should note also that, even if /kih/ is used as a relative pronoun or as an indicator of direct speech, this does not necessarily preclude it also functioning as a logical connective. For example, in (61) the /kih/ functions both as an indicator of direct speech and as connective implying purpose.

4.1.1 /kih/ to signify purpose. Perhaps the best way to proceed at this juncture is merely to list a number of examples in which the /kih/ seems to be acting in a manner indicating purpose.

148 David A. Ross

(62) MC4
iilum, kan-aa uraa Tii aenoo mehmaan-as bas-uunee teenaa bala
xoo-ee kan-ee eet-ee
kih *ta-Tii suu beeT k-eeva*

Brother, today a guest has come to my house, give me your big cooking pot, *(so that)* I will cook meat in it.

There is not much doubt that the speaker is giving the purpose for which he is asking to borrow the pot. It is of note that the first clause quoted gives the background or reason for the request, and yet there is no connective overtly indicating this.

(63) T32

kan-ee	*peen*	*kaariim*	*af*		*naa*	*xizmat*
PRO^1s-OBL	other	work	be^NEG^PRES/FUT^3s		PRO^2s^of	service

caa-eeva		**kih**	*daaR-ee*	*bas-uunuT*
understand-PRES/FUT^1s		that	DEM(near)-OBL	come-PERF^1s

"I have no other work, I know what service you want *(and for this purpose)* I have come here."

This example is satirical, in that the lady speaker is objecting to serving as a waitress for her stepson. (It is cultural for the females of a household to be responsible for meeting the needs of the males.) She is really saying, "I certainly did not come here just to wait on you!"

(64) XND88

akram	*teenaa*	*vas-tee*		*kar-ee*	**kih**	*fariida*	*walaad*	*naa*
Akram	self^of	power-OBL^PL		do-PAST^3s	that	Farida	child	of

xiiaal-ee	*teenaa*	*ust*	*aan*	*kaS-ee*		*vala*
idea-OBL	self^of	heart	from	pull^out-PAST^3s		but

oo	*sar*	*soob*	*ma-t-auu*
PRO^3s(med)	arrival	direction	become-NEG-PAST^3s

Akram used his powers (of persuasion) *(in order that)* Farida might forget about having a child but she did not do so.

We note that (64) is an example of frustrated purpose, in that the intended purpose was not realized.

A Beginning Look at Brahui Connectives

4.1.2 /kih/ as reason. There seems to be clear evidence that /kih/ is also used in some circumstances to indicate reason. You may have noted above that /kih/ can be used to indicate a purpose relationship in both older and newer texts. In the same way, in this section I will give examples from both older and newer texts as appropriate.

(65) MC10.5, 10.6
magar oof-taa cuca aa-ta sambaal-ee k-ees
kih *piD pur oo*

"...but take care of their children, (*because* they) are pregnant."

(66) XND23

niiaaRii	*naa*	*vajood*	*hamoo*	*tam*	*mukamal*
woman	of	existence	DEM(med)	time	finished

mar-eek	**kih** *oo-naa*	*kuT aT*	*oo-naa*	*walaad*
become-PRES/FUT^3s	that PRO^3s-of	lap with	PRO^3s-of	child

parvaraS	*xan-aa*
nourishment	see-PAST^3s

A woman's existence becomes complete in this—*(because)* she has nourished her own child.

The emphasis is not on how a woman's life may be reckoned as complete, but rather, once it is complete, explanation of the reason why it is considered so. The mood is one of dejection and sorrow, since the heroine of the story is at this point barren.

(67) XND48

haraa	*draxt*	*aan*	**kih**	*baram*	*duu*	*ba-f-0*
all	tree	from	that	fruit	hand	come-NEG-PRES^INDEF^3s

oo-naa	*guD-iN*	*juuaan*	*ee*
PRO^3s(med)-of	chop^off-INF	good	be^PRES/FUT^3s

Every tree *which* does not bear fruit should be chopped down.

This example is basically proverbial. The /kih/ is being used to introduce a relative clause, with the /draxt/ 'tree', as head noun. It is also being used in a larger sense to explain why the tree should be cut down; namely, that it does not bear fruit.

150   David A. Ross

4.1.3 /kih/ as result. It does not seem as if we can tie down the morpheme /kih/, within the range of purpose-reason-result, in such a way that it leaves room for other morphemes to fill in gaps. We have so far seen that, in both older and newer texts, /kih/ can indicate both purpose and reason-type relationships. Now we demonstrate that, under the same circumstances, it can also indicate a result-type relationship.

(68) MC3.2, 3.3
       daa baxiil too luc-iias kan-iN zaruur ee
       kih *taa kah-iN-iska ood-ee yaat aan im-p-0*

       It is necessary to do some cheating with this miser *that* he will remember until he dies.

(69) XB5
       *daaf-tee   aa   as   **kih**   kaziiat   kar-ee*
       PRO^3p(near)-OBL to   be^PAST^3s that   die   do-PAST^3s
       It was to them *that* he died.

The example in (69) is almost formulaic, appearing in several forms in the same text. In each case, however, the emphasis is on the result, namely that the person died. Perhaps another instance in (70) will reinforce this.

(70) XB16
       daa   cunaa daa-iskaa   ira saal naa as   kaziiat kar-ee
       DEM(near) child PRO^3s(near)-up to two year of   be^PAST^3s die do-PAST^3s
       When this child was two years old he died.

From another text we have another example of a result-oriented connective, but there are two occurrences of /kih/ in the sentence, and so we need to be careful to sort out the uses of each.

(71) XND107
       *heeraan   mas   **kih** daa   aenoo   kan-ee   ant*
       astonished become^PAST^3s that DEM(near) today   PRO^1s-OBL what

       *mas   **kih** taNg-aan   in-aaT*
       become^PAST^3s that   upset-from   go-PAST^1s
       She was astonished *(musing),* "What has happened to me today that I am no longer upset/sorry?"

A Beginning Look at Brahui Connectives 151

The free gloss should make it clear that the first occurrence of /kih/ in (71) is the direct quotation formula in its briefest form. We know this because the first clause is in the third-person singular, whereas the second and third clauses make reference to the first-person singular.

The result oriented /kih/ is the second occurrence of /kih/ in (71). There is no doubt of its result-type emphasis because it is such a relief to the lady that the stigma of her barrenness has been removed that all other considerations are as nothing.

So then, it seems that /kih/ functions to indicate all three of the relation types commonly referred to as purpose, reason, and result. At first this might seem to be a disappointment, because we had hoped to restrict all connectives except /too/ to mutually exclusive semantic domains. However, I don't really think this is a problem at all. If we are content to use the analogy of /too/, which we termed a general connective, then maybe /kih/ functions as a general purpose-reason-result connective. In other words, the total range of its possible activity as a connective is limited to purpose-reason-result activity, but, within this restriction, it can operate effectively over the functions of purpose, reason, and result. If we posit this as a working hypothesis, then, to confirm it, we will need to demonstrate that other connectives which function in this range of purpose, reason, and result are severely limited, hopefully in a mutually exclusive manner, in their range of application.

As if to prove that language is not so readily describable as this, there is one other use of /kih/ which we must note before passing on to another connective.

4.1.4 /kih/ as amplification. The examples and categories outlined above do not include all the uses noted in the texts. In particular, the /kih/ in (72) appears to be functioning as an amplification marker, indicating that the material which follows further elaborates on the clause just given.

(72)   N79
   oo-naa zind-ee handun gulzaar k-eek
   kih *oo Tii har paara Gaa phul-taa xuuSboo oo gindaar naa raN-ak*
   taalaan mar-eera

   It (good fortune) makes life (like) a field of flowers *(so) that* in it on every side it (is as if) the fragrance of flowers and the colors of the rainbow are spread out...

The free translation seems to indicate a result-type relationship and it may be possible to defend that proposition. It is dubious, however, whether there is semantically an event involved in the first clause of the example. Thus, it seems much more likely that the second clause is elaborative in nature.

152   David A. Ross

I do not propose to make any more comment on this, being content to place this use on the residue pile.

4.1.5 /antae kih/. A special extended form of /kih/, which is used occasionally in the text corpus and frequently in speech, is the expression /antae kih/, usually glossed as 'because'. The expression is actually a juxtaposition of two words and literally could be glossed as 'why that'. It is probably analogous to the Urdu expression /kyuu = kih/ 'because' which could also be glossed literally as 'why that'. This is all the more significant because the expression does not occur in older texts and, thus, is probably the result of relatively recent borrowing and adaptation from Urdu.

The only use yet noted for /antae kih/ is as a reason-type connective. One example will suffice for now.

(73) N54
      iilum naa mark aan guD abdul qaadar gul biibii oo riihaana teen too
          Shar aa al-eesus
      antae kih *daasa oofk xalk aT yak-taniiaa bee dardxoor sal-eesur*

      After his brother's death Abdul Qaadar himself had brought Gul Bibi and Rihana to the city *because* they now had lived in the village alone, without a protector

4.2 Relevant phrases

Example (73) shows that a connective is not always a single word. We will now follow up on this by considering three phrases, each of which occurs only rarely in the text corpus, and each of which has a function which fits somewhere in the range of purpose, reason, and result.

4.2.1 /handaa xaatar aan/. Because of the tendency of Brahui to drop word-initial /h/, this phrase often appears as /andaa xaatar aan/. If translated literally, this phrase would be glossed as 'just this reason from', or, less literally, 'for just this reason'. The expression does not occur at all in the older texts analyzed.

Probably the best approach to this connective is to give several examples and see if we can derive a function for it as we go.

(74) XB8, 9, 10

oo-naa	*kaziiat*	*aa*	*kafaa*	*maka*	*Tii*	*paar-eesus*	*kih*
PRO^3s(med)-of	death	to	heathen	Mecca	in	say-PLUP^3s	that

A Beginning Look at Brahui Connectives 153

muhamad naa ic-oo farzand-as bacee-t-auu
Muhammad of something-INDEF son-INDEF leave-NEG-PAST^3s

daasa oo-naa pin haloo koo kas-as
now PRO^3s(med)-of name call to someone-INDEF

sali-p-aroo **andaa xaatar aan** *daa*
stand-NEG-PROB^FUT^3s DEM(near) reason from PRO^3s(near)

mookah aa suura koosar naazal mas-usas
opportunity to Sura Kosar revealed become-PLUP^3s

At his death the heathen(s) in Mecca had said that, "Muhammad did not leave a son. Now no one will to bear his name." *Thus*, Sura Kosar was given (by God) to meet this opportunity.

In (74), the connective seems to function to indicate some emphasis on the result, i.e., that this particular chapter of the Koran was revealed. The problem with this is that the revelation of the chapter is completely incidental to the story which concerns the life of the Prophet. In this connection, it is far more important that the Prophet was at that point without a son, and that his enemies were ridiculing him for this. Thus, it seems that, while the connective indicates result, the clause marked with the connective is definitely semantically subordinate to its predecessor.

(75) XB35, 36
baaz mo'arix-ak num-aa farzand-tee Tii asi maar husin
many historian-PL PRO^2p-of son-OBL^PL in one son Husin

oo masiR raqiia naa ziiaa-ii-ee kar-einoo oo
and daughter Raqia of great-NN-OBL do-PERF^3p and

naviSta kar-eenoo daa artooma-k cunak-ii Tii
written do-PERF^3p PRO^3s(near) both-PL child-NN in

kaziiat kar-eer **andaa xaatar aan** *daa-taa*
death do-PAST^3p DEM(near)^SG reason from PRO^3p-of

haal tariix Tii af
health history in be^NEG^PRES/FUT^3s

Many historians tell of another son, Husin, and a daughter, Raqia, of the prophet, and they have written (that) they both died in childhood. *Therefore*, their stories are not (recorded) in history.

154 David A. Ross

Here again the final clause indicates a result, and yet the emphasis is not on the clause containing the /andaa xaatar aan/. It is of far greater consequence that the (reputed) children died than that their stories are not recorded.

(76) K55, 56

nan	ham	juuaan	javaab	tin-iN	caa-eena-ta
we	also	good	answer	give-INF	know-PRES/FUT^1p-RESPRO

nii	asi	juuaan-oo	maNgat	see	us.
PRO^2s	one	good-INDEF	asking	concerning	be^PRES/FUT^2s

handaa	**xaatar**	**aan**	nee	maaf	k-eena
DEM(near)	reason	from	PRO^2s^OBL	forgive	do-PRES/FUT^1p

"We also know how to give a good answer (to someone); you are a good person for asking questions. *Therefore,* we forgive you."

The example in (76) is spoken in an ironical manner, where the speaker is deliberately ridiculing the addressee. In this context the final clause professes to be a result clause, but, in fact, it is a negation of the truth. It is of more consequence that the speaker is ridiculing the addressee. A freer translation might be something like 'We also can give smart retorts; you have no right to make such demands of us. Nonetheless, we will forgive your impudence if...'

Thus, in characterizing the use of this connective, we can say that it is result oriented, and yet it reflects the fact that the result is less important than the impetus.

A slightly different form of this /daa xaatar aan/ connective appears once in the text corpus.

(77) K27

gul	xaan	oo-tee	aan	**daa**	**xaatar**	**aan**
Gul	Khan	PRO^3p(med)-OBL	from	PRO^3s(near)	reason	from

haRseeNg-aa	kih	oo-naa	pisTool	ham
turn^oneself^back-PAST^3s	that	PRO^3s-of	pistol	also

ooR-ee	tam-asas
PRO^3p-OBL	fall-PLUP^3s

For this reason Gul Khan returned to them (namely) that his pistol also had (been) dropped at the place.

A Beginning Look at Brahui Connectives

155

This use of the connective seems to be reason oriented, explaining the reason why he returned to his former colleagues.

To be fair we must also include the residue which does not seem to fit nicely into this analysis. In this case, the residue is in the form of an example which seems to be more an elaboration than a result orientation.

(78) XB66.2, 67

xuuaaja *masla* *azam* *mas-eesas* **andaa** **xaatar** **aan**
lord reformer great become-PLUP^3s DEM(near) reason from

xuuaaja *oof-tee* *paar-ee* *daa* *takaluf-tee*
lord PRO^3p(med)-OBL say-PAST^3s this waste^of^money-OBL

eel-boo
take-IMPER^PL

The Prophet had become the great reformer. *Therefore*, the Prophet said to them, "Stop this waste of money."

In (78), a case could be made that the second and third clauses (and the similar ones which follow) are the result of the application of the principle that the Prophet was the great reformer. This seems a little doubtful however, since it could equally well be said that the clauses after the /andaa xaatar aan/ represent an elaboration of what it means to be a great reformer. The data is too little to confirm either approach, but it is still appropriate to note that /andaa xaatar aan/ may have an elaborative function also, much as was noted for /kih/.

4.2.2 The /savab/ expressions. In the N text there are two other expressions based on the word /savab/, Urdu for 'reason'. These expressions in (79) and (80) might also be said to function as connectives within the scope of the purpose-reason-result connectives.

(79) N70: /handaa savab be/

Saaid handaa **savab** *as-aka kih riihaana naa ilah ood-ee teenaa maar hameed naa pin aa kar-ee*

Perhaps this was the *reason* that Rihana's uncle engaged his son Hameed to her.

The sentence in (79) follows a sentence philosophizing on the willfulness of human emotions. The first clause quoted, then, becomes a connective in its entirety. It seems to be focussing on the result aspect of the preceding

156 David A. Ross

sentence. Since the result is the important aspect as far as the story is concerned, we could distinguish the connective from /handaa xaatar aan/ by saying that it introduces an important, or focussed, result.

(80) N76, 77: /handaa savab aan/
asa uraa Tii parda man-iN ma-f-ak. **handaa savab aan** *mana vaxt aan guD asa vaar valdaa asa jaagah tuul-iN baS man-iN-ee Saruu kar-eer*

In one house it is not (possible) to keep purdah. *For this reason*, a little time later they began again to get used to sitting (together) in the same place.

Again, the focus here is on the result orientation given by the connective phrase. Note that the first sentence quoted is a principle (as preceded the previous example), but that the important aspect is the outworking, or resulting application, of that principle.

I note that these expressions only occur in the N text, and that in these texts the connectives involving /xaatar/ do not occur. I am inclined, therefore, to think that the author of the N text merely adopted a different word for 'reason', but that both the /xaatar/ expressions and the /savab/ expressions are essentially identical in that they indicate result orientation. The sample size is too small to support any finer gradation of meaning.

4.2.3 The /vaja/ expression. Yet another word glossed as 'reason', /vaja/, occurs once in the text corpus in a connective phrase.

(81) XB30: /andaa vaja aT/

andaa	**vaja**	*aT*	*hasrat*	*usman-ee*	*(zuulan oreen)*	*naa*
DEM(near)	reason	with	Hasrat	Usman-OBL	(Zulan Oren)	of

xitaab	*raseeNg-aa*	*antae kih xuuaja*	*naa*	*ira*	*jaGar*
title	arrive-PAST^3s	because lord	of	two	liver

naa band	*padar-iisa*	*aT*	*oo-naa*	*ust*
of closed	following-PRES^ADV^PLE	with	PRO^3s(med)-of	heart

puudeen-ii	*naa*	*savab*	*mas-uur*
cold-NN	of	reason	become-PAST^3p

For this *reason*, Hasrat Usman acquired a title (see Zulan Oren's book), because his heart became so peaceful, since he married two of the Prophet's daughters, one after the other.

A Beginning Look at Brahui Connectives
157

The reason for the interest in this expression is that it occurs in the XB text, where there were also three examples of the use of /andaa xaatar aan/. There is no need for confusion here, however, since the expression /andaa vaja aT/ seems to couple with the expression /antae kih/, lending emphasis to the latter.

4.3 'Thus'-type expressions

The morpheme /dun/ 'thus' will be the next focus of our consideration of purpose-reason-result connectives. The morpheme occurs in many forms. It may sometimes link with the pronouns for added emphasis.

(82)   Third-person singular pronoun 'thus' compound

near	/daa/	/dahun/ or /dun/
medial	/oo/	–
distant	/ee/	/ehun/

It may also join with the demonstrative, /han-/, to form /(h)andun/, and with the adjectival definite suffix /-aNgaa/ to form /dunaNgaa/. It should, however, be distinguished from the pure demonstratives /andaa/ and /hamoo/.

4.3.1 Nonconnective uses of /dun/. There seem to be several uses of /dun/, or its derivatives, which do not seem to be used specifically as connectives. One of these is as an indicator of indirect speech as in (83).

(83)   N88
*too **dun** paa-0 kih oo tuG aan samaa kar-ee*

Then she (*thus*) said that she should get up from sleep.

The second clause quoted is an indirect quotation, and the indicator for it appears to be the /dun/ in the first clause.

There also appear to be formulaic uses of /dun/. Perhaps the above use of /dun/ might fit this category. A clear example of this is at the beginning of the WMB text.

(84)   WMB1, 2

vad	*Tii*	*buT-as*	*ee*	*kih*	*kariimdaad*	*GaTii*
Vad	in	hillock-INDEF	be^PRES/FUT^3s	that	Karimdad	Ghati

158 David A. Ross

> *paar-aa*   *daa-naa*   *nakl* **dun** *ee*
> say-PRES^INDEF^3s   PRO^3s(near)-of   story   thus   be^PRES/FUT^3s

In Vad there is a hillock which they call Karimdad Ghati. This is its story.

There seems little reason for the /dun/ in the last clause, except that it preserves a formulaic story introduction. Further, it seems that /dun/ may be used when an application of a principle is being given as in (85).

(85)   N29, 30
har niiaaRii zind Tii asa vaar muhabat k-eek.
*han**dun** riihaana ham hameed toon muhabat kar-eesus*

Every woman loves once in her life. *Thus,* Rihana also had loved Hameed.

In (85), there does not seem to be any result-type emphasis, such as we observed when /andaa xaatar aan/ was used following a principle. Rather, it seems that an example is being given of the principle at work.

4.3.2 /dun/ as result. Somewhat to our chagrin, it seems that /dun/ can function as a connective indicating result, in much the same manner as many of the connectives discussed above.

(86)   N22, 23
ust naa ooG-iN aa kas-as naa nazar tam-p-ak.
*han**dun** maxluuk naa nazar aT riihaana baaz xuuS as-aka vala hakiikat*
    aT oo baaz muunjaa as

No one sees the crying of the heart. *Thus,* people saw (that) Rihana was very happy but in fact she was very sad.

In a similar manner to that in which we saw /andaa xaatar aan/ functioning to indicate the resulting application of a preceding principle, it seems that /handun/ operates in (87) with a result-type emphasis.

(87)   T42, 44

> *abdal*   *dee*   *drust*   *peeSan*   *teenaa jaaiidaar*
> Abdal   PRO^3s(near)^OBL   recognized   in^front   self^of   unsettled^one

> *aa as*   *ood*   *ant*   *xabar*   *0*   *kih*   *uraa*
> to be^PAST^3s   PRO^3p(med)   what   news   be   that   house

A Beginning Look at Brahui Connectives

159

Tii	*naasar*	*too*	*ant*	*man-iN*	*Tii-ee*	***ehun***
in	Nasser	with	what	become-INF	PRES^CONT^3s	thus

ham	*abdal*	*teenaa*	*uraaG-aa*	*handaa-k*	*bar-ook*
also	Abdal	self^of	house-to	DEM(near)-PL	come-ADJ

kasar	*aa*	*leeTa-v-aka*
road	to	lie^down-NEG-IMPF^3s

Abdal recognized that in front of him was someone [his son] who was upset. What new things were happening—what is happening to Nasser in the house? Thus, as he was coming to his house, he did not lie down on the side of the road (viz., as was his custom).

In this example, also, /ehun/ is indicating the result or outcome of Abdul's musings. In particular, he is concerned about the upsetness of his son, Nasser, and the clause beginning with /ehun/ indicates the nonhabitual action this led him to. There is certainly no principle operating here, in the sense that we saw above. However, there is still a result coming from an observation (as opposed to a response to an active stimulus).

4.3.3 /dun/ to indicate manner. As part of the residue it should be noted that /dun/ can sometimes appear to give an indication of manner, which is not really part of this investigation. There are several examples which tend in this direction, but the clearest indication is the response of a man to a threat of physical violence, specifically by punching on the nose.

(88) K53

rahzan-ta		*bala*	*paar-ee*	*na*	*xuuaaja*	***daahun***
highway^robber-RESPRO	big	say-PAST^3s	no	lord	thus	

ka-p-as
do-NEG-PRES^INDEF^2s

The highway robber replied loudly to him, "No, sir, you can't do this."

There seems to be an indication that not just the threat of physical violence is being objected to, but also that the manner in which the violence was proposed (the punching on the nose) is considered inappropriate. The immediately preceding and following sentences confirm this.

160   David A. Ross

4.4 Implied purpose-reason-result relations

We have now examined at least some of the connectives which may indicate purpose-reason-result relationships between propositions. It is possible, however, to imply these relationships. Rather than trying to list circumstances in which this may occur, I will give some examples which illustrate this phenomenon.

(89)   WML4, 5, 6
   cuTav   waam-ee   ti-t-auu   *oo   miirhaajii-ee   kireeN*
   Chutta   loan-OBL   give-NEG-PAST^3s   and   Mirhaji-OBL   abuse

      tis   aaxir   niiaama   Tii-ta   jaN
      give^PAST^3s   finally   middle   in-RESPRO   fight

      mas   oo   miirhaajii   kas-f-iNg-aa.
      become^PAST^3s   and   Mirhaji   die-CAUS-PASS-PAST^3s

      mengal   oo   jadgal   naa   niiaama   Tii   xoon   baS
      Mengal   and   Jadgal   of   middle   in   blood^feud   get^up

      mas
      become^PAST^3s
The Chutta did not return the loan and (instead) abused the Mirhaji. Finally, a fight broke out between them and the Mirhaji was killed. A blood feud arose between the Mengals and the Jadgals.

For our purposes, it is sufficient to note that there are perhaps result-type relationships operating. Between the second and third clauses, one could argue that the /aaxir/ indicates a result-type relationship, because it is quite natural that an argument will escalate into a fight unless there is some other restraining influence. I think there is some doubt about this, but for the moment we will not contest this.

Between the third and fourth clauses the /oo/ indicates another result-type relationship, but we find little to concern us with this, since /oo/ has many different uses, and we noted that, in older texts, a result-orientation was possible, even if not well explained.

The implied relationship which interests us here, however, is the one between the last two clauses in (89). As far as the story goes, it is of vital importance that the feud broke out between the two tribes, the Mengals and the Jadgals, of which the Chuttas and the Mirhajis are subtribes. Furthermore, this feud is a direct result of the death of the Mirhaji, which in turn is

A Beginning Look at Brahui Connectives 161

a direct result of the argument over the loan. There is, nonetheless, no overt connective indicating the result relationship existing between the last two clauses. Rather, the relationship is implied.

Further along in the same text, after the Jadgals had been defeated in battle, we find an implied reason relationship. After the defeat there is a period of negotiation of peace terms. The Jadgal leader proposes an even swap of bodies, which would entail killing more Mengals, since there were more Jadgal casualties in the fighting. The Mengal leader rejects these terms with the proposal in (90).

(90) WLM29.3, 30
 ii   har   mengal kee musi xoon   hal-eeva   mengal oo
 I   every Mengal for three revenge take-PRES/FUT^1s Mengal and

   jadgal   naa xoon   baraabar af
   Jadgal   of   revenge equal   be^NEG^PRES/FUT^3s
 I will take three bodies for every Mengal (killed). A Mengal and a Jadgal are not of equal value.

The second clause in (90) gives the reason or justification for the first clause, and yet there is no overt connective.

5. Conclusions

To enable us to draw conclusions more succinctly, let us summarize briefly what we have found so far about the functions of Brahui connectives.

Coordinating Connectives

 /too/ - newer texts only
     - a facet introducer, with overlap
     - concurrent or subsequent time marker
     - result indicator
     - contraexpectation indicator
     = CONCLUSION: a general, nonconditional, connective

 /oo/ - chronological sequencing
     - a facet introducer, without overlap
      (may sometimes be concessive marker)
     - result indicator (older use)
     = CONCLUSION: probably was an older, general, nonconditional connective, has become more restricted in use

162   David A. Ross

/ham/   - emphasis marker, not coordinating connective

Adversative Connectives

/vala/   - newer texts only [allophones /valee/ and possibly
           sometimes /valdaa/]
         - contraexpectation
         - contrast, with overlap
         - amplification, restatement

/magar/ - in newer texts largely contrast, overlap not required
         - in older texts, contraexpectation

other contraexpectation indicators   - IMPLIED
                                     - /daasa/

occasioners/twist introducers   - /bahar/ 'however' [concessive]
                                     - /neeT/ 'finally'
                                     - /aaxir/ 'finally'

/balka/- negated antonym; Note: may also be IMPLIED
         - maybe contrast/contraexpectation

Purpose-Reason-Result Connectives

/kih/   - purpose
         - reason
         - result
         - amplification
         = CONCLUSION: general purpose-reason-result connective

/antae kih/   - newer texts only
                      - reason

{/handaa savab BE/ } - result, focus on result, application of principle
{/handaa savab ann/}

/andaa vaja aT/   - emphasis on later expression plus /antae kih/

/dun/   - result, application of principle
                      - manner

IMPLIED   - at least reason-result

A Beginning Look at Brahui Connectives 163

The key theoretical assumption which undergirded the previous analysis was that it was possible to define "regions of mutually exclusive influence" for each connective. Without explicitly stating this, it was assumed that these regions would be semantically based. Unfortunately, while there are indications that the trends are in this direction, the Brahui data leads us to the conclusion that this assumption cannot be unquestioningly validated. It seems, rather, that some reference to syntactic and referential concerns will, at a minimum, be necessary. Rather than separate confirming evidence and contrary evidence, I shall discuss the issues in chunks, largely corresponding to the way in which the analysis was conducted, although with some comments of a global nature as appropriate.

The first factor which becomes an obvious complication in validating the assumption of being semantically based is the definite trend to diachronic change in connectives and their use. This appears to be taking place much more rapidly than other changes in discourse markers (see Ross 1987). Clearly, in order to validate the assumption, we need somehow to be able to extract the diachronic influences. There are some encouraging signs that this is possible. For example, the older use of /magar/ to indicate contraexpectation seems to have been largely discontinued as the new morpheme /vala/ usurps this function. Further, the morpheme /too/ seems to be replacing the morpheme /oo/ as a general connective, with the result that the morpheme /oo/ is becoming more restricted in its use. For example, /oo/ seems to be losing its result-indicating capacity.

Even when the diachronic changes are taken into account, however, we still find that sometimes it is difficult to distinguish between the functions of two different connectives. For example, both /magar/ and /vala/ may indicate contrast in newer texts. In order to separate them, one notes that, when /vala/ is used to indicate contrast, there is characteristically a high degree of syntactic parallelism and lexical overlap. When /magar/ is used to indicate contrast, however, this construction is usually not a feature. It seems to me that some theoretical breakthrough is needed here. I suspect that we are treating semantics and syntactics as mutually-exclusive disciplines, whereas their interrelationships might be greater than expected.

As an added indicator of this, we note that both /too/ and /oo/ may function as facet introducers. Exactly where this goes in the semantic scheme of things I do not know yet, but the discussion arose while we were examining coordinating connectives. When /too/ is used in this function, however, it is characterized by syntactic parallelism and lexical overlap, whereas these are not essential characteristics when /oo/ is used in this function.

As a prelude to the next aspect of this discussion, we note that, right from the outset, we had to allow for general connectives which appeared to operate in a wide range of regions, such that it was not possible to define a

164   David A. Ross

cohesive region big enough to incorporate all the uses of such connectives. In itself this is not intuitively very satisfying, although it is possibly excusable if widely enough observed.

The extension of this by analogy, however, seems much more problematic. We discovered that we needed to allow /kih/ to operate as a general purpose-reason-result connective, and even then we were left with its amplification uses not included. This leads us inescapably to the idea of a subgrouping of regions, with some degree of external relatedness (so that the /kih/ can operate over the whole range), and yet with internal distinguishability, so that some connectives operate only on certain smaller regions of connective influence. This does not seem to me to be ideal, but would probably not be a serious objection if there were no other problems.

While discussing the purpose-reason-result connectives, let us note that sometimes the region of use of connectives could only be distinguished by reference to the degree of importance of result and impetus. Maybe this would be better defined in terms of purpose and result, although we had already considered purpose (§4.2.1) in a somewhat more restricted sense.

The final issue which needs to be mentioned in this discussion is the issue of implied connectives, i.e., when there is definitely a semantic relationship between two (usually juxtaposed) propositions, but where there is no overt marker indicating this relationship. It proved almost impossible to define a range of regions within which implied relationships were possible, because it is only possible to validate certain relationships, but very difficult to disprove any at all. It may be that this issue of implied relationships will hold the key to the next breakthrough, but it certainly seems to limit the viability of our initial governing assumption.

One possible approach for extension of this work would be to examine other types of connectives in Brahui using the same basic framework of examining exhaustively the use of connectives one at a time. It would be possible to shift focus to other types of relationships such as conditional, content, amplification and paraphrase, and (possibly) substitution. Such an investigation would certainly help to round out our understanding of Brahui connectives, but would probably contribute little more to the larger theoretical exercise for which this article was conceived.

Leaving aside the obvious need for more theory, which I am not competent to attempt, I wonder whether a look at something a little different might help break the logjam. We have noted in our investigation at certain points the use of expressions which would generally be classified as temporals to indicate some different connection between two propositions. It might help if we were to list all the temporals, and then concentrate on those which can be demonstrated to have uses other than time indication. If we did this we would be moving away from a strict interpretation of "regions of mutually exclusive

A Beginning Look at Brahui Connectives

165

influence", on which this article was based. Rather, we would be considering groups of related words, and finding how unrelated their uses may be.

Appendix A

A miser and a cheat

(1) *maaSed-naa   Saar-Tii   asiT   baxiil-as   as*
Mashed-GEN   city-in   one   miser-INDEF   be^PAST^3s
In Mashed there was a miser

kih   teenaa   umr   paxiir-as-ee   asa   baaxoo-as   iraG
that   self^of   age^in   poor^man-INDEF-OBL   one   morsel-INDEF   bread

naa   ti-taw-asas
of   give-NEG-PLUP^3s
who had never given a morsel of bread to a poor man,

oo   agar   peen   kas-as-ee   xan-aka
and   if   other   someone-INDEF-OBL   see-IMPF^3s
and if he saw someone else

kih   giRa-as   kas-as   tis-aka
that   thing-INDEF   someone-INDEF   give-IMPF^3s
who was giving anything

baaz   xafa   mas-aka
very   angry   become-IMPF^3s
(then he) became very angry.

(2) *hamoo   Saar-Tii   asiT   luc-as   as*
the^same   city-in   one   cheat-INDEF   be^PAST^3s
In that same city was a cheat.

(3) *daa   luc   paar-ee   kih*
DEM(near)^SG   cheat   say-PAST^3s   that
This cheat said,

daa   baxiil   too   lucii-as   kan-iN   zaruur
DEM(near)^SG   miser   with   cheating-INDEF   do-INF   certainly

>   *ee*
>   be^PRES^3s
> "It is necessary to do some cheating with this miser

>   *kih   taa   kah-iN-iska   ood-ee   yaat-aan*
>   that as^long^as die-INF-up^to^time^of PRO^3s(med)-OBL memory-from

>   *im-p-Ø*
>   go-NEG^PRES^INDEF^3s
> that he will remember until he dies."

(4)   *asa   dee-as   oo-naa   paaraG-aa   bas*
          one   day-INDEF   PRO^3s(med)-GEN   side-towards come^PAST^3s
          One day he came to (the miser)

>   *paar-ee*
>   say-PAST^3s
> (and) said,

>   *iilum   kan-aa   uraa   Tii   aenoo   meemaan-as   bas-uunee*
>   brother PRO^1s-GEN house in   today   guest-INDEF   come-PERF^3s
> "Brother, today a guest has come to my house.

>   *teenaa   bala   xoo-ee   kan-ee   eetee*
>   self^of big   cooking^pot-OBL PRO^1s-OBL   give(IMPER^SG)
> Give me your big cooking pot

>   *kih   tah-Tii   suu   beeT   k-eeva*
>   that inside-in meat   on^(fire) do-PRES/FUT^1s
> so that I will cook meat in it

>   *oo   pagar   soob-too   padai   hatar-eeva-ta*
>   and   tomorrow   morning-with back^again bring-PRES/FUT^1s-RESPRO
> and tomorrow morning I will bring it back."

(5)   *baxiil   awal   Tii   na   kar-ee*
          miser   at^first in   no   do-PAST^3s
          At first, the miser did not do so (i.e., lend the pot).

>   *aaxir   luc   ood-ee   mana   paisa   kiraa   tis*
>   finally cheat PRO^3s(med)-OBL few   paisa   hire   give^PAST^3s
> Finally, the cheat gave him a few coins (as) hire

A Beginning Look at Brahui Connectives

oo   paar-ee
and   say-PAST^3s
and said,

ii   nee   peenduuaaR   ham xuuaaS k-eeva
I   PRO^2s-OBL   another^time   also   happy   do-PRES/FUT^1s
"I will also make you happy some other time."

(6)   *baxiil aaxir   xoo-ee   ood-ee   tis*
miser finally cooking^pot-OBL   PRO^3s(med)-OBL give^PAST^3s
Finally, the miser gave him the cooking pot.

(7)   *eeloo dee luc   iraT cuna-oo   xoo   daa*
next   day   cheat two   small-DEF   cooking pot   DEM(near)^SG

bala   xoo   TI   SaaG-aa
big   cooking^pot   in   put-PAST^3s
Next day the cheat put two small cooking pots in this big cooking pot,

hees
bring^PAST^3s
brought (them),

baxiil-ee   tis
miser-OBL   give^PAST^3s
gave (them) to the miser,

oo   paar-ee
and   say-PAST^3s
and said,

iilum   istoo   naa   xoo   kan-aa   uraa   TI
brother last^night PRO^2s^GEN   cooking^pot   PRO^1s-of house in

iraT cuca   jaaR   xan-aanee
two   child   twin   see-PERF^3s
"Brother, last night your cooking pot had two little twins in my house.

daa   naa   xoo   ee
DEM(near)^SG PRO^2s^GEN   cooking^pot   be^PRES^3s
This is your cooking pot,

168   David A. Ross

daa   cuca-aa-koo-tee   arf
DEM(near)^SG child-towards-DEF-ACC^PL lift^IMPER^SG
take these children!"

(8)   *baxiil   ust   Tii   xuuaaS   mas*
       miser   heart in   happy   become^PAST^3s
       The miser became happy (in his heart)

       kih   daa   bala-oo   beeaklii-as   ee
       that   DEM(near)^SG big-DEF   folly-INDEF   be^PRES^3s
       about this folly;

       paar-ee
       say-PAST^3s
       (he) said

       juuaan   nee   Saabaas   ee
       good   PRO^2s^OBL congratulation   be^PRES^3s
       "Good, (I) congratulate you

       oo   daa-aan   guD   har-vaxt   nee   xoo
       and   DEM(near)^SG-from later   every-time PRO^2s^OBL cooking^pot

            bakaar   mar-ee
            necessary   become-PRES^INDEF^3s
       and, after this, every time you need (a) cooking pot

       bar-ak
       come-IMPER^SG
       come,

       oo   dar
       and   take^IMPER^SG
       and take (it).

       daa   uraa   naa   jinda   naa   ee
       DEM(near)^SG house PRO^2s^GEN self   GEN be^PRES^3s
       Treat this house as your own."

(9)   *mana dee aan   guD   luc   padaaii   bas*
       few   day from   later cheat back^again   come^PAST^3s
       A few days later the cheat came back again

A Beginning Look at Brahui Connectives 169

paar-ee
say-PAST^3s
(and) said,

iilum aenoo baaz mehmaan bas-uunoo
brother today many guest come-PERF^3p
"Brother, today many guests have come,

teen-aa kul xoo-tee kan-ee eetee
self-of all cooking^pot-OBL^PL PRO^1s-OBL give^IMPER^SG
give me all your cooking pots."

(10) *baxiil xuuaaS mas*
miser happy become^PAST^3s
The miser became very happy,

paar-ee
say-PAST^3s
(and) said,

kul xoo-k haazir oo
all cooking^pot-NOM ^PL in^attendance be^PRES/FUT^3p
"All the cooking pots are here,

dar-ak-ta
take-IMPER^SG-RESPRO
take them,

magar oof-taa cuca-aa-ta sambaal-ee
but PRO^3p(med)-GEN^PL child-towards-RESPRO care-OBL

   k-ees
   do-PRES^INDEF^2s
but take care of their children

kih piD^pur oo
that pregnant be^PRES/FUT^3p
(because they) are pregnant."

(11) *luc paar-ee*
cheat say-PAST^3s
The cheat said,

170 David A. Ross

xan-tee   *aT*
eye-OBL^PL by^means^of
"By my eyes (i.e., certainly)."

(12) *baxiil   naa   kul   xoo-tee*   *harf-ee*
miser   of   all   cooking^pot-OBL^PL   lift^up-PAST^3s
He took all the miser's pots

daR-ee
go^down-PAST^3s
(and) left.

(13) *baaz   dee   gidreN-a*
many   day   pass^over-PAST^3s
Many days passed,

luc   xoo-tee   *hat-at-au*
cheat   cooking^pot-OBL^PL   bring-NEG-PAST^3s
the cheat did not bring the cooking pots (back).

aaxir   baxiil   baevas   mas
finally   miser   upset   become^PAST^3s
Finally, the miser became upset,

bas
come^PAST^3s
came,

luc-ee   tavaar   kar-ee
cheat-OBL   shout   do-PAST^3s
shouted to the cheat

paar-ee
say-PAST^3s
(and) said,

kan-aa   xoo-tee   *hat*
PRO^1s-GEN   cooking^pot-ACC^PL   bring^IMPER^SG
"Bring (back) my cooking pots."

A Beginning Look at Brahui Connectives

171

(14) *luc*   *paar-ee*
cheat   say-PAST^3s
The cheat said,

oo *xuuaaja ii naa*   *moon* *Tii* *Sarminda* *uT*
Oh! lord   I PRO^2s^GEN face   in   ashamed be^PRES/FUT^1s
"Oh (my) Lord, I am ashamed before you,

kih   *naa*   *xoo-k*   *kask-uunoo*
that PRO^2s^GEN cooking^pot-NOM^PL die-PERF^3p
(but) your cooking pots died."

(15) *baxiil* *paar-ee*
miser   say-PAST^3s
The miser said,

antae *masxara* *k-eesa*
why   jest   do-PRES/FUT^2s
"Why do you jest?

xoo   *ham* *gahas* *kask-uunee*
cooking^pot also never die-PERF^3s
Cooking pots have never died."

(16) *luc* *paar-ee*
cheat say-PAST^3s
The cheat said,

nee   *raast* *paa-va*
PRO^2s^OBL truth say-PRES/FUT^1s
"I tell you the truth."

(17) *aaxir* *jaN* *kar-eer*
finally fight do-PAST^3p
Finally, they fought,

hin-aar   *haakim naa paarAG* *aa*
go-PAST^3p ruler of side   towards
(then) went to the judge

172   David A. Ross

kih   *nan-aa*   *Saraa-ee*   *kar-ak*
that   PRO^1p-GEN   decide^by^Muslim^law-OBL   do-IMPER^SG
(asking), "Decide between us by Muslim law."

(18)   *haakim*   *paar-ee*
       ruler   say-PAST^3s
       The judge said,

       teen-aa   *ahwaal-ee*   *eeti-boo*
       self-of   story-OBL   give-IMPER^PL
       "(Each of you) give your own story."

(19)   *daa-k*   *har*   *asiT*   *teen-aa*   *ahwaal-ee*   *paar-eer*
       DEM(near)-NOM^PL every one   self-of   story-OBL   say-PAST^3p
       Each of them gave his own story.

(20)   *haakim*   *paar-ee*
       ruler   say-PAST^3s
       The judge said,

       har   *vaxt-as*   *kih*   *xoo*   *cuca*   *xan-ik*
       every time-INDEF that   cooking^pot   child   see-PRES/FUT^3s
       "(If) a cooking pot (can) have a child,

       guRa   *xoo-ee*   *mark*   *ham*   *aree*
       then   cooking^pot-OBL   death   also   be^PRES^EMPH^3s
       then it (will) also die;

       nii   *baxiil*   *xoo*   *naa*   *cuca*   *kee*   *xuuaaS*   *mas-us*
       PRO^2s miser   cooking^pot of   child   for   happy   become-PAST^2s
       you, miser, were happy about the pot's child,

       daasa   *mark*   *kee-ta*   *ham*   *xafa*   *ma-f-a*
       now   death   for-RESPRO   also   sorry   become-NEG-IMPER^SG
       now don't be sorry about it's death either;

       Sukr   *kaS-a*
       thanks   eject-IMPER^SG
       (instead) give thanks,

A Beginning Look at Brahui Connectives

173

> *navaa xudaa xafa mar-ee*
> lest God angry become-PRES^INDEF^3s
> lest God become angry

> *naa jind-ee kasf-ee*
> PRO^2s^GEN life-OBL kill-PRES^INDEF^3s
> (and) kill you."

(21) *baxiil Sarminda mas*
miser ashamed become^PAST^3s
The miser was ashamed

> *teenaa kasar-ee halk*
> self of road-OBL seize^AST^3s
> took his own road

> *hin-aa*
> go-PAST^3s
> (and) left.

Appendix B

Nikaah (wedding)

(1) *aenoo hameed naa nikaah naa dee as-aka*
today Hameed of engagement of day be-IMPF^3s
Today was Hameed's engagement day.

(2) *anoo naa dee xuuS-ii oo Saadkaam-ii naa dee as*
today of day happy-NN and elation-NN of day be^PAST^3s
Today was a day of happiness and elation (at success).

(3) *uraa naa har cunk-aa bal-aa xuuS as-aka*
house of all little-DEF big-DEF happy be-IMPF^3s
Everyone in the house, big and small, was happy.

(4) *asa paar Gaa masink diira aa maS-ook xal-iN*
one side to daughter^PL drum to get^up-PRES^PART pull-INF

Tii   as-ura
in   be-IMPF^3p
On one side the girls were starting up to the drum.

too   eloo   paar Gaa uraa   naa piir-angaa   nariina zaaifa-Gak
then   other   side to   house of   old^man-DEF man   wife-PL

nikaah   naa tiiaar-ii Tii lag-ook   as-ura
engagement of   ready-NN in   climb-PRES^PART be-IMPF^3p
And elsewhere, the old people of the house, men and their wives,
were making ready for the engagement.

(5)   *cunk-aa cunaa-k   raN   raNg-ii   oo   puc*
little-DEF child-PL   color color-NN   be^PRES^3p cloth(es)

baen-ook
wear-PRES^PART
The little children are wearing brightly colored clothes

daaN   eeN   gooii   kar-eera
this^way that^way backtrack do-PRES/FUT^3p
(and) running hither and thither.

(6)   *vataax   aT hameed   naa varnaa aa saNgat-ak   oo-naa*
guest^room in Hameed of   youth   to friend-PL   PRO^3s(med)-of

daa   paar-ee paar aan   tuul-ook   as-ura
PRO^3s(near)   side-OBL side from   sit-PRES^PART be-IMPF^3p
In the guest room, Hameed, together with his youthful friends from
here and there, was sitting.

(7)   *baraam-ii   naa uraa   ham paanaad aa   as-aka*
wedding-NN of   house   also near   to   be-IMPF^3s
The wedding house also was nearby.

(8)   *hamooRee   ham   diira oo dukhuR   naa tavaar*
just^there(med)   also   drum and musical^instrument of   noise

as
be^PAST^3s
From there, too, came the noise of drums and (another) musical
instrument.

A Beginning Look at Brahui Connectives

(9) *xuuS-ii naa dee-as har cunk-aa bal-aa xuuS as-aka*
happy-NN of day-INDEF all little-DEF big-DEF happy be-IMPF^3s
On (such a) day of happiness everyone, young and old, was happy.

(9a) *uraa Tii uraa naa goodii-k mehmaan-taa xidmat-ee*
house in house of housewife-PL guest-GEN^PL service-OBL

    kan-iN aT damdar-iN-tav-asa
    do-INF by^means^of tired-PASS-NEG-IMPF^3p
In the house, the ladies of the house were not becoming tired as they served the guests,

    too vataax aT uraa naa xuuaaja-ak nariina-taa xidmat
    then guest^room in house of master-PL man-GEN^PL service

    aT axtajaan as-ura
    by^means^of busy be-IMPF^3p
and in the guest room the men of the house were busy serving the men guests.

(10) *asiT-taa iraG dan-iN Tii ee*
one-GEN^PL bread take^away-INF CONT be^PRES^3s
One of them is taking bread (to eat),

    too eloo-taa suu beediir 0
    then other-GEN^PL meat soup IMPLIED
and another (is taking) meat and soup.

(11) *kas-as brinj naa rakaabii-tee arf-eenee*
someone-INDEF rice of small^plate-OBL^PL ask-PERF^3s
Someone (guest) asked for plates of rice,

    too kas zaRdah naa 0
    then someone sweet^rice of IMPLIED
and another asked for sweet rice.

(12) *iraG kun-ook aa mehmaan-tee aan kas diir*
bread eat-PRES^PART to guest-OBL^PL from someone water

xuuaah-iN   *Tii*   *ee*
be^necessary-INF   CONT   be^PRES^3s

As he is eating bread, someone from (among) the guests is finding it
necessary (to have) water

too   *kas-as-taa*   *beediir*   *Ø*
then   some-INDEF-GEN^PL   soup   IMPLIED

and another (wanted) soup.

(13)   *har*   *paar*   *Gaa*   *ajaaib-oo*   *xuuS-ii-as*   *taalaan*
      all   side   to   wonderful-INDEF   happy-NN-INDEF   spread^out

          as-aka
          be-IMPF^3s

Everywhere wonderful happiness was evident.

(14)   *har*   *asa*   *cunk-aa*   *bal-aa*   *naa*   *ust*   *xuuS*   *ee*
      all   one   little-DEF   big-DEF   of   heart   happy   be^PRES^3s

Everyone, big and small, was happy in his heart.

(15)   *dun-angaa*   *xuuS-ii*   *naa*   *vaxt*   *aa*   *har*   *asiT*   *zeebaa-oo*
      thus-DEF   happy-NN   of   time   to   all   one   beautiful-INDEF

          puuskun-oo   *puuS-aak*   *baen-ook*
          new-INDEF   cloth(es)-PL   wear-PRES^PART

At this happy time everyone is (wearing) beautiful, new clothes.

(16)   *daaN*   *eeN*   *carx*   *k-eek*
      this^way   that^way   walkabout   do-PRES/FUT^3s

(and) is walking hither and thither.

(17)   *vala*   *daa*   *kul*   *naa*   *niiaam*   *aT*   *riihaana*   *naa*   *ust*
      but   PRO^3s(near)   all   of   middle   in   Rihana   of   heart

          muunjaa   *ee*
          sad   be^PRES^3s

But in the middle of all, this Rihana's heart is sad.

(18)   *puuskun-oo*   *puc-oo*   *saat-* *Ø*
      new-INDEF   cloth(es)-INDEF   cherish-INCOMPL

Cherishing new clothes,

A Beginning Look at Brahui Connectives

too riihaana ham baen-aanee
then Rihana also wear-PERF^3s
Rihana also wore them.

(19) oo-naa jooR-tee aa ham biSxanda naa phul
PRO^3s(med)-of lip-OBL^PL to also smile of flower

das-k
SOW-PRES/FUT^3s
Also, on her lips she wore a smile like a flower.

(20) vala ust naa muunjaa-ii Ø
but heart of sad-NN IMPLIED
But the sadness of her heart was (great),

too siina Tii Dak-ook oo giRaa see
then chest in hide-PRES^PART be^PRES^3p thing concerning
and the reasons for this are hiding in (her) chest.

(21) maxluuk baa naa mix-iN-ee ur-ik
people mouth of laugh-INF-OBL look(at)-PRES/FUT^3s
The people watch the smiling mouth;

(22) ust naa ooG-iN aa kas naa nazar tam-p-ak
heart of cry-INF to someone of sight fall-NEG^PRES-PRES/FUT^3s
no one sees the crying of the heart.

(23) handun maxluuk naa nazar aT riihaana baaz
thus people of sight by^means^of Rihana very

xuuS as-aka
happy be-IMPF^3s
Thus, people saw (that) Rihana was very happy,

(24) vala hakiikat aT oo baaz muunjaa as
but fact in PRO^3s(med) very sad be^PAST^3s
but, in fact, she was very sad.

(25) aaxir oo amar ma-tav-aka
finally PRO^3s(med) why become-NEG^PAST-IMPF^3s
At last, why shouldn't she be sad?

178 David A. Ross

(26) *aenoo naa dee ooR-ee kan kiiaamat naa dee aan*
today of day PRO^3s(med)-OBL up^to doomsday of day from

    hic-oo ooR-oo Dool see Tii kam
    something-INDEF PRO^3s(med)-INDEF drum concerning in little

    alav-aka
    be^PAST^NEG-IMPF^3s
Today was no less than doomsday for her, with drums for starters.

(27) *aenoo riihaana naa mahbuub oo ust naa band*
today Rihana of beloved and heart of captive
Today, Rihana's beloved one, who had captured her heart,

    hameed naa nikaah nazoo toon mar-ooii as-aka
Hameed of engagement Nazo with become-NN^OBL be-IMPF^3s
Hameed, his wedding was intended to take place.

(28) *hameed kih oo riihaana naa cunak-ii naa muhabat*
Hameed who PRO^3s(med) Rihana of small-NN of love

    as-aka
    be-IMPF^3s
Hameed, who was Rihana's childhood love,

    aenoo hameeSa kan peen asiT naa mar-ooii as
today always up^to other one of become-NN^OBL be^PAST^3s
was going to be someone else's from today forever.

(29) *har niiaaRii zind Tii asa vaar muhabat k-eek*
all woman life in one time love do-PRES/FUT^3s
Every woman loves once in her life.

(30) *handun riihaana ham hameed toon muhabat kar-eesus*
thus Rihana also Hameed with love do-PLUP^3s
Thus, Rihana also had loved Hameed.

(31) *daa muhabat oo-naa ooliikoo oo aaxir-ii*
PRO^3s(near) love PRO^3s(med)-of first and finally-NN

A Beginning Look at Brahui Connectives

179

     muhabat   as-aka
     love   be-IMPF^3s
This love was her first and last love.

(32)   *hamoo   muhabat*
      this^same(med) love
      This same love,

      kih oo   Tii varnaa-ii   naa xaaxar-ii aa jazbah 0
      that PRO^3s(med) in youth-NN   of fire-NN   to emotion IMPLIED
      which had the fiery emotion of youth

      too   vaar cunak-ii oo masoom-ii naa fatar-ii   aa
      then time small-NN and innocent-NN of natural-NN to

      jazbah   ham   vaar as-aka
      emotion also time be-IMPF^3s
      was combined with the natural emotions of childhood and innocence.

(33)   *baaz-ak phul-ee   Saax   aan   jitaa k-eera*
      very-PL   flower-OBL branch from sort do-PRES/FUT^3p
      Many people shake flowers from the branches

      oo   teenaa zulf aT xal-eera
      and self^of hair in   pull-PRES/FUT^3p
      and put (them) in their hair

(34)   *vala riihaana daa   muhabat naa haneen oo   giceen aa*
      but Rihana   PRO^3s(near) love   of   sweet and choice to

      phul-ee   tiiaar tiiaar Saax   aa   kaSka-tav-eesus
      flower-OBL ready ready branch to draw^out-NEG^PAST-PLUP^3s
      but this flower of love was not fully ready when Rihana had picked it;

(35)   *balka oo   daa   phul-ee teenaa duu   aT*
      rather PRO^3s(med) PRO^3s(near) flower-OBL self^of hand by^means^of

      xar-f-eesus
      grow-CAUS-PLUP^3s
      rather, she had caused the flower to grow by herself.

180 David A. Ross

(36)   *oo-naa*   *xiiaaldaar-ii-ee*   *kar-eesus*
PRO^3s(med)-of thoughtful-NN-OBL do-PLUP^3s
She had cared for (it).

(37)   *daa*   *phul*   *oo-naa*   *baaz* *baaz* *xuuaarii*   *aan*
PRO^3s(near) flower PRO^3s(med)-of very very hard^work from

         guD *aval GuTii-as*   *mas-uusus*
         later first bud-INDEF become-PLUP^3s
This flower, after much hard work, had had its first bud.

(38)   *pad-aa baa*   *mal-uusus*
later-to mouth open-PLUP^3s
Later it had blossomed.

(39)   *daasa zeebaa-oo*   *phul-as*   *jooR* *mas-uusus*
now beautiful-INDEF flower-INDEF made become-PLUP^3s
Now a beautiful flower had been made

    kih oo-naa   *raN* *oo* *xuuSboo aa* *riihaana naa zind*
that PRO^3s(med)-of color and fragrance to Rihana of life

        aT *am* *raN* *oo* *xuuSboo*   *taalaan*   *as-aka*
        in also color and fragrance spread^out be-IMPF^3s
that had a (beautiful) color and fragrance just as Rihana's life also;

(40)   *vala aenoo* *daa*   *phul*   *naaz* *oo-naa*   *zulf-tee*
but today PRO^3s(near) flower pride PRO^3s(med)-of hair-OBL^PL

        Tii *xal-iNg-aka*
        in   pull-PASS-IMPF^3s
but today, this pride of the flower was being pulled in the curls (of married woman) of her hair!

(41)   *hameed* *riihaana* *naa* *ilah*   *naa* *maar* *as-aka*
Hameed Rihana of paternal^uncle of son be-IMPF^3s
Hameed was Rihana's uncle's son.

(42)   *riihaana* *naa* *baava* *abdul kareem* *teenaa* *zaaifa gul biibii*
Rihana of father Abdul Kariim self^of wife Gul Bibi

A Beginning Look at Brahui Connectives

181

oo   cunk-aa   masiR   riihaana   toon   xalk   aT
and little-DEF daughter Rihana   with village in

raheeNg-aaka
live-IMPF^3s

Rihana's father, Abdul Kariim, together with his wife Gul Bibi and little daughter, lived in a village.

(43) *oo   hamooRee   bazGar-ii   kar-eeka*
PRO^3s(med) just^there(med) farming-NN do-IMPF^3s
In this place, he was a tenant farmer.

(44) *riihaana oo-naa   teenaa oo asiT naa walaad as*
Rihana   PRO^3s(med)-of self^of and one of   son   be^PAST^3s
Rihana was his only child and like a son to him.

(45) *hameed   naa baava   abdul qaadar baaz vaxt must   xalk*
Hameed   of   father Abdul Qaadar very time before village

aan   Shar   aa   bas-uusus
from city to   come-PLUP^3s

Hameed's father Abdul Qaadar had come from the village to the city a long time before

(46) *oo   handaRee   jaagah-ii   mas*
PRO^3s(med) just^there(dist) place-NN become^PAST^3s
He was living there.

(47) *too   teenaa iilum   abdul kareem-ee   am   salah   tis*
then self^of brother Abdul Kariim-OBL also advice give^PAST^3s
Then he also advised his brother

kih oo   am   gul biibii oo riihaana-ee   arf-ee
that PRO^3s(med) also Gul Bibi and Rihana-OBL bring-PRES^INDEF^3s
that he should also bring Gul Bibi and Rihana

Shar aa   bar-ee
city   to   come-PRES^INDEF^3s
(and) he may come to the city.

(48) *vala   abdul kareem xalk   naa saada-oo   bandaG-as*
but   Abdul Kariim village of   simple-INDEF   man-INDEF

182   David A. Ross

as-aka
be-IMPF^3s
But Abdul Kariim was a simple village man;

(49) *xalk-ee   hal-iN   kan tiiaar   ma-t-au*
village-OBL seize-INF for ready become-NEG^PAST-PAST^3s
he was not ready to leave the village.

(50) *riihaana naa umr haft   saal   as-aka*
Rihana   of age seven year be-IMPF^3s
Rihana was seven years old.

(51) *oo-naa   baava asa nan jald jik^oo^jooR*
PRO^3s(med)-of father one night fast in^good^health

     mulk-taa   diir   too   naN kan in-aa
country-GEN^PL water then wife for go-PAST^3s
One night her father, in good health, went hurriedly to the watering
place (to get water) for (his) wife,

(52) *vala soob   too   oofk   oo-naa   laaSa-ee   uraa*
but   morning with PRO^3p(med) PRO^3s(med)-of body-OBL house

     Gaa al-eer
    to   bring-PAST^3p
but in the morning they brought his body to the house.

(53) *gul biibii oo riihaana naa bad kismatii   naa bala*
Gul Bibi and Rihana of bad misfortune of beast

     abdul kareem-ee   xalk-oosus
     Abdul Kariim-OBL   hit-PAST^COND^3s
The beast of misfortune belonging to Rihana and Gul Bibi would
have struck Abdul Kariim.

(54) *iilum   naa mark   aan   guD abdul qaadar gul biibii   oo*
brother of death from later Abdul Qaadar Gul Bibi   and

     riihaana teen   too   Shar aa   al-eesus
     Rihana   self with city to   bring-PLUP^3s
After his brother's death Abdul Qaadar himself had brought Gul Bibi
and Rihana to the city

A Beginning Look at Brahui Connectives   183

antae kih daasa oofk xalk aT yak-taniiaa bee
why that now PRO^3p(med) village in one-alone without

dardxoor sal-eesur
protector stop-PLUP^3p
because they now had lived in the village alone, without a protector.

(55) abdul qaadar naa uraa Tii riihaana oo teenaa luma-ee
Abdul Qaadar of house in Rihana and self of mother-OBL

ic-oo takliif-as al-au
something-INDEF trouble-INDEF be^NEG-PAST^3s
In Abdul Qaadar's house nothing was trouble for Rihana and her mother.

(56) hameed riihaana naa hamsar as-aka
Hameed Rihana of same^age be-IMPF^3s
Hameed was the same age as Rihana.

(57) oofk dee drust asa jaagah gooaazii kar-eera
PRO^3p(med) day all one place play do-IMPF^3p
All day they were playing together.

(58) riihaana naa masoom aa zahn mark oo zind naa
Rihana of innocent to memory death and life of

falsafah-ee poo ma-tav-aka
wisdom-OBL understand become-NEG^PAST-IMPF^3s
Rihana's innocent brain did not understand the philosophy of life and death,

(59) vala oo-naa luma teenaa ariG naa jitaa-ii
but PRO^3s(med)-of mother self of husband of different-NN

naa Gam-ee ust aa tix-aasas
of grief-OBL heart to place-PLUP^3s
but her mother had placed in her heart the grief at separation from her husband.

(60) daa Gam ood-ee xoora aan baar kun-asa
PRO^3s(near) grief PRO^3s(med)-OBL borer from like eat-IMPF^3p
This grief was eating her like a borer.

184 David A. Ross

(61) *in-aa*
go-PAST^3s
Time passed.

(62) *riihaana naa noo-miikoo saal aa raseeNg-aa*
Rihana of nine-ORDINAL year to arrive-PAST
Rihana arrived at her ninth year,

    too oo-naa luma am daa
    then PRO^?s(med)-of mother also PRO^3s(near)

        duniiaa-ee faanii aa al-aa
        worldly^possessions-OBL mortal to bring-PAST^3s
then her mother too found that this worldly life is transitory (i.e., she died).

(63) *oo yatiim oo yak-taniiaa sal-iis*
PRO^3s(med) orphan and one-alone stop-PAST^3s
She was (then) an orphan and alone.

(64) *vala na*
but no
But no.

(65) *abdul qaadar oo oo-naa zaaifa riihaana naa kaaTum*
Abdul Qaadar and PRO^3s(med)-of wife Rihana of head

    aa Safkat naa seexaa kar-eer
    to kindness of protection do-PAST^3p
Abdul Qaadar and his wife gave the kindness of protection to Rihana('s head).

(66) *hameed ood-ee yak-taniiaa-ii naa ahsaas man-iN*
Hameed PRO^3s(med)-OBL one-alone-NN of perception become-INF

    kan alee-t-au
    for be^NEG-NEG^PAST-PAST^3s
Hameed did not allow her to feel lonely.

(67) *oof-taa saNgat-ii peen ziiaada mas*
PRO^3p(med)-GEN^PL friend-NN other great become^PAST^3s
Their friendship became very great;

A Beginning Look at Brahui Connectives
185

(68)   *masoom aa dimaaG-ak asa eloo Raan dee padee xurk*
       innocent to brain-PL one other from day later near

     mar-eesa   in-aar
     become-PRESˆADVˆPART go-PASTˆ3p
     their innocent minds were becoming closer day by day.

(69)   *jazbah-ak am dariiaa-oo   naa diir   aan   baar teen kan*
       emotion-PL also river-INDEF of water from like self for

     teen   aT   kasar kar-eesa   kaa-ra
     self   byˆmeansˆof road do-PRESˆADVˆPART go-PRES/FUTˆ3p
     Emotions are like the water of rivers in that they go where they will.

(70)   *Saaiid   handa   savab   as-aka*
       perhaps justˆhere reason be-IMPFˆ3s
       Perhaps this was the reason

     kih   riihaana naa ilah   ood-ee   teenaa   maar
     that Rihana   of   paternalˆuncle PROˆ3s(med)-OBL selfˆof son

     hameed   naa pin   aa   kar-ee
     Hameed of   name to do-PASTˆ3s
     that Rihana's uncle made to her (the engagement) of his son Hameed.

(71)   *masoom aa dimaaG-taa paak   oo   saaf   aa jazbah   asa peen*
       innocent to brain-GENˆPL holy and clean to emotion one other

     daaR-oo   Dool see   Tii   haRseeNg-aa
     PROˆ3s(near)-INDEF way concerning in turnˆoneselfˆback-PASTˆ3s
     This pure and holy emotion of innocent minds was turned back to
     another way.

(72)   *daa   jazbah*
       PROˆ3s(near) emotion
       This emotion

     kih   ood-ee   hic-oo   pin-as   tin-iN
     that PROˆ3s(med)-OBL something-INDEF name-INDEF give-INF

186   David A. Ross

ma-tav-aka
become-NEG^PAST-IMPF^3s
for which it was not possible for her to give a name,

balka beerav   mahsoos   kan-iNg-aka
rather returned   perceived   do-PASS-IMPF^3s
rather it was only felt,

daasa muhabat naa jazbah   aT   badal   mas
now   love   of   emotion   in   change   become^PAST^3s
now was changed into the emotion of love.

(73)   *riihaana   naa   xan-tee   Tii   hiiaa   naa raN   oo*
      Rihana   of   eye-OBL^PL in   shyness of   color   be^PRES^3p
      In Rihana's eyes is the color of shyness.

(74)   *hameed   naa   ust   aT   teenaa   mahbuub-ee haasil   kan-iN*
      Hameed   of   heart   in   self^of   beloved-OBL   product   do-INF

         Garoor Ø
         pride   IMPLIED
      She was proud to become the beloved of Hameed's heart.

(75)   *zaahir   aT   asa   eloo   Raan   mur man-iN   naa*
      outward^condition   in   one   other   from   far   become-INF   of

         kooSiS Ø
         try   IMPLIED
      Outwardly they tried to remain far from each other

      vala baatan aT   asa   eloo   naa   diid   naa
      but   heart   in   one   other   of   meeting^of^loved^ones of

         talabgaar   Ø
         seeker   IMPLIED
      but in their hearts they sought out meetings of loved ones.

(76)   *asa   uraa   Tii   paRda   man-iN   ma-f-ak*
      one   house   in   purdah   become-INF   become-NEG^PRES-PRES/FUT^3s
      In one house it is not (possible) to keep purdah.

A Beginning Look at Brahui Connectives 187

(77) handaa   savab   aan   mana vaxt aan   guD asa vaar valdaa
    just^here(near) reason   from   few time from   later one time again

     asa jaagah tul-iN   baS   man-iN-ee   Saruu   kar-eer
     one place   sit-INF get^up become-INF-OBL start   do-PAST^3p
For this reason, a little time later they began again to get used to
sitting (together) in the same place.

(78) kasmat kih   ansaan aa   mherbaan   mar-ee
    destiny that human to   loving   become-PRES^INDEF^3s
Luck, which may be loving to a person,

     too oo-naa   daamun-ee   har xuuS-ii   aan   pur
     then PRO^3s(med)-of skirt^of^garment-OBL all happy-NN from   full

     k-eek
     do-PRES/FUT^3s
(as if) it fills the hem of one's kamiz with happiness.

(79) oo-naa   zind-ee handun gulzaar   k-eek
    PRO^3s(med)-of life-OBL thus   field^of^flowers do-PRES/FUT^3s
It makes life like a field of flowers

     kih oo   Tii har paara Gaa phul-taa   xuuSboo   oo
     that PRO^3s(med) in   all side to flower-GEN^PL fragrance and

     gindaar naa raN-ak   taalaan   mar-eera
     rainbow of color-PL   spread^out   become-PRES/FUT^3p
(so) that in it, on every side, it (is as if) the fragrance of flowers and
the colors of the rainbow are spread out.

(80) hameed oo riihaana naa zind   am   andun-oo zind-as
    Hameed and Rihana   of life   also thus-INDEF life-INDEF

     as-aka
     be-IMPF^3s
The lives of Hameed and Rihana were like this.

(81) kasmat oof-tee   aa   mherbaan as-aka
    destiny PRO^3p(med)-OBL^PL to   loving   be-IMPF^3s
Luck was loving to them

188   David A. Ross

(82) *vala kasmat kih aasmaan naa baland-ii-taa*   *rase-f-iN*
but   destiny that sky   of height-NN-GEN^PL arrive-CAUS-INF
"but luck, which causes one to arrive at the height of heaven

aan   guD bandaG-ee DaGaar naa paara Gaa yala
from   later man-OBL   land   of   side to   loose

    k-eek
    do-PRES/FUT^3s
later looses a man (to fall back) to earth,

too bandaG naa vajood   hazaar Tukur mar-eek
then man   of   existence 1,000   piece   become-PRES/FUT^3s
and then a man's body will become a thousand pieces."

riihaana sooc   kar-ee
Rihana   think   do-PAST^3s
Rihana thought.

(83) *asa   giRaa-as   bandaG-ee duu   ba-f-Ø*
one   thing-INDEF   man-OBL   hand come-NEG-PRES^INDEF^3s
(If) something is not available to a man

too   oo   sabar   k-eek
then   PRO^3s(med) resigned^to^fate do-PRES/FUT^3s
then he accepts it.

(84) *vala duu   naa giRaa kih duu   aan   peeS   tam-aa*
but   hand of   thing   that hand from (in)^front fall-PAST^3s
But when it became (no longer) available,

too   bandaG-ee baaz armaan bar-eek
then   man-OBL   very   yearning come-PRES/FUT^3s
then a great desire comes to a man.

(85) *riihaana am hameed-ee duu-ii   kan-iN aan   guD*
Rihana   also Hameed-OBL hand-NN do-INF   from later

    padaa   gooh-aa
    back^again lose-PAST^3s
Rihana also, after gaining Hameed, lost him again.

A Beginning Look at Brahui Connectives

189

(86) *riihaana baraam naa tavaar tavaar aan baaz mur*
Rihana wedding of noise noise from very far

    xiiaal-taa daniiaa Tii gum as-aka
    thought-GEN^PL world in lost be-IMP^3s
Rihana was lost in a dream world far from the (big) noise of the wedding.

(87) *riihaana*
Rihana
"Rihana,"

    hameed naa luma ood-ee tavaar kar-ee
    Hameed of mother PRO^3s(med)-OBL noise do-PAST^3s
Hameed's mother made a noise to her.

(88) *too dun paa-∅*
then thus say-IMPLIED
Then she (thus) said

    kih oo tuG aan samaa kar-ee
    that PRO^3s(med) sleep from get^up do-PRES^INDEF^3s
that she should get up from sleep.

(89) *jii*
yes
"Yes,"

    riihaana javaab tis
    Rihana answer give-PAST^3s
Rihana answered.

(90) *daa uraa Tii mehmaan-tee diir eete*
PRO^3s(near) house in guest-OBL^PL water give^IMPER^SG
"Give water to the guests in this house,"

    hameed naa luma paar-ee
    Hameed of mother say-PAST^3s
Hameed's mother said.

(91) *riihaana jag-ee arf-ee*
Rihana jug-OBL lift-PAST^3s
Rihana lifted up a jug,

samaavaar naa kunDa aa in-aa
samovar of corner to go-PAST^3s
(and) went to the corner (where the) samovar (was).

(92) *jag-ee diir aan pur kar-ee*
jug-OBL water from full do-PAST^3s
She filled the jug with water.

(93) *oo uraa naa darvaaza Gaa raseeNg-aa*
PRO^3s(med) house of door to arrive-PAST^3s
She arrived at the door of the house,

too naa gumaan tuufak naa Tuk aa mas
then of sudden rifle of shot to become^PAST^3s
then suddenly there was the sound of a rifle shot.

(94) *riihaana xal naa but aan baar hamoo jaagah aa*
Rihana stone of idol from like this^same(med) place to

jik^aan^jik sal-iis
stationary stop-PAST^3s
Rihana remained stationary at the same spot like a stone idol.

(95) *oo-naa veeraan xan-tee Tii ust naa ditar*
PRO^3s(med)-of uninhabited^land eye-OBL^PL in heart of blood

safaa xan-iNg-aka
clearly see-PASS-IMPF^3s
In the desolation of her eyes, the emotions of her heart were clearly being seen.

(96) *hameed naa nikaah mas*
Hameed of engagement become^PAST^3s
"Hameed's engagement has happened,"

oo sooc kar-ee
PRO^3s(med) think do-PAST^3s
she thought.

A Beginning Look at Brahui Connectives

(97) uraa   naa taha aan   mubaarak-badii   naa tavaar baS
      house   of   room from congratulation-song   of   noise   get^up

     mas
     become^PAST^3s
From the room of the house came the sound of the wedding song.

(98) mehmaan aa niiaaRii-k hameed naa luma-ee   hameed naa
      guest   to woman-PL   Hameed of   mother-OBL Hameed of

     nikaah   naa mubaarak-badii   tis-ura
     engagement   of   congratulation-song   give-IMPF^3p
The lady guests were giving Hameed's mother the wedding song for Hameed's engagement.

(99) kanaa   paara Gaan   am   lakh   vaar mubaarak
      PRO^1s^of side from   also 100,000   time congratulation

     mar-ee   num-ee
     become-PRES^INDEF^3s   PRO^2p-OBL
"100,000 congratulations may come to you from me,"

     asa niiaaRii-as   hameed naa luma-ee   paar-ee
     one woman-INDEF   Hameed of   mother-OBL say-PAST^3s
     one woman said to Hameed's mother.

(100) riihaana araaRee Ø
      Rihana   where   IMPLIED
     "Where is Rihana?"

(101) ood-ee   am   uraa naa-ta   iraT-miikoo   baraam   naa
      PRO^3s(med)-OBL   also house of-RESPRO   two-ORDINAL   wedding of

     mubaarak-badii   eet-in
     congratulation-song   give-PRES^INDEF^1p
"We may give to her, in his house, the wedding song for his second wedding,"

     asa niiaaRii-as   paar-ee
     one woman-INDEF   say-PAST^3s
     one woman said.

(102) *vala   riihaana   xaRiiNk-ii   aa xan-tee   too   teenaa   ust   aT*
but   Rihana   tears-NN   to eye-OBL^PL with self^of heart in

     duaa   xuuaan-asaka
     prayer   read-IMPF^3s
But Rihana, with tears in her eyes, was praying,

     kih   yaa   alah
     that oh   God
"Oh God,

     naazoo-ee   hameed   aan   walaad   eet-ees
     Nazo-OBL   Hameed   from son   give-PRES^INDEF^2s
may you give Nazo a son by Hameed.

(103) *kan-ee   aan   baar   bee   walaad   ka-p-ees*
PRO^1s-OBL   from like   without son   do-NEG-PRES^INDEF^2s
May you not make (her) like me, without a son.

(104) *agar   oo   am   kan-ee   aan   baar   bee   walaad*
if   PRO^3s(med) also PRO^1s-OBL from like   without son

     mas
     become^PAST^3s
If she also (will be) became like me, without a son,

     too   dun   maf   0
     then   thus   forgive IMPLIED
then forgive (him, us)

     kih   hameed   naa   musiT-miikoo   nikaah   am
     that Hameed   of   three-ORDINAL engagement also

     mar-ee
     become-PRES^INDEF^3s
that Hameed may have a third engagement also."

References

Andronov, Mikhail S. 1980. The Brahui language (English translation). U.S.S.R. Academy of Sciences, Institute of Oriental Studies, Moscow. (First published in 1971.)

Arif Zia. 1984. Zaraab (Flame). Quetta, Pakistan: Brahui Adabi Society.

Bray, Denys D. 1907. The Brahui language, Part 1: Introduction and grammar. Reprinted by the Brahui Academy, Quetta, 1977.

———. 1934. The Brahui language, Part 2: The Brahui problem, and Part 3: Etymological vocabulary. Reprinted by Brahui Academy, Quetta, Publication No. 11, 1978.

Elfenbein, J. H. 1982. Notes on the Balochi-Brahui linguistic commensality. Transactions of the Philogical Society.

———. 1983a. The Brahui problem again. Indo-Iranian Journal 25:103–32.

———. 1983b. A Brahui supplementary vocabulary. Indo-Iranian Journal 25:191–209.

Ghulam Hedar Hasrat. 1981. Xuuaaja baava naa haesyat aT. In BandaGii naa xeer xooaah. Brahui Academy, Quetta, 27–38.

Godi Aminah Yosef. 1985. Kick! Talar, March 1985, 8–11. Quetta, Pakistan: Brahui Adabi Society.

Hussein Bakhsh Sajid Asani. 1985. Teardrop. Talar, September 1985, 11–12. Quetta, Pakistan: Brahui Adabi Society.

Jamait Rai and Bahadur Diwan. 1907. Notes on the study of the Brahui language. Quetta. Second edition, 1917. Reprinted by Brahui Academy, Quetta, Publication No. 31, 1985.

Larson, Mildred L. 1984. Meaning-based translation. Lanham: University Press of America.

Longacre, Robert E. 1983. The grammar of discourse. New York: Plenum Press.

Mann, William C. and Sandra A. Thompson. 1987. Rhetorical structure theory: A theory of text organization. ISI reprint series; ISI/RS—87–190 (Reprinted from The structure of discourse); Marina del Rey, California.

McAlpin, David W. 1981. Proto-Elamo-Dravidian. Transactions of the American Philological Society 71, part 3. Philadelphia: University of Pennsylvania Press.

Ross, David A. 1987. A pilot study of diachronic discourse features. M.A. thesis. University of Texas at Arlington, Arlington, Texas.

———. 1988. Another sketch of Brahui grammar. Unpublished ms.

———. 1989. A brief sketch of Brahui phonology and its orthographic implications. Unpublished ms.

'If' in Capanahua

Eugene E. Loos

Capanahua has no 'if' morpheme but speakers can express both real mode and hypothetical mode conditional statements. Sequential timing morphemes that serve as subordinate clause markers are important for expressing conditional statements; the relation between the clauses can be interpreted as a conditional by language processing principles that take account of both linguistic and paralinguistic factors.

If we take a truth table view of a conditional 'if...then...' expression in natural language, we would presumably describe a listener's language processing of the conditional statement as a two step operation. First, the listener determines the value of the protasis (the 'if' clause), and then draws a conclusion concerning the truth value of the apodosis (the 'then' clause): '*if* the protasis is true *then* the apodosis is true'.

The essential factor in a conditional is that the status of the protasis must be ascertained in order to determine the status of the content of the apodosis. The difference between a conditional statement and a cause-result statement is that in the cause-result statement the status of both the causing clause and the result clause is a given; in the conditional the result in the apodosis depends on a protasis for which the current status must yet be determined.

(1)   If it rains the frogs chirp.

(2)   Because it rains the frogs chirp.

The relation of the cause (rain) to the effect (chirp) is stronger in the cause-result statement (2) because the statement leaves no doubt about whether it is raining and the frogs are chirping. Example (1) would not make

196 Eugene E. Loos

much sense if it is already raining and 'rains' were taken to refer to the current event; (2) would be readily understood.

While in both (1) and (2) there is a cause and effect relation, with (1) it is up to the listener to process the condition to discern what the result in the apodosis is and from that what the speaker's intent for him is. However, the relation between a truth table result, if there is one, and the speaker's intended meaning may be practially undiscernable, as in (3).

(3)   If you are cold put this coat on.

A speaker's intended meaning, i.e., the protasis-to-apodosis relation, is often apparent. Some of the principal types of protasis-to-apodosis relations identified in Capanahua conditional statements are:

1. sequential timing—the event of the apodosis follows that of the protasis chronologically.
2. predictable regularity—the event in the apodosis predictably follows that of the protasis.
3. propriety—the propriety of the statement in the apodosis depends on the content of the protasis.
4. natural cause and natural consequence—the state in the apodosis is the result of the state of the protasis.
5. logical cause—the state of the apodosis is the logical outcome of that of the protasis.
6. natural incentive—the protasis is not the direct natural cause of the apodosis but provides an incentive for the apodosis.
7. direct provocation—the protasis directly provokes the action in the apodosis.
8. indirect provocation—the protasis indirectly provokes the action of the apodosis.
9. psychological motive—the protasis is a psychological motive for the apodosis.

What the above means is that for each type, in processing a conditional rather than finding a truth table value, the task of the listener is to discern the belief concerning the protasis that the speaker wants to communicate, and thereby infer from the apodosis what the speaker intends. In some cases the relation is the inverse: if the conversing pair are seeking to find a cause, they may have readily discerned the value of the apodosis first and may be seeking to find a suitable protasis. Obviously, a listener's factual knowledge is important for determining which type of relation the speaker intends.

A distinctive of an English IF clause is that it is explicitly tagged as inferential by the particle 'if', but even without 'if', a feature common to all conditional statements, there is a precedence of the protasis to the apodosis. The precedence may be that the protasis is temporally prior to the apodosis,

'If' in Capanahua 197

is logically necessary for the apodosis event, is a cause of the apodosis event, etc. A conditional in which the condition of the protasis is subsequent to or the result of the apodosis would be a logical contradiction. Even in an expressly future protasis subsequent to the apodosis as in 'if this seed is going to bear fruit, then it must be planted now' the condition must be read as a present tense 'if it is the case that...'

1. Processing factors

A typical conditional like (4) is very dependent on pragmatic inferences that supply implicit structure.

(4)   If you call me a toad I'll swat you.

The structure that is implicitly supplied would be something like '*If it is ever the case that* you call me a toad, then *I assure you that* I will swat you'. The protasis 'if *it is ever the case that*' roughly follows the form of the protasis of a truth table proposition, but the apodosis 'then *I assure you that*' does not; 'I assure you that' is not readily resolved by a truth table evaluation.

The implicature that the listener derives depends on many factors, including the language categories available or used, how much he knows, the circumstantial evidence and indicators of the speaker's intended illocutionary force such as to teach, lead to draw a conclusion, blame, explain facts observed, to threaten, etc. For (5) the context in which the utterance is made, the intonation with which the utterance is expressed, and the mode of the sentence would be crucial cues. For example, if (5) is said sarcastically by a supervisor to chide a subordinate for going ahead with mistaken ideas, the implicature of the apodosis would be quite different from what it would be when spoken to bystanders by a disenchanted computer user who has been trying to install software with telephone on-line help.

(5)   If you call for help you might receive it.

2. Evidence that no 'if' morpheme is available in Capanahua

In Capanahua many morphemes are used to link propositions, but none of them is a condition marking particle. There are five verb suffixes that create participle-like subordinate clauses that are used in constructions

198   Eugene E. Loos

interpeted by listeners as conditional statements. There are questions that
come to mind.

1. How do we know that one or more of these suffixes is not a homophonous form of 'if'?
2. If the morphemes do not mean 'if', how is it that listeners agree on
   the meaning?
3. Why are these morphemes and not others pressed into service to express conditional statements?

The five suffixes are described below. Each of them always signals a
unique combination of switch referent and event timing relation between the
subordinate clause and the main clause. The subordinate clauses produced do
not always function as a conditional statement; in fact, they most often do
not. If lexicalization had taken place so that one or more of them could be
utilized as 'if' outside their ordinary usage restrictions, we would have a
usage different from the accepted pattern for that morpheme and that would
allow for an analysis of polysemy, but we do not find such. The switch referent conditions, for example, are never violated and the timing sequence
called for between the subordinate clause event and the main clause event
always holds.

The particular switch referent marking morphemes that occur in conditional statements have one feature in common: they indicate that the subordinate clause event begins before or simultaneously with the event of the
main clause. Given the precedence relation of protasis to apodosis in conditional statements, it is no surprise that none of the various subordinate clause
marking morphemes that indicate that the timing of the subordinate clause is
SUBSEQUENT to the event of the main clause ever serve to communicate
conditional statements.

First we present an overview of the switch referent marking morphemes
to show how they are used in nonconditional sentences, then we show how
their characteristics are used to express conditional statements.

The verb suffix -ya indicates that the subject referent of the subordinate
clause is different (DS) from that of the subject of the main clause. The action of the subordinate clause is initiated before that of the main clause. (In
all references to main clause we refer to the clause to which the subordinate
clause is subordinated. The main clause is not necessarily the independent
clause of the sentence; it may itself be subordinated to another clause.)

'If' in Capanahua   199

(6) bahoh-i   choyotai-ya jascaja-quin nonti hohca-quin
     flexible-become soft-DS   so^doing-TNS canoe spread^open-TNS[1]
     When the canoe becomes flexible and soft, one spreads it open in that
     way.

The verb suffix -xon indicates that the subordinate clause subject has the
same referent (SS) as the subject of the main clause, the main clause is
transitive, and the action of the subordinate clause is initiated before that of
the main clause as in (7).

(7) jonon   mera-xon   pi-quin
     peccary   find-SS   eat-TNS
     When a peccary finds it, he eats it.

The verb suffix -ax indicates that the subordinate clause subject has the
same referent (SS) as the subject of the main clause, the main clause is in-
transitive, and the action of the subordinate clause is initiated before that of
the main clause as in (8).

(8) xenisca-ax   behmequeht-i
     old^become-SS   break-TNS
     When it becomes old, it breaks.

The verb suffix -ah indicates that the object or indirect object of the subordinate clause is coreferential (OS) with the subject of its main clause, and
the action of the subordinate clause is initiated before that of the main clause
as in (9).

(9) hinan-ah   bih-quin
     give-OS   take-TNS
     He accepted what she offered him.

The verb suffix -ton indicates that the subject of the subordinate clause is
coreferential with the object (SO) of its main clause which will be transitive
(thus ruling out coreference between the subject of a subordinate clause and

---

[1] Abbreviations: DECL, declarative modal; DIST, distantive; DS, different subject referent;
EVID, evidential; FUT, future tense; IFF, if and only if; IMPV, imperative; INSTR, instrumental;
MD, modal; NEG, negative; OS, object referent same as subject referent of main clause; PL,
plural; POT, potential; REP, reportative; SEQ, sequence; SO, subject referent same as object
referent of main clause; SS, same subject referent; SUP, suppositional; TNS, substitute form of
tense; VERIF, verification.

200   Eugene E. Loos

a reflexive main clause). The action of the subordinate clause is in process at the time of the initiation of the action of the main clause as in (10).

(10)   *siritai-ton   sca   rabe-quin*
        good^become-so   then   invert-TNS
        When it is ready, you turn it over.

These morphemes occur very frequently. Their function in identifying referents allows nouns and pronouns to be omitted as can be seen in examples (11) through (14) which are blocks of sentences taken from vernacular texts.

(11)   *jihui hani baxo. queyani. bimi chaho-hax   naman*
        tree   big   baxo tall   fruit soft^become-ss below

        miracahtai-ton sca   jonon   mera-xon pi-quin
        earth^on^lie-so then peccary find-ss   eat-TNS
        The baxo tree is huge, very tall. When its fruits become soft and fall to the ground, the peccary eats them when he finds them.

(12)   *nonti behna   hohc-ah-ma caroja-xon   chihi queteja-xon*
        canoe new   open-OS-NEG firewood-make-ss fire   light-ss

        jihui qui queyan-xon chihin xanaja-ha siriscai
        tree on   elevate-ss   fire   get^hot-os well-be-TNS

        bahohi   siritai-ton sca   rabe-xon   jihuin
        become^flexible good^be-so then   turn^over-ss post-INSTR

        nonti quexa qui nichin-xon. jaxbaja-quin.   bahoh-i
        canoe edge on   stand-ss   open^mouth-TNS flexible-TNS

        choyotai-ya jascaja-quin   nonti hohca-quin
        soft-DS   so^doing-TNS   canoe open-TNS
        When you have an unopened canoe, you make firewood, build a fire, raise the canoe up on posts, and when you have heated it, it becomes ready, flexible. When it is ready, you turn it over, stand log props on its edges and spread it open. That is the way you spread a canoe open, when it is soft and flexible.

'If' in Capanahua   201

(13) *mai quenti qui cobinja-ha bi   qui xenisca-ax behmequehti*
      clay pot   in   cook-os   but REP old^get-ss crack^TNS
      They say when you cook in a clay pot, it cracks up when it gets old.

(14) *pehin   cahuaquin quesaja-ha   behmequehti*
      leaves^in wrap^TNS poorly-os   crack^TNS
      If you wrap things in leaves poorly, the package disintegrates.

For the sake of brevity, in the remainder of this presentation the data
chosen will focus on examples formed on the morpheme *-ya*. The language
processing principles that apply to *-ya* apply also to conditional statements
formed on the other morphemes listed above.

3. Capanahua IFF (if-and-only-if)

The most readily identifiable conditional in Capanahua is an if-and-only-
if statement. The basic form is shown in (15). The format of the statement is
simple: a pair of clauses is used to open one possibility and another pair of
clauses is used to close the alternative. The narrator has explained that the
treed white-faced monkey has gray fur. It runs in groups of four without
calling, and sleeps in the hollow of a tree. Its appearance is predictable according to specific conditions.

(15) *bari xanahi-ya picoti,   hoi behi-ya   picoyamahi*
      sun hot-DS   emerge^TNS^DS rain come^TNS-DS emerge^NEG^TNS
      When the sun is hot it comes out, when it rains it doesn't come out.

The second protasis-apodosis pair (which contains the alternative that is
to be closed) can simply be a negated version of the first pair, producing the
Capanahua counterpart to an if-and-only-if (IFF) truth table condition, as in
(16).

(16) *mia cahi-ya tah   hen ca-tihi. min cayamahi-ya cahen hearihbi*
      you go-DS   DECL I   go-FUT you go^NEG-DS   SUP   I^also

      ca-yama-hi
      go- NEG-TNS
      If you go, I go. If you do not go, I do not go.

The protasis always has an imperfect tense, and the tense of the apodosis
is present or future. The Capanahua tense system is asymmetrical having

202   Eugene E. Loos

four past tenses (roughly for time countable in hours, days, months, and
years) and four future tenses (today, tomorrow or next day, later, indefinite).
The imperfect tense (otherwise called the present tense) serves for presently
ongoing or imminently impending action and for any incomplete time spans.

If the main clause has a past tense, the listener does not question when it
might be realized; no conditional interpretation is called for because the
pasts represent fairly concrete time even when not modified by adverbial
time constructions as in (17).

(17)   *hen tah hen ca-ha-qui*   I went (just now).
       hen tah hen ca-hipi-qui   I went (yesterday).
       hen tah hen ca-ho-qui   I went (a month ago).
       hen tah hen ca-ni-qui   I went (a year ago).

It is worth noting that the temporal clause marker *-tian* 'at the time that,
at any time that' can be used to communicate the time of an event. It differs
from *-ya* and the other suffixes listed in that it indicates bounded time, not a
sequence of time. As exemplified in (18) it is not used for conditional statements.

(18)   *mia   cahi-tian   tah   hen   hearihbi catihi*
       you   go-at^the^time   DECL   I   I^also   go^will
       At the time that you go I will also go.

As was observed earlier, in a conditional statement the protasis must
have a precedence relation to the apodosis. Chronological timing of the protasis to the apodosis is one kind of precedence. Therefore, subordinate
clause markers having an imperfect (incomplete) tense in the protasis must
have a present or future tense in the apodosis. For a conditional interpretation it is essential that the tense of the main clause indicate that the state or
event has not concluded. Hence, any Capanahua construction with a past
tense in the main clause is ineligible for interpretation as a conditional.

4. Pragmatic processing defines interpropositional meaning

In factual statements of chronologically sequential events, a subordinate
clause marked by *-ya* has a main clause in REALIS mode. Realis is used in
sentences that the listener will readily interpret as expressions of present or
past fact. Realis sentences are marked by the declarative mode indicator *-ta,*
and if the verb is not in first or second person and imperfect tense, the verb
terminates with the evidential verb suffix *-qui.*

'If' in Capanahua   203

IRREALIS sentences on the other hand, express events that have not yet been and might not be realized and are marked by an irrealis mode indicator which will be described later.

As we have noted, the verb suffix -*ya* in a subordinate clause marks an action that begins before or at the same time as the action of the main clause. The intended relation expressed between the subordinate clause and main clause may be little more than a matter of chronological timing, whether coincidental or intentional.

Example (19) comes from a short autobiographical note. The -*tanai* ending of *rehtetanai* indicates that the speaker has just come from the hunt; the realis nature of the main clause is marked by *tah*. The timing of the action of the subordinate clause with respect to the action of the main clause suggests a 'while' gloss for the subordinate clause. Indeed, given the sociocultural context of a jungle scene, a causal or motivational relation between subordinate clause and main clause is not logical. The hunter wants to get the birds when they have settled down on the roost; the birds are then quiet and more easily hunted. Therefore, the speaker intends for the listener to infer from -*ya* only that the timing of the event of the subordinate clause precedes the event of the main clause.

(19) *coma*   *paichai-ya* *tah*   *hen* *rehtetanai*
      pheasant   roost-DS   DECL I   shoot^DIST
      I just shot a pheasant while it was roosting.

Though a past tense in a main clause can be an indicator of realis mode, the tense does not have to be in the main clause itself; it can have been provided in the previous context. In (20) the main verb *becani* ends with -*i* which substitutes for a tense in discourse. Strings of sentences in discourse typically carry no tense once the mode and tense have been established in the narration. Instead of a tense, a tense substitute is used, its value being whatever has been established earlier. To the extent then that in discourse the realis mode of a sentence is determined by discourse factors, in order to interpret conditional statements the listener must be aware of extensive contextual information outside the immediate sentence.

The emphasis marker -*bi* in (20) focuses attention on the timing of events as simultaneous, but there is no conditional or causal relation. The participants simply waited until dawn to come home.

(20) *janobi* *racashina-hax* *qui,* *xaba* *paquetai-ya* *bi* *becani* *can,*
      there   lie^nocturnal-SS REP   dawn   fall-DS   just came   well

204 Eugene E. Loos

> *jaton xoboho hihcohi*
> their house^in enter

Having laid there all night, *right at* dawn they came on to their homes.

Realis is not limited to verifiable real-life accounts. In (20) as well as (21), the reportative morpheme *qui* indicates that the information is not first-hand; though the speaker attributes the information to other sources it is presented as realis.

Example (21) comes from a legend. A deity departs, taking the low-hanging sky with him in stages as he rises. The legend explains the origin of the moon in the sky, for the deity becomes the moon. The coincident timing of the events is the only significant relation from which one can deduce that the deity took the sky up with him.

(21) *jaa jan cahi-ya bi qui hahbe nai qui hahbetanbi cahi*
 he he go-DS just REP with^him sky REP with^him go
 As he ascended, the sky lifted up with him.

In (22) the purpose of the protasis is to frame the time precisely within the period that the past tense encompasses; there is no way to interpret a causal relationship between 'uncle going' of the subordinate clause and 'I saw' of the main clause.

(22) *xaba paquetai-ya bi huenixon coca tenaman cahi jisquin*
 dawn fall-DS just rising uncle port go saw
 Just at dawn I got up and saw uncle going to the canoe landing.

Apart from switch reference functions, the preceding examples have shown how *-ya* is used to indicate chronological timing between a subordinate clause and main clause in a realis mode sentence. Since without a specific conditional marker like 'if' any conditional reading a listener might give to a sentence depends on pragmatic processing, the role of concrete tense in a main clause is an important filter factor. If the tenses in the main clauses had not signalled completed actions, these examples would have been instances when a relation of chronological sequence as a conditional would be a possible interpretation. We examine next some cases where more than the core chronological meaning of *-ya* is intended.

'If' in Capanahua   205

4.1 Natural consequence

As can be expected when meanings depend on pragmatic interpretation, ambiguities arise according to the listener's understanding of the speaker's intentions. The *-ya* clause of (23) could be interpreted as 'whenever' if the speaker is expressing the sentence as a summary of sequential conditions; but if the speaker refers to current conditions only, he intends a logical relation 'since'. Knowledge of natural phenomena leads the listener to associate a cause and effect timing relation between the clauses.

(23) *hihti   mehcha ta   mai   jaiqui,   baquen.   huasibo rihbi   mehcha*
      very   wet   DECL earth is   son   grasses also   wet

      hoi   behi-ya   jatihibi   mehchati
      rain   come^when-DS   all   be^wet
      The ground is really wet, Son. The grass too. *Whenever* it rains, everything gets wet. *or Since* it has rained, everything is wet.

In (24) we find the same type of construction but the tense of the main clause refers to a single instance that can be interpreted as a natural consequence of the event in a causal subordinate clause, hence 'because'.

(24) *tiscohax janobi   tsahotai.   bicopai-ya tiscotani tah   hen*
      slipping   there   sit   slimy^DS   slipped   DECL I

      tsahorenenai
      sat^suddenly
      I slipped, fell, and remained sitting there. *Because* it was slimy I slipped and suddenly sat down.

The result expressed by the main clause may only be an accident instead of a purely natural consequence, as in (25) where a man cuts his hand on a sharp machete because it has been stuck upright in the ground without him realizing it was there.

(25) *heen   machito   quehshoha   nichi-ya   ta   mesemehtaxqui*
      my   machete   sharpened   stand-DS   DECL   hand^cut
      Because my machete was very sharp and standing up, he cut himself on it.

206 Eugene E. Loos

4.2 Indirect provocation

We consider now cases in which the relation between the clauses that the speaker intends to convey is that the events of the subordinate clause may be construed as an indirect provocation (26) or motivation (27) for the action of the main clause. The tense of the apodosis still eliminates interpretation as a conditional statement.

(26) *pejoxni   pecaya   tah   min qui,   chahin,   hihqui. peca*
     back^blanched back^with DECL you EVID cousin   says   back

      hihti   joxotai-ya   papan coca jascajaquin
      very   white^become-DS Papa uncle said
"You have a white back, cousin!" said Papa to my uncle because my uncle's back has become very white.

(27) *janobihax   qui bitsari bitsarihcani. bitsatai-ya* **bi** *qui*
     there^being REP laugh   laughed   laugh-DS just REP

      sinajascaquin
      scolded
Standing there, they reportedly giggled on and on. *Because* they laughed, he scolded them.

Examples (23) through (27) have subordinate -*ya* clauses that signal a temporal relation of one event to another with a fairly evident causative factor in the subordinate clause, producing a result on the main clause. Many -*ya* clauses are used when the timing of the event in the subordinate clause has only a weak causal effect such that the event in the main clause is simply suitably timed given the preceding event in the subordinate clause. The reason we identify for the reader such interclausal relationships is that for a listener to identify a conditional protasis-apodosis relation there has to be a reasonable way for him to associate the clauses with other than the core meanings of the switch referent suffixes. If we know what the associations are between nonconditional clauses, we can anticipate that we will find the same relations between clauses in statements interpeted as conditional statements.

4.3 Sequential suitability

The cooking instruction of (28) is different from the other examples up to this point in that it carries the expectation that as the cooking is done, the

'If' in Capanahua   207

sequential stage comes about that the fruit becomes tender and suitable for food. Though the main clause is present tense imperative, the explanation of the cooking process leaves the subordinate clause more in focus than the final main clause.

(28)   *quenti qui bohasaxon jene   machixon   chihin   xanajaquin,*
          kettle   in   filling   water   pouring^over   fire^with   heat

         choyonon.   choyotai-ya   sca   piquin
         to^be^tender   tender-DS   SEQ   eat
         First fill a kettle with the fruit, then pour water over it and heat it until they are soft. *After* they become soft, eat them.

In some cases, a subordinate clause marked by *-ya* is ambivalent; it does not make much difference to the sense of the sentence whether the main clause is interpreted as just sequential to the subordinate clause or suitably timed. Nevertheless, looking ahead we can see that the suitability of timing can also be the implicature in a conditional based on constructions like (29) which describes the characteristic habits of a bird, indicated by the verb suffix *-nica* 'characteristically'. The *-ya* clause refers not to one event but to a tendency, with two timing conditions: that it be raining and that it be dusk. The speaker indicates by the verb ending of the subordinate clause that he intends the statement of the facts that he has observed to be a generalization verifiable by anyone; the meaning is the same whether we take *queonica* as an activity suitably timed or simply a sequential event.

(29)   *jaa rihbi ta   hoi behi-ya   bi   yantanai-ya   queo nica*
          he   also   DECL   rain come-DS   just   dusk^become-DS   singer

         qui
         VERIF
         That (bird) is also one that sings *when* it rains *at* dusk (*when* it becomes dusk).

4.4 Regularity of timing

Some events happen with such regularity that 'whenever' generalizations can be made regarding their occurrence. We can anticipate that when such events are represented by subordinate *-ya* clauses, those clauses may form the protasis of conditional statements. The regularity expressed can be understood as a natural, e.g., (30) and (31), or motivated, e.g., (32), causal relation. The greater the listener's knowledge of jungle travel and tropical

208   Eugene E. Loos

conditions, the more likely that he will process the statements as observed regularities rather than as simple temporally sequential events.

(30) *nonti jihui peracahtihi, huean janin. huean hihti tsosinai-ya*
      canoe log   lies^on   creek in   creek very dries^up-DS

          benesen peracahti
          shallow   lies^on
      The canoe gets stuck on a log in the creek. *Whenever* the creek becomes very shallow, the canoe runs aground (on a log).

(31) *mai poto potohi bari xanahi-ya potohax nihuehi-ya sca*
      earth dust dusty^be sun heats-DS dusty^be windy^be-DS then

          poto potohi nihuen hahca
          dust dusty^be wind^by blown
      Whenever the sun is hot and wind comes, ground dust rises and scatters, blown by the wind.

(32) *hoi penesai-ya pitso queoti, xapo jihui mebin*
      rain fades-DS parakeet sings huimba tree branch

          cahtsahotax nai bejisahnan
          sitting^on sky looking^at
      Whenever the rain fades away the pihuichos sing, sitting on the limb of a huimba tree and looking at the sky.

5. Real mode conditional statements

Many real mode Capanahua conditional statements do not differ greatly from temporal statements. We can usually take them as either 'if' or 'whenever' statements. The principal requirement is that the tense of the main clause be imperfect (present or future tense) so that when the sentence is processed the possibility remains of interpreting the subordinate clause as a condition (the protasis) for the main clause (its apodosis).

Example (33) is a narrator's definition of a lexical entry in a dictionary. The three *-ya* clauses contrast three semantic relations between a subordinate clause and each subordinate clause's main clause: (a) natural cause, (b) suitability of fit, and (c) timing. If uttered in a different context, any of the subordinate clauses could be interpreted as a conditional with the same

'If' in Capanahua   209

interclausal semantic associations as when not conditional, shown by the slashed options in boldface.

(33) a. *mani   pehi pehuahi, bari hihti   xanatai-ya*
      banana leaf withers   sun very   heats-DS
      Banana leaves wither *because/if* the sun is very hot.

    b. *pehi   hotsihi   yohihi,   mahuatima   bi   xanahi-ya*
       leaf   shrink   says   dies^ NEG   but   dries-DS
       To wither means that the leaves shrivel *when/if* they don't die but are dry.

    c. *bari   xana   huinotai-ya   roharihbihi*
       sun   heat   passes-DS   recovers
       After/if the sun's heat has passed, they recover.

Nevertheless, not all temporally related *-ya* clauses are either 'if' or 'whenever' statements even though they satisfy the requirements. Example (34) shows a sample 'when' or 'whenever' relation that is not amenable to a conditional interpretation. The example provides local wisdom about how to seek a wife. The logical relation of the potential protasis to the apodosis we might describe as 'when the conditions are right'.

(34) *haibo   honanti jaquin,   hestipishcabi   xontacoscai-ya   sca*
     woman tags   very^small though   adolescent-DS   then

     bihyanoxon
     get^FUT^to
     We take note of a girl though she be very young, then take her later *when* she begins to enter womanhood. (We take note of a girl to marry her in the future.)

Though the conditions given in the protasis must precede those of the apodosis to be the right conditions, and the factual main clause 'we take note of her' above is future in tense, the subordinate clause *bihyanoxon* 'in order to take her later' leaves no interpretive ambiguity about taking her. Only the time is in question; no conditional interpretation is intended.

Example (35) comes from a native speaker's explanation of when it is appropriate to use the expression *huehrohi* to describe the condition of a lake. The suitability or appropriateness of the expression in the apodosis to the conditions described in the protasis seems to make sense to the listener who deduces pragmatically from contextual information that a causal

210   Eugene E. Loos

relation or timing is inappropriate, but suitability is. Given the context, either
a temporal or conditional interpretation relation of protasis to apodosis is
possible.

(35) *jene   huehroti,   honaxonbi pishca behchonai-ya rahma*
      water shimmers   slowly   small   wave^be-DS   now

      huehro huehrohi
      wave   waves
      The water shimmers *whenever/if* it is just barely moving with minis-
      cule waves.

In the examples to follow we examine progressively stronger conditional
relationships.

5.1 Direct natural cause

We can identify a more direct causal force in the subordinate clause
having natural consequences in the main clause in (36). The listeners' fa-
miliarity with natural phenomena will enable them to interpret the cause-
and-effect relation intended. If the tense of the main clause is changed to
future so that the statement becomes a prediction, a conditional cause-and-
effect interpretation is obtained, as in (37).

(36) *nihue coshin   jahui-ya   ta   hoa jihui   tehquecahinipishqui*
      wind strongly   come-DS   DECL that tree   broke^apart
      When a strong wind came, that tree broke apart.

(37) *nihue coshin   jahui-ya   ta   hoa jihui   tehquecahinyaxihquiqui*
      wind strongly   come-DS   DECL that tree   break^apart^will
      If a strong wind comes, that tree will break apart.

5.2 Indirect cause as motivation

In order for a realis statement to be interpreted as a conditional, there has
to be a plausible relation between the protasis and apodosis. When the relation is indirect, more cultural knowledge is called upon to find a reasonable
association. In (38) the first sentence is plainly descriptive; the following
sentences provide cultural information intended to explain the first sentences, and the *-ya* clause of (38) also provides cultural information to explain its main clause. The third sentence can therefore be interpreted as a

'If' in Capanahua   211

conditional by an acculturated Capanahua who is not aware of local habits. If the subordinate clause had not provided the necessary cultural information, a conditional interpetation might not be attained. We conclude that the imperfect tense aspect of the main clause ALLOWS interpretation as a conditional but does not REQUIRE it to be so interpreted.

(38) *metoti   metsohihqui.   mequeman   pihax metoti   metsohihqui.*
      finger   wipes   hand^by   eating fingers wipes

      jano   xeni   hueotai-ya   metsohihqui
      there grease sticks-DS   wipes
      He wipes his fingers. Having eaten with his fingers, he wipes them off *if* grease has stuck to his fingers.

Given a context in which the narrator describes what an ideal Capanahua woman is like, in (39) the first sentence describes a characteristic rather than a specific event. The -*ya* clause can then be interpreted as a conditional.

(39) *caro   pexaquin.   caro   yamahi-ya carojaquin*
      firewood splits   firewood be^ NEG-DS firewood^makes
      She splits firewood. *If* she has no firewood, she cuts some.

The association of the protasis to the apodosis may be that the protasis is to be taken as a PSYCHOLOGICAL PROVOCATION for the event in the apodosis, as in (40)

(40) *nea risbi ta   hihti terehi pecatimahiqui, baquen. hihti*
      this rope   DECL very   tight untie^ NEG   son   very

      nexetai-ya jascari coca
      tangle-DS   said   uncle
      This rope is so knotted that I can't untie it, son. That's what uncle says *if* it is all knotted up.

Example (41) was offered as an explanation for why more men than ever before will be intruding from outside the community. Intruders used to come singly hunting peccary hides but they will come in droves to hunt tiger hides. The event in the protasis is an INCENTIVE for the event in the apodosis.

(41) *hashoan copitai-ya   ta   hashoan hicha   sca   jaa*
      more   expensive-DS DECL more   much   then that

212   Eugene E. Loos

     benahi   *benayaxihcaniqui*
     search^to   come^they
If tiger hides become worth more, they will come in much greater
numbers.

The *pesabin* is a tall jungle tree with very sweet, edible fruit. The tree
trunk is huge, the fruit small and round, hard to grasp. When asked how one
gets the fruit, the respondent replied that it is necessary to chop the tree
down, then supplied (42a). Without changing the form of (42a) but by putting it in a context where the substitute tense *-quin* is understood to be a
substitute for a future tense and imperative mode, it will be understood to be
a conditional (42b).

(42) a. *jenquetsax*   *hinatimahi-ya*   *reraquin* *yamin*
         how^doing   climb^able^ NEG-DS chop   axe^with
         When there is no way to climb the tree, we chop it down with an
         axe.

      b. *jenquetsax*   *hinatimahi-ya reraquin yamin*
         way^finding climb^ NEG-DS chop   axe^with
         If there is no way to climb the tree, chop it down with an axe.

Similarly, the descriptive context of (43a) and (44a) leads to a nonconditional reading that could easily be conditional. If the context supplies imperative mode and present or future tense to indicate incomplete action, the
very same sentence structures are interpreted as conditional statements, provided here in similar versions (43b) and (44b) of the same sentences.

(43) a. *hen mani*   *papixon* *beha*   *bi*   *hihuepai-ya tah*   *hen*
         I   banana carrying brought but be^heavy-DS DECL I

         potabehnanai
         left^behind
         I came bringing a racimo of bananas, but *when* it got heavy I left
         it behind.

      b. *min*   *mani*   *papi-xon beha*   *bi*   *hihuepai-ya*
         your bananas carry-ss brought but heavy-DS

         potabehnanhue
         leave^behind^IMPV
         If you bring bananas and they get heavy, leave them behind.

'If' in Capanahua   213

(44) a. *hea hishtohi bahin   cahi. hoi behi-ya hishtohi*
          I   hurry   path^in · go   rain come-DS hurry

          hotahi   cahi
          shelter^take   go
          I was hurrying along the trail. *Because* rain was coming I
          hurried, in order to take shelter.

      b. *hoi behi-ya   hishtohi hotahi   cahue*
          rain comes^when-DS running   sheltering go^IMPV
          If it rains, run to take shelter

We have shown how a switch referent marking verb suffix *-ya* that indicates a sequence in action can also be used pragmatically to associate additional semantic relations between the clauses. The associations range from
appropriateness of the event in the main clause to suitability of its timing;
going further we have seen that various degrees of cause and effect between
the clauses is intended.

Examples have shown how, if the main clause has an imperfect tense,
the context invites or allows the listener to determine what the event's outcome is and the conditional protasis-to-apodosis relations have the same
range of association as nonconditional statements. These have all been in
realis mode; we have not yet examined hypothetical conditional statements.
We turn now to the way hypothetical statements are expressed.

6. Hypothetical mode conditional statements

In a hypothetical statement the event expressed has not yet happened in
real time but the possibility of it happening is contemplated. The sentence
must be marked so that the listener will understand that there is no claim
that the event has happened whether the aspect be imperfective or perfective.
One way of marking the sentence is to indicate that the event is a potential
event; the other way is to mark the sentence as hypothetical by inclusion of a
suppositional modal.

Potential events are indicated by the verb suffixes *-quehan* 'almost,
might, could have' for events in perfect aspect or *-han* 'would' for events in
imperfect aspect.

The suffix *-quehan* signals completive aspect for an unrealized event. It
is used to indicate that the action of the verb though completive falls short of
being realized. The action or state is initiated or intended but its full realization is averted.

214 Eugene E. Loos

(45) *tabara huenijaqueha bi qui xaco, neatihopa qui sanatan.*
board lift^up but REP worm this^size REP struck

 *bero chahchi-**quehan**-quin*
 eye poke-POT-TNS
When she lifted the board, a worm about this size sprang out from under it and struck at her and *almost* hit her in the eye. *or* When she lifted the board, a worm about this size sprang out and struck and *could have* hit her in the eye (but missed).

(46) *heen xobo ta mapo-**quehan**-ipishqui*
my house DECL burn-POT-PAST^EVID
My house *almost* caught fire. *or* My house *could have* caught fire.

The suffix -*quehan* may be in the verb of either a subordinate clause, e.g., (47), or the main clause, e.g., (48) and (49). The modal is the real mode declarative *ta* or its substitute -*quin/i* in embedded sentences.

(47) *jonoyabi paque-**quehan**-ax rahte rahtescai, coca*
peccary^with fall-pot-ss startle startled uncle
My uncle got startled when he almost fell with the peccary.

(48) *hea paranxon hea caaro rehtema-**quehan**-ai*
me deceive^ss me firewood kill^cause-POT-TNS
By deceiving me he *almost* killed me with the firewood (i.e., by dumping the load of firewood on me).

(49) *jahuerohajaquin ta mia bihyamacanaxqui. mia*
fortunately DECL you grab^NEG^they you

 *bichibosca tah min janobi-**quehan**-ai*
 grabbed^by^PL DECL you remain-POT-TNS
Fortunately they didn't receive you. Had they received you, you *would have* had to remain there.

The verb suffix -*han* signals unrealized, incomplete aspect. No evidential suffixes occur with it. It occurs in a sentence that contains a hypothetical modal and is used to make suppositional statements as in (50). The background of (50) is that a young Capanahua boy and his father are walking along the street of the provincial capital and pass a jail. The boy asks what kind of building it is, and the father replies that it is a jail. When asked what a jail is, the father explains a jail's function by describing a suppositional event.

'If' in Capanahua   215

(50) *nesca tah   qui,   jise.   mia **cah**   min nonti yometsot-**an**.*
     thus   DECL   EVID   look   you DECL   you canoe steal-POT

        jaatian, porisia jahui
        then   police   come
It's like this, see. *Suppose* you steal a canoe. Then the police come.

-*han* is also used to express wishful thinking and speculation as in (51) and (52).

(51) *jahuen quencha jan jispaquehabi   qui jaaribi   qui*
     his   plate   he looked^but   REP that^also REP

        bochohi,   jaa   pichan   jahuen yoha
        became^full the^same cooked^yucca his   yucca

        *mahuahah.   jaa **ca**   hompa nomi-**han***
        cooked^soft he DECL beer   drink-POT
He looked down at his plate and saw that it had refilled itself with the same cooked yucca. He was hoping to drink beer (i.e., he *would* have preferred beer).

(52) *jaa joi   nincayamahibo cahhen jenenencanya ca-han*
     that message   hear^NEG^PL   DECL   water^in   go-POT
Those that do not obey the message *would* of course drown in the water.

The HYPOTHETICAL MODE itself is indicated by one of the suppositional modals such as *ca*. In this mode the speaker indicates that he offers the sentence as a supposition; it needs no evidencial suffix to support its credibility. In some cases the hypothetical mode is used to indicate that the speaker supposes that the listener already knows the information; in other cases he offers the information as an aside or as fill-in to complete, semi-redundantly, a notion already made.

(53) *nihnibahinai.   jaaban **can**   jaton jahuequi*
     went^walked^all^day they   suppose their   things

        *hahbehini-**han***
        bring^up-POT
We walked all day. *Of course*, later they *would* be bringing their things by themselves.

216   Eugene E. Loos

(54) *jaabo yohuanquihnyamanoxon cah   man nea mai potabahini*
      them speak^with^NEG^in^order DECL you this land leave

      ca-han
      go-POT
      In order to avoid speaking with them you *of course would* have to
      leave this land completely.

(55) *jahueranon   ra   can mia ca-han   xomanquenen mia*
      where   perhaps DECL you go-POT   spirit   you

      xehanon
      swallow^that
      Where *would* you go by yourself so that the spirit would swallow you
      up?

At this point the reader will already have anticipated that Capanahua
constructions used to express potential and hypothetical STATEMENTS can
readily be adapted to express hypothetical CONDITIONAL STATEMENTS simply
by the inclusion of switch-reference marked subordinate clauses. As before,
the subordinate clause becomes the protasis, and the main clause becomes
the apodosis. It is frequently but not necessarily the case that the hypothetical event is formulated on a negated version of the real event. Examples (56)
and (58) have positive statements in both protasis and apodosis; (57) has a
negated protasis.

In (56) a man has accidentally gone to the land of the dead without dy-
ing. He is not welcomed by the defunct citizens, rather is avoided by them.
Finally, he comes to the house of his deceased sister, and she explains why
he was not welcomed. It is the requirement in that land that its citizens be
dead before arriving.

(56) *min yamaquihrani jahui-ya ta   mia nomimacan-quehan-i-qui*
      you dying^first   come-DS   DECL you drink^cause^they-POT-TNS-EVID
      If you had died before coming, they *would* have given you beer to
      drink.

Two female spirits come upon two boys fishing. One spirit is offered a
fish which she eats immediately. Her manner of eating it causes the boys to
flee, whereupon the first spirit says to the fish eater:

'If' in Capanahua 217

(57) *non tah non jato   texte-**quehan**-ai, mian min piyamahi-**ya***
      we   DECL we   them behead-POT-TNS you   you eatˆNEGˆTNS-DS
      We *would* have been able to behead them if you hadn't gone ahead
      and eaten.

It is the plan of these spirits that if they are patient and engage the young
men amiably, they will have them for dinner. The listener of the story recognizes the logic: the apodosis contains the predictable result of the negation
of the protasis.

In (58), an elderly midwife helps a woman deliver a baby girl; the midwife exclaims how lovely the baby is by hypothetically engaging herself to
the baby had it been a boy.

(58) *heen bene   hihqui-**ya** heanbi   bih-**quehan**-ai*
      my   husband be-DS   Iˆmyself grab-POT-TNS
      If she had turned out to be related as (eligible) husband for me, I
      would have married her myself.

The purely contrary-to-fact, hypothetical statements in the preceding examples of conditional statements show how a language that has no 'if' morpheme can express hypothetical conditional statements: the protasis must
have a hypothetical mode and a tense that precedes that of the apodosis;
pragmatic processing that enables the listener to discern the temporal,
causative, logical, or psychological progression from protasis to apodosis
does the rest.

A Noncategorical Approach to Coherence Relations: Switch-Reference Constructions in Mbyá Guaraní

Robert A. Dooley

Mbyá Guaraní, a South American Indian language of the Tupí-Guaraní family,[1] is a switch-reference language; a common way to attach subordinate clauses having an adverbial role is by means of switch-reference markers. Such markers, occurring enclitic to an adverbial clause, indicate whether or not that clause has the same or different subject as its matrix clause ($\beta\dotplus$ 'same subject' or $ram\tilde{o} \sim r\tilde{a}$ 'different subject').[2] There do exist conjunctions with specific semantic content such as 'after' and 'in order to', but

---

[1] The Mbyá dialect of Guaraní belongs to the Tupí-Guaraní family of the Tupí stock (Rodrigues 1984/85). In Brazil, it is spoken by 2,250 to 3,500 people in the states of Rio Grande do Sul, Santa Catarina, Paraná, São Paulo, Rio de Janeiro, and Espírito Santo; it is also spoken by indigenous groups in Paraguay and Argentina. Other dialects of Guaraní, including Paraguayan Guaraní (Avañeém) are spoken in Argentina, Bolivia, and Paraguay, as well as in other parts of Brazil. The present study is based on fieldwork carried out since 1975 at or near the Posto Indígena Rio das Cobras, Paraná, under the auspices of the Summer Institute of Linguistics and with the cooperation of the Fundação Nacional do Índio.

[2] Phonemic transcription is used in this article. Mbyá has six vowels: i, $\dotplus$, u, ε, a, o ($\sim$ $[\mathfrak{o}]$). It has fourteen consonants: p, t, k, k^w, $\mathfrak{f}$, $\jmath\!\!\!\!\!\!\!\!\!\!\!\!\!/$ ($[d\mathfrak{z}]$ preceding oral vowels), m ($[{}^mb]$ preceding oral vowels), n ($[{}^nd]$ preceding oral vowels), η ($[{}^ng]$ preceding oral vowels), η^w ($[{}^ng^w]$ $\sim$ $[g^w]$ preceding oral vowels), r, $t\mathfrak{f}$ ($\sim$ $[ts]$), h, β ($\sim$ $[w]$ $\sim$ $[v]$). Nasalization occurs regressively throughout (roughly) a word whose final syllable is nasal, and is also regressive from any of the consonants m, n, η. Syllables are V or CV. Roots which are lexical items have a single syllable which can accept primary stress; for most, this is the final syllable. Within the stress group (generally corresponding to a clause constituent), primary stress falls on the last syllable that can accept it, with secondary stress on alternate syllables counting back from the primary stress.

220   Robert A. Dooley

these are mutually exclusive with switch-reference markers, and occur only
about thirty-five percent as often.

'After' and 'in order to' are examples of coherence relations. A
COHERENCE RELATION is a meaning relation that is perceived as holding
between two (or more) propositions in text interpretation.[3] These propositions may derive from clauses in a switch-reference construction or, more
generally, from any type of clause combining; they might also arise as sum-
maries of larger segments of text. In this article, we will speak of
(COHERENCE) RELATIONS BETWEEN CLAUSES as a brief way of referring to
coherence relations between the propositions represented by those clauses.

"Functionally, switch reference is a device for referential tracking"
(Haiman and Munro 1983b:ix), not for signalling coherence relations. Therefore, when switch-reference markers are used in Mbyá (and this happens in
twenty percent of all clauses), coherence relations between the two clauses
must be interpreted on the basis of something besides the conjunction.

This brings up the question: In switch-reference constructions (or more
generally, when clauses are combined without semantically specific conjunctions), in what sense are coherence relations present? In this article, it is
assumed that by combining clauses syntactically, the speaker is conveying
his intention that the interpreter recognize the existence of something like a
coherence relation between them. It is not assumed, however, that the
speaker always intends to communicate a specific relation by means of such
a construction; the possibility is left open that his communicative intentions
may be less than specific. Nevertheless, even when there are no indications
that the speaker has a specific relation in view, the interpreter will have
available certain clues which constrain (limit, narrow down) his interpretation. In some cases, linguistic constraints—morphemic or syntactic—are
present. Extralinguistic constraints, especially deriving from the textual and
cultural context, are assumed to be operative in all cases.

Thus, instead of asking the question, "Which coherence relation is the
speaker intending to communicate in a given construction?" this article asks,
"On what evidence, if any, should we suppose that the hearer's interpretation is being constrained?" An approach reflected by the first question assumes discrete categories of coherence relations, hence is said to be
CATEGORICAL; an approach reflected by the second is referred to as
NONCATEGORICAL, since it makes no such assumption. Interpretations of

---

[3] The term "coherence relation", originating with Hobbs 1979 (and used in Blakemore
1987, 1988, Blass 1986, and Sanders, Spooren, and Noordman 1990), corresponds to
"relations" in Thompson and Mann 1987 and Mann and Thompson 1988, as well as in Longacre 1983; to "rhetorical predicates" in Grimes 1976; and to "rhetorical relations" in Grosz
and Sidner 1986.

coherence relations can also be spoken of as categorical (specific) or non-categorical (nonspecific, general). Noncategorical interpretations, this article argues, are a natural and predictable result of text processing under typical conditions.[4] Categorical interpretations, however, are not uncommon either.

This article, then, is an investigation, beginning with a noncategorical perspective, of common constraints on the interpretation of coherence relations for switch-reference constructions in Mbyá Guaraní.[5] The exposition is organized as follows. Section 1 briefly discusses the theoretical basis for a noncategorical approach to coherence relations, based in particular on RELEVANCE THEORY (RT), and compares this with a categorical approach as represented by RHETORICAL STRUCTURE THEORY (RST). Section 2 examines extralinguistic constraints on interpreting coherence relations, §3 examines morphemic constraints, and §4 syntactic constraints.

1. Categorical and noncategorical approaches to coherence relations

The approach taken in this article illustrates a major difference between two approaches to discourse interpretation: Rhetorical structure theory (Thompson and Mann 1987, Mann and Thompson 1988) and relevance theory (Sperber and Wilson 1986, Blakemore 1987).

1.1 Rhetorical structure theory as a categorical approach

Rhetorical structure theory deals with cases where, between two given parts of a text, the operative coherence relation can be identified categorically as being of one type rather than another. This condition is a prerequisite for an RST analysis. By means of such categorical judgments, a fairly small list of relations (CIRCUMSTANCE, JUSTIFY, ANTITHESIS and twenty others in Mann and Thompson 1988) has been defined and is reported to be adequate for many texts, as judged by multiple interpreters.[6]

---

[4] Proponents of relevance theory (Blakemore 1987, 1988, Blass 1986) have generally argued for that theory by showing its superiority in text situations where coherence relations (and cohesion relations) do not hold. The present study deals precisely with situations where coherence relations can be assumed to exist, but comes to a similar conclusion.

[5] The grammar of Mbyá switch reference is described in Dooley 1989.

[6] The RST listing of coherence relations is not closed in principle; "We see it as an open set, susceptible to extension and modification for the purposes of particular genres and cultural styles" (Mann and Thompson 1988:250). In a similar categorical treatment (Sanders, Spooren, and Noordman 1990), however, there is an apparently closed system of classification consisting of twelve categories determined by values for four parameters; within this classification, seventeen relations are listed.

222   Robert A. Dooley

When experienced interpreters fail to agree in a certain place, RST speaks of "multiple analyses": each interpreter is assumed to have a categorical relation in mind, but the interpretations fail to agree (Mann and Thompson 1988:265). It is certainly an impressive result that "virtually every text [of various types of written monologue] has an RST analysis" according to consensus interpretation (pp. 244, 259). However, it is also true that "certain text types characteristically do not have RST analyses" (p. 259). This fact suggests that the assumption of categoricality cannot be taken to underlie a theory of coherence relations that aims at maximum generality.

Before proceeding to a more general approach, it should be made clear that in RST, there is no claim that the categoriality of relations is dependent on their being linguistically coded: "recognition of the relation always rests on functional and semantic judgments alone" (p. 249f.). I take this to mean that even when there is apparent linguistic coding of a relation, other, extra-linguistic factors must serve as the final arbiters in its identification. Notice that this is the case for the preceding sentence: the expression 'even when' cannot simply be taken to code a temporal relation, since it could be para-phrased by nontemporal, concessive expressions like 'even under the condition that/even in the case that'. RST does not assume that relations are linguistically coded, but it does assume that they have a categorial interpretation.

1.2 Relevance theory as a noncategorical approach

Relevance theory (Sperber and Wilson 1986) is more general in the sense that it offers an explanation of how there can be an effective discourse connection even without a specific, categorical relation. The basic idea underlying the theory is that "in processing information, people generally aim to bring about the greatest improvement to their overall representation of the world for the least cost in processing" (Blakemore 1988:238). Sometimes this involves one striking improvement (an addition, correction, etc.) of one's representation of the world, a modification carrying a high degree of certainty; but it may instead involve several small improvements, with lower degrees of certainty, dealing with a loose cluster of related ideas. Sperber and Wilson (1986:59f.) call a result of this latter type WEAK COMMUNICA-TION: "We might think of communication...as a matter of degree. When the communicator's informative intention involves making a particular assumption strongly manifest, then that assumption is strongly communicated. When the communicator's intention is to marginally increase the manifestness of a wide range of assumptions, then each of them is weakly communicated." Note that whereas RST begins with the assumption of categoriality, relevance theory begins with scalarity: "communication...as a matter of degree."

Switch-Reference Constructions in Mbyá Guaraní 223

The first example of weak communication given by Sperber and Wilson is nonverbal communication:

> Mary and Peter are newly arrived at the seaside. She opens the window overlooking the sea and sniffs appreciatively and ostensively. When Peter follows suit, there is no one good thing that comes to his attention: the air smells fresh, fresher than it did in town, it reminds him of their previous holidays, he can smell the sea, seaweed, ozone, fish; all sorts of pleasant things come to mind, and while, because her sniff was appreciative, he is reasonably safe in assuming that she must have intended him to notice at least some of them, he is unlikely to be able to pin her intentions down any further. Is there any reason to assume that her intentions were more specific? (1986:55)

The varied and open-ended list of possible "meanings" of Mary's ostensive sniff illustrates "the communicator's intention...to marginally increase the manifestness of a wide range of assumptions" or ideas, rather than to make one specific idea "strongly manifest." There is apparently no requirement to seek a more specific interpretation. This is the essence of weak communication.

Sperber and Wilson's next example is verbal:

(1)   Peter: What do you intend to do today?
           Mary: I have a terrible headache. (p. 56)

With regard to (1), the authors ask, "What does Mary implicate? That she will not do anything? That she will do as little as possible? That she will do as much as she can? That she does not yet know what she will do?" These are all stated as categorical possibilities, but since none of them is actually indicated by Mary, her utterance, though specific in one sense, is quite vague as an answer to Peter's question. She is communicating weakly, and Peter may not be intended to interpret her utterance, as an answer, in any specific sense. For this particular exchange, there may be no need to.

Weak communication can apply to coherence relations as well. Consider the Mbyá switch-reference construction in (2) where the marking clause—the one containing the enclitic switch-reference marker—is enclosed in brackets. In the context, an Indian had gone hunting and killed some coatis. On his way home he stopped to drink at a river and laid them down.

224   Robert A. Dooley

(2)   *[o-+-ʔu-pa   βɨ   ɲɛ]   o-upi   ɲɛβɨ   tʃĩʔɨ   haʔɛ   o-o*
      3-water-eat-all SS   HSY   3-raise again   coati   and   3-go[7]
      After he had finished drinking, he picked up the coatis again and left.
      (9.13)[8]

At issue in (2) is the coherence relation translated 'after', but which in the Mbyá data corresponds to the switch-reference conjunction *βɨ* (same subject). Certainly it would be reasonable to suppose that a temporal relation (SEQUENCE) is in some sense there. But also a logical relation, such as ENABLEMENT (he would need to pick up the coatis again in order to go, since he was taking them home) or VOLITIONAL CAUSE (he picked up the coatis and left because he had finished drinking) could be considered to be there as well (these last two relations are taken from Mann and Thompson 1988). Should we consider that these different meaning components are included in a categorical interpretation of the coherence relation?

At this juncture, an RT-type question seems relevant: Is there any reason to believe that the narrator's communicative intentions are specific, so that the hearer would need to interpret the coherence relation categorically? If not, then what we find in (2)—a loose cluster of possible interpretations, some more probable than others—is a typical example of weak communication. We do not question that something like a coherence relation is there, since that is assumed to be the reason behind the switch-reference construction in the first place. What we question is whether there is any reason to suppose that a specific and categorical relation is there. Examples like (2) show why the notion of weak communication is an attractive alternative to categorical approaches.[9]

---

[7] Abbreviations: ABL, ablative; ANA, anaphoric expression; BDY, constituent boundary marker; CAUS, causative marker; COLL, collection; COM, comitative; COND, condition; DIM, diminutive; DS, different subject; EP, epenthetic segment; FUT, future; GER, gerund; HSY, hearsay particle; INSTR, instrument: 'by means only one'; NEG, negative; NR, nominalizer; PAST, past tense; PL, plural; PURP, purpose; REFL, reflexive; REL, relativizer (marker of relative clause); RESP, indicator of response; SG, singular; SS, same subject; TR, transitivizer; 1s, first-person singular; 1Sˆ2O, first-person subject and second-person object; 1+2, first person plus second person, (first person inclusive); 1+3, first-person plural exclusive of second person; 2, second person; 2s, second-person singular; 2p, second-person plural; 3, third person.

[8] Many examples in this article bear an index of the form mm.nn, where mm refers to text number and nn to line number in a version available as part of Arquivo Lingüístico. These texts, along with others in Mbyá, may be ordered from: Summer Institute of Linguistics, SAI/No, Lote D, Bloco 3, 70770 Brasília, DF, Brazil.

[9] Besides RT, there are other approaches to coherence relations that are at least potentially less categorical than, say, RST. The artificial intelligence approach of Grosz and Sidner 1986 produces a hierarchical analysis of discourse that is similar to RST, but on the basis of "discourse purposes" which have a much higher level of generality than coherence relations: "a claim of the theory...is that a discourse can be understood at a basic level even if the

Switch-Reference Constructions in Mbyá Guaraní

How commonly does weak communication occur? Sperber and Wilson (1986:60) state: "Often, in human interaction, weak communication is found sufficient or even preferable to the stronger forms." Blakemore (1987:133) concurs: "Speakers do not always have specific expectations as to the way their utterances will be interpreted. In many cases the hearer is free to recover any of a range of contextual effects." This article, therefore, does not claim that Mbyá is different in kind from other languages with respect to noncategoricality; it simply uses Mbyá as an illustration of this phenomenon. It takes as its starting point the high incidence of switch-reference constructions, which raise the issue of noncategoriality and weak communication in a forcible way.

1.3 Factors affecting categoriality

The approach to coherence relations taken in this article is noncategorical in the sense that we do not assume that the speaker intends, for each case of clause combining, to communicate a relation categorically. But we are also prepared to recognize categorical interpretations when evidence for them is available, evidence which, for example, could be linguistic, cultural, inferential, or experimental. In this way, a theory of categorically interpreted coherence relations might be considered to be embedded as a subtheory within a more general, noncategorical theory. One of the tasks of the general theory would be to specify when the subtheory would be invoked, that is, when categorical interpretations arise. Or rather, since it would not do to state the difference between categorical and noncategorical interpretations in categorical terms, the general theory would need to specify factors or conditions which affect the degree of categoriality.

It seems intuitively clear that factors of different kinds would be involved. Certain kinds of factors would be highly context-specific, as will come out in the discussion in §§2, 3, and 4. Others would be of a more general nature, having to do, for example, with type of text and conditions under which interpretation is done; some factors of this latter type are mentioned here. Although these suggestions are both partial and tentative, particularly in the absence of relevant experimental data, they should all be immediately recognizable from personal experience.

[hearer or reader] never does or can construct, let alone name, such rhetorical relationships" (p. 202). The psycholinguistic approach of Sanders, Spooren, and Noordman 1990 presents a taxonomy of categorical relations on the basis of four primitive binary parameters ("cognitive primitives"); these could possibly be exploited to define relations—or rather, "natural classes of coherence relations"—at higher levels of generality. Both of these approaches, however, are intrinsically categorical in their own way.

226 Robert A. Dooley

Certain genres of text would be expected to give rise to different indices of categoriality. Scientific treatises and legal opinions, for example, could well have a higher overall index of categoriality than a folk tale. Degree of planning could also be expected to correlate in a positive way with categoriality. We note that the major effort in RST has centered on nonnarrative texts which are highly planned and tightly argued.

Another relevant parameter of text type is the medium of communication. Written communication gives the interpreter an open-ended time frame in which to examine points of interpretation, and even the opportunity to go back over them a second or third time from the vantage point of a later understanding of the text. Interpretation of a spoken text must be largely done linearly and in real time, hence almost instantaneously.

In regard to conditions under which text processing is done, it would be predictable, for example, that the index of categoriality will be higher when the interpreter is at each point being asked (or is asking himself) "Which relation is meant here?" An experimental procedure such as this is used in theories like RST,[10] and a field linguist focusing on coherence relations would be likely to have the same question in mind. The present study could certainly be expected to show certain effects of this mindset. When, on the other hand, analytical results are not the primary goal of text processing, but are subordinated to some other goal such as enjoyment or human interest, a lower index of categoriality would be expected.

Conditions of text processing also include attention level of the interpreter. A low level of attention means that a small amount of the potential processing resources are being allocated to the task at hand. According to RT, an interpreter is always assessing likely communicative payoffs against processing costs: "The key problem for efficient short-term information processing is thus to achieve an optimal allocation of central processing resources. Resources have to be allocated to the processing of information which is likely to bring about the greatest contribution to the mind's general cognitive goals at the smallest processing cost" (Sperber and Wilson 1986:48). On the other hand, an interpreter who for some reason is not concerned with high communicative payoff on a particular occasion will not be likely to make a heavy allocation of processing resources. This could result in a low index of categoriality in interpreting coherence relations. From a slightly different viewpoint, we could say that an interpreter who is devoting a high degree of attention to, say, the interpersonal aspects of a communicative situation may devote correspondingly less to the analytical, content-oriented aspects.

---

[10] Mann and Thompson (1988) include SEQUENCE, but not SIMULTANEITY, among their coherence relations.

Switch-Reference Constructions in Mbyá Guaraní

As has already been suggested, when a text analyst is concentrating on coherence relations in RST-type experiments or a field investigation, most or all of the above conditions which make for a high index of categoriality are likely to hold. Such conditions of interpretation are arguably different in degree, if not in kind, from those of a more typical hearer. This does not mean that an approach like RST has no value; especially when the judgments of multiple interpreters are found to converge, that is a significant result. But when an atypically high index of categoriality occurs, that fact should be recognized in both theory and applications.

2. Extralinguistic constraints

In this article it is assumed that, while there may or may not be linguistic constraints on an interpretation, there will always be extralinguistic constraints. This assumption derives from the very nature of text interpretation.

2.1 Internal and external contextualization

The interpreter of a text is engaged in an ongoing effort "to construct an image, or maybe a set of alternate images. The image that the interpreter creates early in the text guides his interpretation of successive portions of the text, and these in turn induce him to enrich or modify that image. While this image-construction and image-revision is going on, the interpreter is also trying to figure out what the creator of the text is doing—what the nature of the communication situation is. And that, too, may have an influence on the image-creating process" (Fillmore 1974:IV–5). "The nature of the communication situation", includes (among other things) possible goals it might have, such as informing, entertaining, solidifying interpersonal relationships, etc., which generally occur in some combination. In another article, Fillmore (1981:149) calls the process of image construction/revision INTERNAL CONTEXTUALIZATION, and that of figuring out why the text is being given as EXTERNAL CONTEXTUALIZATION. As the interpreter processes sentence n, for example, he will have on hand provisional contextualizations through level $n-1$ as at least initial constraints on his interpretation.[11]

The way the interpreter goes about internal contextualization may depend in part on what he perceives the external contextualization to be. For example, in a joke beginning "There was this guy who...," it would not be particularly

---

[11] For the internal contextualization of a text-initial sentence, the interpreter may have no extralinguistic constraints available; however, the speech situation will generally furnish him with clues for external contextualization.

appropriate for the interpreter to try to pin down the reference. A similar observation can be made for coherence relations: when the goals of the communicative situation are not perceived as involving a heavy element of analysis—or put another way, when a specific coherence relation is not seen as crucial for the purposes which the interpreter is pursuing at that point— then it may not be necessary to fine-tune the interpretation (see also §1.3). In a similar way, the interpreter may be satisfied with a noncategorical interpretation if a particular coherence relation is not focal or crucial to an internal contextualization (done at a level that satisfies the interpreter). That is, noncategorical interpretation of a given coherence relation is a priori more likely if a specific interpretation is not in focus for the purposes of either external or internal contextualization.

Since internal and external contextualizations are mental constructs or representations rather than the simple output of a decoding process, they are treated here as extralinguistic constraints on text interpretation.

2.2 Expectation structures

In arriving at contextualizations, the interpreter will make repeated attempts to apply "off-the-shelf" expectation structures, rather than to construct representations "from scratch." Expectation structures, often referred to as frames, scripts, schemata, and scenarios, come from the interpreter's experience and often from the collective experience (culture) of the society of which he is part (see Brown and Yule 1983 for a clear overview). Commonly, they are representations of stereotypical events and situations. For example, an expectation structure in western society would be 'at the supermarket': in this, we hardly need to be told that there are check-out registers and stockers placing goods in orderly displays on shelves so that customers can easily pick out what they want. Interpreters commonly make heavy use of expectation structures in both internal and external contextualization. In particular, such structures provide strong extralinguistic constraints on interpreting coherence relations.

This is not to say that expectation structures actually provide categorical interpretations of coherence relations in all cases. On the one hand, expectation structures can function as a repository of coherence relations that can be looked up or brought to consciousness as needed, but as long as a narrative, say, is clearly following a certain expectation structure, there may be little motivation to look up each coherence relation. That is, the fact that a certain expectation structure is activated could well mean that the interpreter of a text feels little need himself to calculate the coherence relations; he can take it on faith that they are there in the expectation structure. On the other hand, expectation structures sometimes mask the absence of categorical coherence

Switch-Reference Constructions in Mbyá Guaraní   229

relations. Many language groups have myths which at certain points are illogical, even to the members of the group: "We don't know why it was done like that," they say, "it just was." When such a myth is told, the fact that it is familiar to the hearers means that they have a complete expectation structure available for it, but instead of that expectation structure containing a complete set of categorical coherence relations, it may lack some at certain points.

2.3 Examples from Mbyá texts

In this section we will briefly examine some examples of switch-reference constructions from Mbyá texts which contain few if any linguistic clues of specific coherence relations. Although we cannot go into the mind of the typical interpreter to see what contextualizations he has constructed up to a certain point, we can note common expectation structures from Mbyá culture. Since we are not assuming that the speaker intends to communicate a categorical coherence relation in each case, we are free to stop short of such, depending on how far the evidence takes us.

As the first example, we return to (2), which has the free translation 'after he had finished drinking, he picked up the coatis again and left'. The nature of the coherence relation here is greatly clarified when we consider a familiar expectation structure among the Mbyá. When one is hot and thirsty from carrying a load through the woods and comes upon a stream, one can be expected to lay down the load in order to drink. That is the basic coherence relation involved in the expectation structure. One picks up the load again when one is finished drinking, simply because the need for laying it down no longer exists. That is, the expectation structure provides a coherence relation between the two propositions in question, but since the relation it provides is nonfocal as well as being complex (involving a previous action and a previous coherence relation), the interpreter would presumably have little motivation to look it up, much less come up with one himself. This means that even though an expectation structure is activated, this particular coherence relation may not be interpreted categorically.

A further example, one with a more culture-specific clue, is provided by (3). In the context, the narrator has been talking about how it would be much better if the Mbyá would be generous with the crops that they harvest and share freely rather than selling to one another.

(3) *[ɲanɛ-poriau-kʷɛ-ʔi   ɲanɛ-kʷai   ßaʔɛ   ßɨ]   na-ɲa-ßɛnɛ-i*
     1+2-poor-COLL-DIM 1+2-beˆPL REL   SS   NEG-1+2-sell-NEG

230   Robert A. Dooley

ßaʔɛ-rã-gʷɛ
REL-FUT-PAST
Since we are poor, we shouldn't sell things to one another. (73.18)

In (3) the coherence relation, which in the free translation appears as 'since' (VOLITIONAL CAUSE in Mann and Thompson 1988), may not be obvious to one outside the culture. There are few if any purely linguistic clues here. From a western cultural point of view, it might make sense to interpret the coherence relation as 'although' (Mann and Thompson's CONCESSION), since selling would provide cash to alleviate the poverty. However, the Mbyá (and Guaraní in general) world view contains the following elements: (a) the Guaraní are meant to be poor, it is part of the destiny they are born with; (b) the way that Guaraní are intended to get by is by sharing with one another. Given these two elements and the expectation structure (the culture) in which they are found, it is clear that VOLITIONAL CAUSE is a fair interpretation; it may well be interpreted categorically here, since the coherence relation is more focal than in (2). The point of this example, then, is not to illustrate a noncategorical interpretation, but to illustrate how expectation structures can provide crucial extralinguistic constraints on coherence relations.

A final example in this section illustrates how expectation structures can be present alongside linguistic clues, not just to reinforce them, but to furnish a twist in the interpretation of coherence relations that would not otherwise have been the case. In the context of this example, the narrator and his nephew had happened on a rattlesnake in a canebrake. They tried to kill it with a stick, but because of the thick stand of cane they could not.

(4) [*arɛ*   *rã*   *oro-mo-potʃɨ*   *ta*   *mã*   *ramõ*
        long^time   DS   1+3-CAUS-violently^angry   about^to   already   DS

       mã-aɛ   *mã]*   *moka*   *pɨ*   *a-ɲuka*
       already-exactly   BDY   rifle   INSTR   1s-kill
       After some time, only when we were about to get him angry, I killed
       him with my rifle. (71.6)

As will be further explained in §3.1, the morphemic structure of (4) provides strong clues for the temporal relation 'only when', i.e., not before that particular time. But an additional constraint comes in extralinguistically, via a culture-based expectation structure, which explains why it is relevant to be so specific about the time frame. A rifle is for killing large game, and killing a snake with one is considered a waste of ammunition. The narrator here is making an excuse for having used his rifle; his next sentence is, 'If I hadn't done that, I wouldn't have been able to kill him at all.' Thus, in (4) we have a

Switch-Reference Constructions in Mbyá Guaraní 231

coherence relation—perhaps a categorical one—which is temporal in regard to its internal contextualization, but whose external contextualization has a strong interpersonal element (an excuse for the benefit of the hearers), one which is only comprehensible in the light of a culture-based expectation structure.

3. Morphemic constraints

Morphemic constraints on the interpretation of coherence relations may include lexical or grammatical morphemes. These constraints come perhaps the closest of any to functioning by simple coding and decoding, but, as will be seen, this takes place only rarely. Hence, we may speak of linguistic clues, although without the connotation that a specific "correct" interpretation is in view. We will consider first morphemic clues of temporal relations, then of logical relations. The question as to whether a given relation is interpreted categorically is not always in focus in this section.

3.1 Morphemic clues of temporal relations

Certain particles and other adverbial elements whose meaning includes some temporal component, when present in the **marking clause** (the clause containing the enclitic switch-reference marker), indicate that the coherence relation probably has some temporal dimension.[12] That is, the presence of a morpheme with a temporal component of meaning in the marking clause typically suggests a temporal component in the coherence relation as well.

These temporal morphemes include the postverbal aspect markers *mã* 'already' and *ʔɛβɨ* 'again'.

(5)   *[pɛtɨ   o-mo-ʔi-pa   mã   βɨ   mã   ɲɛ] o-mo-nɨẽ*
         tobacco 3-CAUS-DIM-all already SS   BDY HSY 3-CAUS-full

        o-pɛtɨ-gʷa
        3ˆREFL-tobacco-NR
        After finishing cutting the tobacco into pieces, he filled his pipe. (26.13)

In (5), the coherence relation translated 'after' has plausible logical as well as temporal components; it could also have been translated 'since'. However, a temporal component of the coherence relation is suggested by

---

[12] Sanders, Spooren, and Noordman (1990) argue against including temporal relations among coherence relations; I do not find their argument convincing. As noted earlier, Mann and Thompson (1988) include SEQUENCE but not SIMULTANEITY.

232   Robert A. Dooley

mã 'already'. This is reinforced by the occurrence of the suffix *-pa* 'all, completely', which along with *mã* forms an idiomatic expression translated 'finishing'. The temporal aspect might be brought out in a (macro)expectation structure: After finishing one task, another is begun. A more specific expectation structure, having to do with preparing to smoke a pipe, suggests logical as well as temporal components of the coherence relation: one normally cuts all the tobacco that he intends to smoke before putting any of it into his pipe.

The coherence relation in (6) also has logical and temporal components.

(6) *[okẽ r-ɛ o-mota ɲeßɨ rã] o-ɲɛ-pe?a okẽ*
   door EP-ABL 3-hit again DS 3-REFL-open door
   When he knocked on the door again, it opened. (88.36)

The logical aspect of the coherence relation could be translated 'because', alongside the temporal one translated 'when'. The point here is that the occurrence of *ɲeßɨ* 'again' appears to contribute to the temporal aspect of the coherence relation. The relation in (6) is, like (5), a simple but noncategorical one.

This is also the case for (7), a commonplace construction.

(7) *[ka?aru mã ramõ mã ɲɛ] o-u ɲeßɨ mã ka?agʷɨ*
   late already DS   BDY HSY 3-come again already woods

   gʷi ŋ-oo   katɨ
   from 3ˆREFL-house toward
   When it was late, he came again from the woods to go home. (9.6)

One categorical temporal relation, combining SUCCESSION and IMMEDIACY, can be coded using the enclitic *-ße* 'more, same' following the switch-reference marker. The translation is typically 'as soon as', as in (8).

(8) *[oro-ßaẽ ɨpɨ   ßɨ-ße] pɨaßɨ-ße i-kãgʷɛ*
   1+3-arrive beginning ss-more atˆnight-more 3-bone

   mi-mo-ĩ-?i   oro-?u
   NR-CAUS-beˆlocated-DIM 1+3-eat
   As soon as we arrive, even at night, we eat a cooked [cow's or pig's] head. (75.13)

In (8), the same enclitic *-ße* occurs with *pɨaßɨ* 'at night' to give a slightly different meaning: 'even at night, on the same night'. It is also used in locatives:

Switch-Reference Constructions in Mbyá Guaraní   233

haʔɛ pɨ-ßɛ 'in the same place' (cf. (10) and (21)). Only when *-ßɛ* occurs enclitic to a switch-reference marker does the construction have a consistently temporal meaning.

There is another expression which, following the switch-reference marker, can give the coherence relation the temporal meaning 'only when'. This is the sandhi form *mã-aɛ [mã'ɛ̃]* 'already-exactly'.

(9) *[a-pɨrõ   rai-ʔi   mã   ramõ mã-aɛ   mã]   o-ɲa*
     1s-step^on   almost-DIM   already DS   already-exactly BDY   3-run

     o-ßɨ   ɲai   r-ɛ
     3^go-GER   underbrush   EP-ABL
     It was only when I almost stepped on [the snake] that it went off into the brush. (67.3)

A coherence relation with *mã-aɛ* typically includes a logical as well as temporal component; in (9), for example, 'only because' would be a plausible translation as well. This is also the case in (4). When *aɛ* 'exactly' occurs following the switch-reference marker without *mã* 'already', the chances of a strong logical relation are increased, as will be seen in §3.2.

When the coherence relation in a switch-reference construction takes on a temporal component because of morphemic elements such as the above, this component is typically SEQUENCE, with the action or situation of the marking clause preceding that of the matrix clause. The only exceptions found thus far are cases, such as (7), where the action or state of the marking clause both precedes and overlaps the action of the matrix clause.

3.2 Morphemic clues of logical relations

When in a switch-reference construction there are no morphemic clues of a temporal component in the coherence relation, the relation can generally be taken to include some logical component of meaning, without excluding the possibility that a temporal component may be present as well. This was seen to be the case in the discussion of (2). But it is also possible to indicate categorical logical relations by means of enclitics. One such is *ri* (condition) in the marking clause.

(10) *[nɛɛ ri   ɛrɛ-ɲuka ramõ] orɛ   oro-ɲuka   ta   apɨ-ßɛ*
      2s   COND   2s-kill   DS   1+3   1s^2o-kill   about^to   here-more
      If it was you that killed [your wife], we are going to kill you right here. (10.80)

234 Robert A. Dooley

In (10), the position of *ri* after the subject *nee* 'you' indicates the locus of conditionality.

Another categorical logical relation is indicated when the enclitic *ɲɛpɛ* 'overcoming' follows the conjunction.

(11) *[ɲa-r-ɛko   r-ɛta   ɛ ʔɨ̃-ʔi   ßɨ ɲɛpɛ]   ɲa-ɲo-tĩ*
    1+2-COM-life EP-many NEG-DIM SS overcoming 1+2-TR-plant

    paßɛ̃-ʔi   ßaʔɛ-rã
    all-DIM   REL-FUT
    Even though we don't have a lot, all of us should plant. (76.6)

In (11), the thought is that even if a person has little seed to spare, he should invest it in planting. *ɲɛpɛ* following the switch-reference marker can be taken as coding the CONCESSIVE relation.

One morphemic signal of logical relations was present in (4) and (9): the adverbial element *aɛ* 'exactly'. Earlier, the combination *mã-aɛ* 'already-exactly' followed a switch-reference marker and signalled 'only when'; that is, *aɛ* 'exactly' was applied to the temporal realm. Here, *aɛ* occurs after a switch-reference marker without *mã* 'already', and the meaning is primarily logical.

(12) *[ɲa-ɲo-tĩ   ßaʔɛ-kʷɛ-ʔi   ɲa-ɛtʃa ßɨ aɛ]   ɲa-ßɨʔa-ʔi*
    1+2-TR-plant REL-PAST-DIM 1+2-see SS exactly 1+2-be^happy-DIM
    We have a little happiness only when we see a little something that we have planted. (76.22)

The coherence relation in (12) is predominantly logical, despite the free translation 'only when'.

In this brief survey of the more common morphemic constraints on coherence relations of switch-reference constructions, we have seen some cases where the morphemic constraint goes so far as to instruct the interpreter to interpret a categorical relation of a certain type. Other morphemic signals do not go that far, but only indicate that a meaning component of some specified type should be included in the interpretation; in this way, the possibility of a less-than-categorial interpretation is left open.

4. Syntactic constraints

All examples of switch-reference constructions presented thus far have shown the marking clause preceding the matrix clause. This is by far the most frequent ordering, occurring in eighty-seven percent of all switch-reference

Switch-Reference Constructions in Mbyá Guaraní 235

constructions. A similar percentage holds for adverbial subordinate clauses in general, of which switch-reference marking clauses are just one type. The decision to prepose or postpose a given subordinate clause is made largely on the basis of the coherence relation (although, as will be seen, discourse-pragmatic factors can change the typical order). Therefore, in the case of switch-reference constructions, the relative order of clauses can provide a clue as to the relation. In particular, since postposing the marking clause is much less common, it provides a stronger, more ostensive clue.

4.1 Preposed marking clauses

When the relation has a strong temporal component, either of SIMULTANEITY, e.g., (13), or SEQUENCE, e.g., (2) repeated as (14), the subordinate clause is typically preposed.

(13)   [SITUATION₁] SIMULTANEOUS SITUATION₂

    [o-u   ßɨ   rimã   ɲε]   parito   ramĩ-gʷa   o-mo-ĩ
    3-come   SS   RESP   HSY   coat   like-NR   3-CAUS-beˆlocated

    o-u-ßɨ
    3-come-GER
    When he came back, he was putting on a kind of coat. (8.32)

(14)   [SITUATION₁] SUBSEQUENT SITUATION₂

    [o-ɨ-ʔu-pa   ßɨ   ɲε]   o-upi   ɲεßɨ   tʃiʔɨ   haʔε   o-o
    3-water-eat-all   SS   HSY   3-raise   again   coati   and   3-go
    After he had finished drinking, he picked up the coatis again and left. (9.13)

The order of the clauses in (14) reflects a natural iconicity: the first event is narrated first. Temporal iconicity underlies much relative ordering of clauses, as well as the ordering of larger sections in narrative and procedural discourse.

Inasmuch as cause normally precedes effect in the real world, the same kind of iconicity shows up when logical components are involved in the coherence relation. In particular, the orderings REASON-RESULT, CONDITION-RESULT, and MEANS-RESULT are commonly observed, with REASON, CONDITION, or MEANS represented by a preposed marking clause.

236   Robert A. Dooley

(15)   [REASON] RESULT

> *[ɛrɛ-nu-tʃɛ   rã]   tʃɛɛ a-momɛʔu ʔrã*
> 2s-hear-want DS 1s 1s-tell   FUT
> Since you want to hear it, I'll tell it. (85.3)

In (15), the marking clause is interpreted as reason, since the other interlocutor had previously said *aɛnutʃɛ* 'I want to hear it'. If the content of this marking clause had not been already realized, (15) would have served as an example of CONDITION-RESULT; this possibility is shown in (16).

(16)   [CONDITION] RESULT

> *[ɛrɛ-nu-tʃɛ   rã]   tʃɛɛ a-momɛʔu ʔrã*
> 2s-hear-want DS 1s 1s-tell   FUT
> If you want to hear it, I'll tell it. (85.3)

MEANS-RESULT is illustrated in (17).

(17)   [MEANS] RESULT

> *[aroi-ʔi   haʔɛ   nuⁿga   ɲa-ɲo-tĩ-ʔi   ßɨ aɛ]   ɲa-ʔu*
> rice-DIM 3^ANA sort 1+2-TR-plant-DIM SS exactly 1+2-eat
> Rice and that sort of thing, it's only as we plant a bit of it that we'll have it to eat. (76.10)

The means clause in (17) could also be freely translated 'it's only by planting...'. The 'only' derives from *aɛ* 'exactly', as discussed in §3.2.

4.2 Postposed marking clauses

In §4.1 we observed iconicity with preposed marking clauses. It can also be observed with postposed subordinate clauses in the MEANS-PURPOSE relation: what is meant to take place later (purpose) is postposed to what is done to bring it about. The subordinate purpose clause very commonly has the content-specific conjunction *agʷã* 'in order to', as in (18).

(18)   MEANS [PURPOSE]

> *ɲa-i-poka   [ɲa-mo-tʃã   agʷã gʷɨrapa]*
> 1+2-3-twist   1+2-CAUS-attached^cord PURP bow
> We twist [palm fibers] to make the bowstring. (68.8)

Switch-Reference Constructions in Mbyá Guaraní   237

However, purpose is not always coded by agʷã. In particular, (a) when the means clause has a verb of motion, (b) when the purpose clause has no change of subject, and (c) when the particular MEANS-PURPOSE sequence is part of a well-known expectation structure, then the conjunction agʷã is often omitted. This is seen in (19).

(19)   MEANS [PURPOSE]

> *a-a   ta   [a-maʔɛ-apo]*
> 1s-go   aboutˆto   1s-thing-make
> I'm going in order to work.

Alternatively, when the above three conditions hold, *agʷã* can be replaced by the same-subject switch-reference marker *βɨ*.

(20)   MEANS [PURPOSE]

> *a-a   ta   [a-maʔɛ-apo   βɨ]*
> 1s-go   aboutˆto   1s-thing-make ss
> I'm going in order to work.

Regardless of the subordinating conjunction or the lack thereof for a purpose clause, its postposing serves iconically to suggest a MEANS-PURPOSE relation, subject of course to extralinguistic constraints (contextualizations).

Another typical type of postposed subordinate clause has (a) the same subject as the matrix clause and (b) a lexical element of mental process.

(21)   RESULT [MENTAL-PROCESS REASON]

> *oka   pɨ-βɛ   ɲu   a-ɲatɨ   [n-a-mo-mo   riβɛ-tʃɛ-i*
> yard   in-more   again 1s-bury   NEG-1s-CAUS-jump merely-want-NEG
>
> *βɨ]*
> ss
> I buried [the snake] right there in the yard [where I had brought it to show it to Robert], since I didn't want to just throw it away. (67.12)

In (21), the enclitic *-tʃe* 'want', or rather its negation, indicates a mental-process type of reason for the content of the matrix clause. MENTAL-PROCESS REASON, like purpose, involves a thought process by which an action is motivated. This may be related to the fact that clauses of these two types are typically postposed. Contrast (21) with (22) (repeated from (15)), which has a preposed reason clause.

238   Robert A. Dooley

(22)   [REASON] RESULT

> *[ɛrɛ-nu-tʃɛ   rã]   tʃɛɛ   a-momɛʔu   ʔrã*
> 2s-hear-want   DS   1s   1s-tell   FUT
> Since you want to hear it, I'll tell it. (85.3)

Although the marking clause in (22) contains the same mental process morpheme *-tʃɛ* 'want' as (21), it is not considered to involve MENTAL-PROCESS REASON. This is because there is a change of subject in (22), so that the mental process does not belong to the subject of the main clause.

4.3 Perception as a coherence relation

One other type of coherence relation is mentioned here, involving the perception of a phenomenon (seeing, hearing, discovering/knowing, etc.). The dominant order is PERCEPTION-PHENOMENON. In (23), the perception clause is subordinated to the phenomenon clause.

(23)   [PERCEPTION] PHENOMENON

> *[haʔɛ   pɨ   o-maʔɛ̃   rã   ɲɛ]   ɨɨ   ramĩ-gʷa   o-ĩ*
> 3ˆANA in   3-look   DS   HSY   water   like-NR   3-beˆlocated
> When he looked there, there was something like water. (27.13)

However, the phenomenon clause can be subordinated instead.

(24)   PERCEPTION [PHENOMENON]

> *pɨtʃaĩ   o-ɛtʃa mã   o-u-pɨ   [kama   kʷɛrɨ   tʃakã*
> ToeˆStumper 3-see   already 3-lying-GER   black   COLL   firewood

> *o-gʷɛr-u   ramõ]*
> 3-COM-come   s
> Toe-Stumper had seen when the blacks brought the firewood. (20.125)

That is, whether the perception clause or the phenomenon clause is subordinated, the order PERCEPTION-PHENOMENON typically holds. Example (25) provides a further example, with a very common construction type.

Switch-Reference Constructions in Mbyá Guaraní 239

(25) [PERCEPTION] PHENOMENON

[tʃɛɛ a-i-kʷaa ɾã] haʔɛ ɛʔɨ̃]
1s 1s-3-know DS 3ˆANA NEG
In my opinion (lit., as I know), he's not the one.

4.4 Discourse-pragmatic reverses of typical clause ordering

As commonly happens with conventional associations of meaning and form, they can be overridden by context-motivated considerations. In particular, the preposing or postposing of marking clauses in switch-reference constructions is not entirely determined by coherence relations. It appears that any coherence relation can, under the right discourse-pragmatic conditions, occur with an ordering of clauses that is different from its typical one.

Two discourse-pragmatic configurations that can reverse conventional orderings involve FOCUS and CLARIFICATION. For example, a purpose clause, which is typically postposed (§4.2), can instead be fronted, hence preposed, as an utterance-initial focus element (Dooley 1982:328f.). This is shown in (26) (cf. (20)).

(26) [PURPOSE] MEANS

[a-maʔɛ-apo ββ̵] a-ɲu
1s-thing-make SS 1s-come
It's in order to work that I've come.

Simultaneity typically involves a preposed subordinate clause. Example (27), however, shows simultaneity with a postposed clause, apparently as a clarification or afterthought (p. 312) (cf. (13)).

(27) SITUATION₁ [SIMULTANEOUS SITUATION₂]

o-mo-ĩ ɲu piɾɛ [o-u ββ̵]
3-CAUS-beˆlocated again skin 3-come SS
He put on his skin again as he was coming. (27.88)

In the brief survey provided by this section, we have seen that switch-reference marking clauses are postposed only in cases of PURPOSE, MENTAL-PROCESS REASON, PERCEIVED PHENOMENON, and discourse-pragmatic CLARIFICATION. These factors account for only thirteen percent of all switch-reference constructions. In the eighty-seven percent of switch-reference

240   Robert A. Dooley

constructions in which the marking clause is preposed, the possibilities for interpreting the coherence relation are much greater (less constrained).

5. Concluding remarks

The high incidence of switch-reference constructions in Mbyá Guaraní, coupled with the fact that they contribute nothing to the interpretation of specific coherence relations, forcibly raises the question: In what sense are coherence relations present when they are not explicitly signalled? Do they exist in the mind of the speaker, in the mind of the interpreter, in the text, in all three, or in none? This article can be understood as an exploration into one type of answer to these questions, an answer which, however, involves a complex interaction of factors.

In regard to the speaker, the assumption here is that when clause combining occurs, it can be taken as an indication that the speaker intends that two clauses be considered as linked by some coherence relation. We have not assumed, however, that the speaker always intends to communicate a specific relation. A theoretical basis for this approach is provided by relevance theory, and in particular by the notion of weak communication.

As evidence bearing on the interpretation of coherence relations, we have considered both extralinguistic and linguistic constraints. Extralinguistic constraints, including previous contextualizations and "off-the-shelf" expectation structures, can be considered a contribution of the interpreter to coherence relations. Another factor based on the interpreter is degree of attention devoted specifically to coherence relations. The major part of the article deals with the contribution of the text itself, that is, linguistic constraints, both morphemic and syntactic. Morphemic signals sometimes instruct the interpreter to render a categorical interpretation. Other morphemic signals only indicate that a certain meaning component should be included in the interpretation, leaving open the possibility of a less-than-categorial interpretation overall. The only syntactic phenomenon investigated in this article is the relative order of the marking clause and the matrix clause; postposed marking clauses are less frequent and more suggestive as to the intended coherence relation (although the typical clause order may be reversed because of discourse-pragmatic factors).

An examination of the above kinds of clues leads to the following observation: although in certain places it is arguable that the coherence relation will be interpreted categorically (under typical processing conditions), often the available clues only serve to suggest that its interpretation (a) is merely circumscribed within a general area or (b) is composed of a loose cluster of related relations. That is, in many cases there is little evidence that would

Switch-Reference Constructions in Mbyá Guaraní

lead one to expect that the typical interpreter will arrive at a specific and categorical interpretation.

The assumption of noncategoricality in interpretation, or rather the non-assumption of categoriality, is not simply a theoretical approach, but one which suggests a definite methodology for investigating coherence relations. Rather than coming to a switch-reference construction with the question, "Which coherence relation is intended here?", we ask, "What evidence is there that the interpretation of the coherence relation is being constrained?" This same approach should be equally valuable for applications, such as translation, that involve text interpretation. The present study is intended to demonstrate that this approach is both principled and viable.

References

Blakemore, Diane. 1987. Semantic constraints on relevance. Oxford: Blackwell.
———. 1988. The organization of discourse. In Frederick J. Newmeyer (ed.), Linguistics: The Cambridge survey. Language: The socio-cultural context 4:229–50. Cambridge: Cambridge University Press.
Blass, Regina. 1986. Cohesion, coherence and relevance. Notes on Linguistics 34:41–64.
Brown, Gillian and George Yule. 1983. Discourse analysis. Cambridge: Cambridge University Press.
Dooley, Robert A. 1982. Options in the pragmatic structuring of Guaraní sentences. Language 58:307–31.
———. 1986. Sentence-initial elements in Brazilian Guaraní. In Joseph E. Grimes (ed.), Sentence initial devices. Summer Institute of Linguistics and the University of Texas at Arlington Publications in Linguistics 75:45–69. Dallas.
———. 1989. Switch reference in Mbyá Guaraní: A fair-weather phenomenon. In Robert A. Dooley and J. Albert Bickford (eds.), Work papers of the Summer Institute of Linguistics, University of North Dakota Session 33:93–120. Dallas: Summer Institute of Linguistics.
Fillmore, Charles J. 1974. The future of semantics. In Charles J. Fillmore, George Lakoff, and Robin Lakoff (eds.), Berkeley symposium on syntax and semantics 4:1–38. Berkeley: University of California.
———. 1981. Pragmatics and the description of discourse. In Peter Cole (ed.), Radical pragmatics, 143–66. New York: Academic Press.
Grimes, Joseph E. 1976. The thread of discourse. The Hague: Mouton.
Grosz, Barbara J. and Candace L. Sidner. 1986. Attention, intentions, and the structure of discourse. Computational Linguistics 12:175–204.

242 Robert A. Dooley

Haiman, John and Pamela Munro. 1983. Introduction. In John Haiman and Pamela Munro (eds.), Switch-reference and universal grammar, ix–xv. Amsterdam: John Benjamins.

Hobbs, Jerry. 1979. Coherence and coreference. Cognitive Science 3:67–90.

Longacre, Robert E. 1983. The grammar of discourse. New York: Plenum.

Mann, William C. and Sandra A. Thompson. 1988. Rhetorical structure theory: Toward a functional theory of text organization. Text 8(3):243–81.

Rodrigues, Aryon Dall'Igna. 1984/85. Relações internas entre as línguas Tupí-Guaraní. Revista de Antropologia 27/28:33–53.

Sanders, Ted J. M., Wilbert P. M. S. Spooren, and Leo G. M. Noordman. 1990. Towards a taxonomy of coherence relations. ms.

Sperber, Dan and Deirdre Wilson. 1986. Relevance: Communication and cognition. Cambridge: Harvard University Press.

Thompson, Sandra A. and William C. Mann. 1987. Rhetorical structure theory: A framework for the analysis of texts. International Peace Research Association Papers in Pragmatics 1(1):79–105.

Proposed Tests
for the Validity of an Analysis
of Logical Connectives

Eugene E. Loos

1. Background

Whether one is undertaking to compile a dictionary for a hitherto unwritten and undocumented language, write a grammar of it, or translate into it a passage containing relations between propositions that we have not yet mastered in the target language, it would be useful to have available a set of interpretive rules or operations that would assure that the results we come up with would be unchallenged. A concrete set of interpretive rules, if even possible, is not yet forthcoming. Lacking that, it would at least be useful to have a set of heuristics that, when used to test the claimed relationships or support the claims to others who might challenge the conclusions, might help in discovering plausible relationships, and that would be accepted as contributing to the probability of a correct analysis. The present article attempts to propose a tentative set of such heuristics.[1]

---

[1] I owe special thanks to Barbara Meyers, Bill Mann, Tom Payne, Regina Blass, Dan Tutton, and Ernst August Gutt for contributions to this article. Any misstatements or errors are my own.

244   Eugene E Loos

1.1 What the heuristic might be

Supporting a claim may be done with less than proof. Suppose that I suspect that in a particular text, not my native language, a specific logical relation between certain propositions is communicated. Further, suppose we admit that I cannot know for sure whether or not the relation is communicated. The question we seek to answer is "What can I do so that my judgment that the relation obtains in that context will at least be more likely to be true?"

1.2 A first approximation

The following questions are proposed as a beginning set to summarize the heuristic challenge that an expositor may encounter upon making claims for a specific language.
1. How do I recognize that a logical relation is intended between a pair of propositions?
2. How do I test to determine that the identified connective is the clue to the meaning?
3. How do I test to determine whether more than one relationship is signaled by the logical connective?
4. How do I determine which of several possible relationships is signaled in a particular instance?
5. What test can I offer to show that my analysis is correct?

It is not unusual to find many instances of homophonous morphemes. A single form may be logged into the lexicon as having different meanings, each meaning coincidentally having identical form. For example, suppose that the Capanahua verb suffix -ya were glossed as having six meanings: 'when', 'if', 'provided that', 'about the time that', 'with', 'after'. The similarity in meaning between these renderings would lead one to suspect that the glosses might be incorrect, due to improper morpheme identification. "If a new meaning has to be assigned for each context, then the proper, more general meaning for the morpheme has not been found."[2] If the meaning of -ya is really a very general 'when' with local interpretations to be determined by the context, some guiding principles for interpretation are needed.

Starting from a different perspective, using relevance theory one can claim that when a meaning has been assigned to a form but that meaning is dependent on the context, then the meaning is derived from the context and is not essentially a part of the form.[3] The listener derives the meaning by a

---

[2] The formulation of the principle is my recollection of how Ivan Lowe expressed it during a lecture at the workshop. Any misrepresentation, though not intended, is mine.
[3] This is my informal summary drawn from Regina Blass's presentation of relevance theory.

Proposed Tests for Logical Connectives

language processing ability that involves his knowledge of the language, his interpretation of the speaker's intended illocutionary force, his knowledge and assumptions about the universe, his experience, etc.

The issue then is (a) whether the usage has been conventionalized (grammaticalized) so that there is a discrete, limited set of possible meanings that can be described in the grammar, or (b) whether the usage is to be accounted for by a theory of communication rather than a theory of grammar.

If the meaning is conventionalized usage, then a further question is asked: Is that morpheme the only signal used to convey the claimed logical relation? If it is the only signal present, the morpheme would be included in the lexicon since the lexicon is the inventory of forms which have meaning assigned to them. If there are also nonmorphemic ways of signaling the same relation, they would be described either in the grammar or in a pragmatic account of reasoning processes in the language.

Either way, two considerations help define what may be expected in searching for indicators or tests to identify logical relations:

1. Logical connectives are signals (morphemes) that the speaker uses so that the hearer will know how to associate propositions.
2. The relations cued by logical connectives are interpreted by the hearer in a cognitive processing of the propositions he has received.

Indicators contained in the linguistic context are a subset of those available to the listener, so a search of the context is a reasonable place to start looking for clues.

2. Clues from obvious etymological composition

2.1 Morphemic composition

Morphemic composition might lead one to suspect that a literal (nonextended) meaning is the basis for an extended meaning. We can also expect to find that locative, temporal, and other extended meanings are synchronically or diachronically derived from basic noun, verb, or prepositional forms.[4]

For example, it is evident that the following Capanahua prefixes (derived from nouns) are related to locatives, and some locatives are related to corresponding temporals. Given that a temporal relation can signify a kind of logical-precedence relation, in some languages it would not be too surprising to find logical relations cued by temporal constructions.

---

[4] As presented by Tom Payne during the workshop.

246 Eugene E Loos

(1) | Nominal | | Locative | | Temporal | |
|---|---|---|---|---|---|
| *cah-* | back | *cah-chi qui* | behind | *cah-chi qui* | after |
| *be-* | face | *bebon* | in front | | |
| *rabet-* | two | *hah-betan* | with him | *betan bi* | simultaneously |

Traugott (1989) traces the process of grammaticalization and shows that there is a remarkably well-attested development from the meanings of Old English descriptive verbs to later deontic and epistemic meanings. Some of those deontic and epistemic meanings are included in the broad category that we are treating as logical connectives. The pattern is so well established that a researcher can expect to find that the source of currently used deontics and epistemics in other languages might be found in earlier verb forms of those languages.

To turn Traugott's important observation into a heuristic we simply seek the inverse of the noted pattern: if we find verbs used to express propositional content, we might also find the use of those verbs extended to encode cohesion-making and presuppositional or other pragmatic meanings. Verbs with such meanings might appear to be so natural that we fail to recognize them as logical connectives.

2.2 Detecting grammaticalized forms

To answer the question, how does one distinguish between a somewhat innovative, dynamically interpreted occurrence and a grammaticalized form, the following points suggest themselves.

Frequency of occurrence. Assuming that an innovative rendering in a particular context effectively communicates an intended logical relation, it is easy to conjecture that such a construal might be wanted in other contexts, hence the construction would re-occur. If repeated often enough, it could become conventionalized to convey that meaning. Others would use it similarly, and its use would be strengthened, leading to still more frequent uses of it.

Hence, statistical counts might be used as evidence for the grammaticalization of a logical connective.

Predictability of occurrence. The most reliable indicator of grammaticalization is when it can be predicted that a form or construction will be used, and then find that the prediction is confirmed. Possible methods of making the prediction:

Proposed Tests for Logical Connectives 247

1. upon hearing others dialog, intuitively predict that the form will be used in certain contexts and listen for the occurrence;
2. set up situations in dialog such that naive addressees might be prompted to supply a meaning and see if the grammaticalized form occurs; and
3. examine texts to see if given certain contexts, a fair percentage of the time the meaning anticipated is indicated by the grammaticalized form.

Contextual and analytical conflict. A conflict between the meaning that the analysis assigns and the meaning that would most likely be contextually motivated is useful. If it can be deduced that the meaning conveyed by the signal cannot have been provided by the context, the basis for the deduction constitutes a measure of strength for affirming that the meaning is conventionalized, not dynamically construed.

Variation in meaning according to context. This is the converse of the principle of contextual meaning conflict above. If it can be shown that the meaning of the morpheme or clue in question varies according to the context, and the variation is quite different, such as 'and' in English meaning 'both and', 'and then', 'if you do...I'll...', etc, then the meanings are derived from the context rather than being carried by the morpheme, and a more basic meaning for the morpheme should be sought.

3. Acceptability tests

3.1 Native speakers

If native speakers are available and the researcher has enough command of the language to elicit judgments about acceptability, some of the following tests can be made to help confirm or refute an analysis.

Inclusion and omission. Test to see if the purported logical connective is essential for the meaning attributed to it in that context by alternately omitting the connective to see if every omission of the connective means that the logical relation is no longer present. For example, *rahan* is a Capanahua particle attached to sentences. Inclusion and omission tests show that it is a response form.

(2) a. *bahquish tah hen cahi*   Tomorrow I'm going.
     b. *min cahin*   You're going?
     c. *cahi rahan*   Going, indeed. (Yes, I'm going.)

248   Eugene E Loos

In a nonresponse form *rahan* is unacceptable as shown in (3).

(3)   *bahquish tah hen cahi rahan*   *Yes, tomorrow I am going.

Responses in (4)–(6) show that the particle confirms that the addressee
was right in the assumptions behind the question or affirmation that
prompted the reply.

(4)   a. *min cayamahin*   Aren't you going?[5]
       b. *cahi rahan*   Yes, I'm going.

(5)   a. *yotihopa ra joni*   What a huge man!
       b. *hani rahan*   Yes, (he is) big.

(6)   a. *jaa ta hihtihosi joni qui* He is a monstrous man.
       b. **hanitahma rahan*   *Yes, he is a small man.

The response in (6b) would draw puzzled looks from the speaker of (6a).
Conclusion: a *rahan* sentence must be a response form to confirm what the
other has expressed, since otherwise the first speaker by gesture or expression indicates lack of understanding upon hearing the *rahan* response.

In conversational situations where rahan is accepted, it is not obligatory
and may be omitted. Hence, we can conclude that it is either redundantly
supplied to help the addressee process the utterance correctly, or it adds an
optional meaning and perhaps otherwise helps in pragmatic processing, such
as supplying indications of courtesy and amiableness.

Permutation of major constituents. Swap the position of clauses or
sentences with respect to the connective to seek to isolate the role of the
constituents with regard to one another. Incorrect collocation will sometimes
produce an ungrammatical sentence or a complete change in meaning.

(7)   a. (husband, in hammock)
          hahrai. hen yora jatihobi tah hen hisinai.
          Oh my! My whole body aches!

       b. (wife, offering a drink)
          hisini rahan, jihui hiabahinahipish **cahron**
          Of course (you) ache, *since* you carried logs all day yesterday.

---

[5] In Capanahua a negative form of question is used when an affirmative reply is expected.

Proposed Tests for Logical Connectives 249

She could say (8), or else (9) if she had helped carry the logs and also aches. But she could not say (10) or (11).

(8) *hisini, jihui hiabahinahipish*
    You ache, (because) you carried logs all day yesterday.

(9) *jihui hiabahinahipish hisini rahan*
    Sure (you) ache, (*because*) (you) carried logs all day yesterday (lit., having carried logs all day yesterday, sure you ache).

(10) **jihui hiabahinahipish hisini **cahron****
    *Having carried logs all day yesterday *since* you ache.

(11) **jihui hiabahinahipish rahan hisini **cahron****
    *Yes, having carried logs all day yesterday *since* you ache.

Other tests can be used with *cahron* to determine that the speaker uses *cahron* 'since' only when she means to indicate that it is reasonable for the speaker to expect to ache. It is a particle that communicates expectedness. There is a reasonable cause and effect relationship between the propositions.

Observance of reactions. Make trial efforts with native speakers while observing their reactions, watching to see if the reactions are consonant with what would be expected if the presumed logical connections were correctly understood by the addressees.

3.2 Native texts

Lacking opportunity for interaction with native speakers to test their reactions, one can examine native texts to see if predictive statements of the distribution of specific contextual parameters match what would be expected. The strength of the test will depend of course on the rigor with which the definition of a suitable context is expressed.

For example, *hicahisen* in Capanahua is a particle used both in arguments, in dismissals, and in granting permission. In each case it is possible to see that the speaker who uses *hicahisen* hopes to terminate the argument, is sending someone off, or wishes to stop harassment by granting a request. The common denominator is that it is used to terminate a topic. In (12) this is shown by the narrator's explanation for the protagonist's response.

250 Eugene E Loos

(12) *nea tah qui hicahisen bichihue. mina tah qui miin coa, hahquin.*
yocacah bi hinanyamaxon sinataiton sca jascajaquin hinanquin

"All right, here it is, come and get it. It's yours," he said. The one who held the spear said that as he returned it to its owner, because the owner had gotten angry when he didn't give it back soon enough.

4. Interviews

Since logical relations are closely linked to the assumptions of speaker and addressee, we can expect that it will be fruitful to make tests to discern the assumptions of the speaker or addressee of a text.

4.1 General principles

The listener's understanding. Question native speakers about aspects of the text; why, when, what next, what were the circumstances, what was the actor's intention, what had happened immediately previous, etc. to determine features of the extended linguistic context and assumptions in the mind of speaker or listener that might not be evident from the text alone. The goal of enriching the information about the text in this way is to provide comparative information that will reveal determining factors.

Adverbial questions in some languages make it possible to probe psychological contexts in the mind of speaker or listener without suggesting them explicitly. It is desirable to explore obliquely because explicit mention of a possible purpose, etc. might prejudice the reply. For example, Capanahua has no general adverb for why. Each of the specific forms of the interrogative adverbs in (13) can elicit a different response because it focuses on a different aspect of the activity.

(13)
jahuejanoxon	in order to do what
jahuejanon	with the result that x do what
jahuejahi	with what purpose
jahuejanon hihxon	with the intention that x do what
jahua copi	what is the cause
jahuejaxon	having done what
jahuejahax	having been what, done (intr)
jahuejahiya	when x does what
jahuejahiton	when x is doing what...to him
jahuejahah	having been done what by x
jahuejahahbo	in order that x2 do what
jenques jaiya	what are the circumstances

Proposed Tests for Logical Connectives   251

jenquetsahpa	what sort of
jahue qui	what, how
jahuerahnon	where
jahuerahnoxon	being where
jahuentian	when
jahueraho	in which direction

Identification of assumptions. Attempt to identify by query what the speaker assumes the listener does not know. Using the vernacular to ask what was in the mind of the speaker may require a level of language command that is out of reach for the investigator, but by attaining that level one can gain insights for pragmatic explanations that are inaccessible otherwise. Circumlocutions to achieve the queries might be: what was x thinking that y knew, what did x think that y did not know, what did x think that y was going to do if x said nothing, etc.

Supplied contexts. Supply suitable psychological contexts and re-examine rejected possibilities. In some cases the reason for the rejection of first explorations might not be grammatical problems but lack of suitable context, as I found in B's answers in (14). Initially the respondent B did not include an airplane when thinking about flying.

(14) A: *yohuanahnan, bahquish ta hea noyaquihnyaxihquiqui* **hihqui**
      hueotimahin
      Would it ever be appropriate for me to say, Tomorrow he will fly me? (lit., Tomorrow he will make me to fly by flying with me).

    B: *hihyamahi, rahan. jaa ta jahuenbi hueotimahiqui*
       No, you couldn't say that. That wouldn't fit any context.

    A: *pilotonen hea jahuen ranchan boyaxihqui shinanax cahran*
       What if I think that the pilot is going to take me in his plane?

    B: *jaatian pari*
       Only then [could you say it].

Felicity tests. Query native speakers concerning the felicity of an acceptable expression. This is the inverse of the previous suggestion. An acceptable expression is tested to see when contextual features cause the expression to be unacceptable. The result might enable one to specify the conditions or assumptions that are required for the expression to be acceptable.

Redundance incongruity. When a redundancy that seems to be implied is denied by a native speaker, it indicates an incongruity between the tested assumption and the addressee's assumptions.

4.2 Confirmation of presumed logical relations

The following are some specific ideas on how to confirm the presence of a presumed relation in a text.

The bilingual test. Speak to a bilingual speaker or author in his second language concerning one of his own native texts and ask him if he communicated in the vernacular the relation that you suppose exists between a pair of propositions in that text. If he confirms that he did, there is some likelihood that the relation is indeed communicated in the text.

Paraphrase tests. Ask a native author to paraphrase or restate his text. Then test to see if the relation still seems to be present in the paraphrase. If it is still present, then it is probable that the relation is communicated in the text.

Via paraphrase ask a native speaker or hearer of the text if the author communicates the supposed relation in the text. If he confirms, then there is some probability that the relation was indeed communicated.

Ask a native speaker or hearer to paraphrase or restate the text to see if the relation shows up in the paraphrase. If so then it is probable that it was present in the original text.

Consistency tests

Contextual consistency. Examine closely the situation in which the text was uttered: when uttered, where uttered, to what audience, with what beliefs, attitudes, concerns, with what expectations of the audience. If after doing so, it still seems consistent with the situation that the relation was communicated in the text then there is some probability that it was.

Immersion and reevaluation. Get immersed in the subject matter of the text. If possible, witness what the text talks about. Seek to participate in the experience described. Compare with other texts on the same subject. Then consider again whether the supposed relation is communicated by the text. If it still seems to be, the probability that it was communicated is strengthened.

Proposed Tests for Logical Connectives 253

Coherence. Assume that the text is coherent, that there are no illogical implications, each element of the text having some evident function in the text as a whole. Seek any counter-indications. Then consider whether the relation that you suppose is communicated would have some pertinent function in the text as a whole. If the relation seems to be intended, then the probability that the relation is implied in the text is strengthened.

Responsibility. Try to detect contexts or occasions when the author is 'blamed' for having communicated the supposed relation. If so, then there is a very good probability that the relation is to be inferred.

Composition. If you suspect that a connective communicates a particular logical relation, compose an utterance that includes the connective but in which the relation if communicated would significantly disturb the sense of the passage. Then test it with native speakers, or read it to yourself and relying tentatively on your own competence in the language judge whether it makes sense or not. If it does not make sense, guess that you may not have identified the relation correctly.

Coincidence. If you suppose there are two (or more) different relations (for example temporal sequence and purpose) that one could posit between a pair of propositions, examine to see if those two relations are often, or usually, possible alternative interpretations in other linguistic contexts. If they are alternatives elsewhere then it is probable that they are valid alternatives in the current instance.

Recurrence. Try to record the text again when it is told to another audience. If the logical relation is in the second text, the probability is strengthened that it is also in the first.

Genre typicality. Assume that in a particular genre of texts some logical relations are more likely to appear than others. For a specific text determine if the supposed relation is more or less frequent than in other texts of that genre. If it is more frequent, then it is probable that the relation is really communicated in the text. If it is less frequent, it may not necessarily follow that the logical relation is less probably communicated.

New compositions. If you think a particular relation is communicated in the text and you think a specific grammatical form marks it, then using subject matter of a foreign or new situation compose a text which uses that form to communicate that relation and see if the relation gets across to native speakers.

254   Eugene E Loos

Redundancy. Add to the text an explicit statement of the supposed relation. Then reconsider the text and ask yourself if it seems redundant. If it does then the supposed relation is probably present in the original version.

Conflicting cues. Add to the text an explicit denial of the supposed relation. Then test the text and determine if it significantly damages the coherence of the text. If it does, then the supposed relation is probably present.

5. Observation in a cross-cultural context

Observed appropriate responses or lack thereof can be important indicators of the interpretations made by listeners. Use a video recorder to monitor a speaker's tracking of listeners for subsequent study:

> ...particularly in the case of face-to-face interactions, the speaker is able to gauge the responses of the listener and modify his/her style accordingly. This is possible mainly by taking account of cues given by the latter. Even when monologuing, narrators look for and expect to find cues that the members of the audience are still attending; such cues may include eye contact, head nodding, paralinguistic responses such as laughter, grunting, and so on, and linguistic responses such as interjections, questions, and the like— see for instance Muecke [1983:v], Schegloff [1982:73–74] and Tedlock [1983:66]. Indeed, the absence of such cues may rapidly lead to the speaker concluding his/her turn and abandoning the floor, or actively seeking a response from the audience—for instance by asking whether or not they are still listening. (McGregor 1988:136)

6. Loans

Loan words can be an indication that there was felt to be a need in the mother tongue to express something that was hitherto ambiguously expressed or expressed in less distinctive terms.

For example, I deduce that in Capanahua, before contact with Quechua and Spanish speaking populaces, only *-non* as a terminal verb suffix was used to indicate 'until', 'that', 'result', 'subsequently'.

Proposed Tests for Logical Connectives 255

(15) *jaa   hani-non   jise*
      he   grow-that   watch

Any of the following meanings can be communicated by (15):

> Watch him *until* he grows up.
> Watch him *so that* he grows up.
> Watch him *then* he will grow up.

After contact with Quechua speakers, the Quechua word *caman* 'until' was usually added when Capanahua speakers intended the first meaning. The Quechua word did not replace the Capanahua suffix *-non*.

(16) *jaa   hani-non   caman   jise*
      he   grow-that   until   watch
      Watch him *until* he grows up.

After contact with Spanish, the Spanish adverb *hasta* 'until' was also added to the same constructions.

(17) **hasta**   *jaa   hani-non   caman   jise*
      until   he   grow-*until* until   watch
      Watch him *until* he grows up. (Care for him until he is grown.)

Presumably the Quechua *caman*, still recognized as an intrusion, did not fully satisfy the felt need to disambiguate, given the pressure of prestigious Spanish where the same ambiguity did not exist.

7. Illocutionary alertness

When as analysts we are working in a language not our own, we may feel that we have missed implied logical relations; perhaps we do not even suspect that a logical relation exists in a statement. By observing specific aspects of the communication we can seek to become more sensitive to hidden cues. The following proposals are offered as possible check points.

7.1 Oblique facets

Questionable oblique facets of communication are those that the hearer can query or challenge in addition to the propositional content of the spoken

256   Eugene E Loos

text; the facets may enable one to discern factors relevant to interpreting
interpropositional relations. Seek to discern:

The emotive state of the speaker
  a. drunk
  b. happy
  c. angry
  d. tired
  e. worried

Interpersonal registers
  a. Condescending: My little children
  b. Respectful: Sir
  c. Intimate: Cousin
  d. Friendly: Pal
  e. Conventional: Mate
  f. Endearing: My dear

The intent of the speaker
  a. to inform of something new
  b. to remind
  c. to cause one to act
  d. to empathize
  e. to express feeling
  f. to entertain
  g. to persuade

Presupposition indicators
  a. motivating events in the linguistic or nonlinguistic context
  b. intonational contours
  c. facial expressions
  d. demeanor
  g. gestures

Epistemological status
  a. shared knowledge
  b. inadequate knowledge
  c. unshared knowledge
  d. verificational support
  e. conflicting evidence

Cultural propriety. The assumed reasonableness of a supposed logical
relation might depend on cultural factors that the investigator needs to
examine. For example, when a young Capanahua said to his father, "You are

Proposed Tests for Logical Connectives

going to make one for me," the father afterward explained that the seemingly rude demand was in reality a polite form of request suitable for intimate relations.

7.2 Confirmation

A speaker usually monitors indicators of the addressee's attention. If the addressee fails to provide the signals that are expected that show his progress in processing the discourse is keeping up with the speaker, the speaker may alter the discourse.

Note cues that the speaker is monitoring the receptor's processing of the discourse:

1. 'echo' responses are provided by the receptor or are expected by the speaker;
2. nonverbal responses are picked up;
3. a lack of responses is associated with distinctives in the text; or
4. repair mechanisms are resorted to.

7.3 Distribution patterns

Patterns of occurrence can lead one to make hypotheses that can be verified empirically and that can, therefore, lead to more general hypotheses.

In Capanahua, the verb suffix -*quin* only occurs on verbs that do not have the expected tense or mood marking suffixes. If one studied legends only, it would appear that verbs ending in -*quin* are thereby marked as being in past tense, but examination of a wider genre of discourse shows that -*quin* also occurs on verbs with imperative meaning and on verbs of future indicative and interrogative meaning. The -*quin* suffix, therefore, cannot mean only past tense. The pattern of its distribution shows that part of its function is to serve as a pro-form substituting for tense and mood of sentences in discourse when the mood and tense has been established by previous sentences. It, therefore, indicates 'same tense, same mood'; the tense is either past, present, or future, and the mood is declarative, interrogative, or imperative, all depending on what has already been established.

Patterns of usage can be indicators of speaker-listener empathy. In tape recordings of Capanahua legends, the particle -*can* occurs in texts by some narrators much more frequently than when the same texts were related by other narrators. The heaviest occurrence showed up in texts provided by narrators who were not well acquainted with the listener. The particle indicates that the speaker supposes that the listener should know that the event mentioned was to be expected. Not knowing how well the listener might be processing the narration, the speakers tended to provide -*can* as a signal to give assistance to the listener.

258   Eugene E Loos

8. Agreement among analysts

If there is agreement among analysts that a logical relation exists between a pair of propositions, though there might not be certainty about the
judgment, there might at least be a high degree of plausibility to it. When
there is no agreement or there is doubt to overcome, the analyst may question the argument to see how well basic analytical issues have been attended
to. They are offered here without elaboration:
1. Have nonlinguistic criteria as well as linguistic criteria been examined?
2. Are all data accounted for? How much is relevant data?
3. What are the (distant) consequences if the hypothesis is valid?
4. Is there a simpler analysis that covers more data? Chapter 3 of Blass
   (1990) is an example of how increasing the explanatory power of an
   analysis by simplifying it accounts for more data.

9. Introspection and imagination

9.1 Redundancy

You might have a feeling that syntactic components as logical connectives are inappropriate because they are superfluous. Ask if the redundancy
might overcome an ambiguity.

For example, in Capanahua -*ya* can signal a conditional 'if' but it can
also mean 'when' or 'after'. To eliminate ambiguity, Capanahua speakers
sometimes express the negative of the condition as well. Though the negative phrase is redundant, it eliminates the temporal meanings as shown in
(18).

(18)   *mia cahiya cahi mia cayamahiya cahen cayamahi*
       If you go, I'll go; if you don't go, I won't go.

9.2 Feeling

There can be times when the analyst has only a feeling for the meaning
and somewhat imagined circumstances are adduced to support the identification of the meaning component. Feeling is the weakest of bases on which
to make a claim, but worth investigating because you might find that tenuous
ideas can be substantiated with more and different data.

References

Blass, Regina. 1990. Relevance relations in discourse: A study with special reference to Sissala. Cambridge Studies in Linguistics 55. Cambridge: Cambridge University Press.

McGregor, William. 1988. Joint construction of narrative in Gooniyandi. La Trobe working papers in linguistics 1. La Trobe University, Australia.

Muecke, Stephen, ed. 1983. Gularabuli. Fremantle: Fremantle Arts Centre.

Schegloff, Emanuel A. 1982. Discourse as an interactional achievement: Some uses of 'uh huh' and other things that come between sentences. In Deborah Tannen (ed.), Analyzing discourse: Text and talk. Georgetown University Round Table on Languages and Linguistics 1981:71–93. Washington, D.C.: Georgetown University Press.

Tedlock, Dennis. 1983. The spoken word and the work of interpretation. Philadelphia: University of Pennsylvania Press.

Traugott, Elizabeth. 1989. On the rise of epistemic meanings in English: An example of subjectification in semantic change. Language 65(1):31–55.

Printed in the USA
CPSIA information can be obtained
at www.ICGtesting.com
LVHW021127261023
762202LV00015B/754